TW.

Twelve Cases of Love Gone Bad

by JoAnne Myers

TWISTED LOVE

Twelve Cases of Love Gone Bad

by JoAnne Myers

ISBN-13: 978-1987902501
ISBN-10: 1987902505

www.RJPARKERPUBLISHING.COM

Published in United States of America

Copyright 2018
All rights reserved

TWISTED LOVE is a short story collection based on actual crimes and entwined within historical and authentic settings for the sole enjoyment of the reader. No part of this publication may be reproduced, stored in a retrieval system, or transmitted in any form or by any means, electronic, mechanical, photocopying, recording, or otherwise, without the prior permission of the author.

All parts of this book are the sole works and property of JoAnne Myers and RJ Parker Publishing, and any portions used without written permission will be considered plagiarism and copyright infringement and subject to prosecution. All information was gathered from newspaper clippings, witness and police statements, news reports and case files.

Book Links

AUDIOBOOKS at RJ Parker Publishing
http://rjparkerpublishing.com/audiobooks.html

Our collection of **CRIMES CANADA** books on Amazon.
http://www.crimescanada.com/

TRUE CRIME Books by RJ Parker Publishing on Amazon.
http://rjpp.ca/TRUECRIME-RJPP-BOOKS

Follow on *BOOKBUB*

Appreciation

Thank you to my editor, proofreaders, and cover artist for your support:

~ JoAnne

Aeternum Designs (book cover)
Bettye McKee (editor)
Katherine McCarthy
Robyn MacEachern
Sandra Miller
Kathi Garcia
Lorrie Suzanne Phillippe
Lana Cisinski
Tina Bates
Karen Spear
Kristal Grimsley Baker
Sharon Lehrmann
Kimberly Keen
Angel McCall
Steve Campbell
Kim Jackson
Barbara Kolb-Cieslewicz

Table of Contents

Book Links..3
Appreciation...4
End of Summer..7
The Death of Innocence............................48
Deadly Rival..63
The Possession...74
Home Town Hero.....................................104
The Girl Not Forgotten............................140
The Spell Casters Murders.......................181
All for The Family....................................190
Thicker than Water?................................226
Mail Order Murder...................................240
3381 Market Street.................................260
A Senseless Killing..................................300
About the Author....................................333

End of Summer

March 22, 2013, could have been just an ordinary Tuesday evening for the small industrial town of Logan, Ohio, population 7,152, if it were not for the glass-shattering screams from a female emanating from the alley next to the Century National Bank in downtown Logan.

The first witness was a twenty-one-year-old named Richard. He told police he was walking in the area of the bank when he saw a girl curled in a ball on the ground, with two grown men standing above her, tasing her.

When he got approximately one foot away from the woman and the men, a woman driver yelled to the men that someone was behind them. He was then pepper-sprayed by one of two male attackers when he tried to intervene. He raced off to an adjoining business, the North Fitness Center, who called 911.

A woman named Rachel, who was outside the fitness center, called 911 to report that a man was pepper-sprayed while attempting to help a woman who had been kidnapped. According to Rachel, Richard was in severe pain when he ran up to her while holding his eyes and yelling for help.

Richard gave the descriptions of the attackers as being two large dark-haired men, with the driver of the white Buick or Crown Victoria being an older female with "bleach blonde" hair.

The author knew Bob, an architect working in his upstairs office in the adjoining building next to the alley. Bob relayed that he heard the commotion, telling the persons to "keep the noise down."

At this same time, two female joggers witnessed a

young woman being shoved into a white Crown Victoria. Reportedly, they were near the Century National Bank when they heard a girl scream and heard a Taser go off. They proceeded to cross the alley beside the bank, noting that as they neared the commotion, the woman being tased seemed to be in a violent struggle with her attackers.

They, too, described the young woman as screaming while two men stood over her with a Taser. The men were dressed in black and had ski masks covering their faces. The woman on the ground wore her hair, which they described as being a dirty blonde color, in a ponytail. Then a woman's voice from the driver's seat yelled, "'Get the hell in the car.'"

From there, the joggers witnessed the girl being tossed into the backseat of the vehicle which then frantically sped away in a desperate hurry. The woman driving the vehicle was "frenzied," and "the blinkers and turn signals" were being used erratically.

After talking with Richard, officers located the area of the attack, finding the young woman's car in the bank parking lot; inside they discovered the back of her phone, a box of Tic-Tacs, a used container of Mace, a Mountain Dew bottle, and a ball cap that did not belong to her, as well as a set of keys on the asphalt. Found in soft soil behind a hedge were what appeared to be foot and knee prints "as if someone lay in wait," said one officer. Inside the bank, instead of finding the woman, all they found was her iPod.

Not until 11 o'clock p.m. that evening did police identify the kidnap victim as twenty-five-year-old Summer Cook Inman. The green-eyed Culinary Arts student, who stood five-foot four-inches tall, was reported missing by her stepfather and mother, Mike and Debra Cook, when she failed to returned home around 9:30 that evening after her cleaning position at the Century National Bank.

Shortly after arriving at the bank and seeing no sign

of Summer, the Cooks contacted the Logan Police Department. Two officers responded to the scene of the parking lot of the bank, as well as North Fitness Center. It was from Mrs. Cook that authorities discovered Summer was a mother of three and was involved in a tumultuous pending divorce with her estranged husband of six years, twenty-six-year-old William "Willy" Inman II.

    The center of the couple's disagreements was custody of their three children, all under the age of five. Debra told police that Willy wanted custody because he did not want to pay child support for three kids.

    Debra received a phone call from Willy around 8:30 p.m. that night, during which he stated he would not be picking up the kids for visitation tomorrow. The tall muscular dark-haired and dark-eyed man claimed he was broke down on the freeway near Cleveland, Ohio, even though he and his parents owned four vehicles.

    According to her Facebook account, Summer was born December 31, 1985, in Logan, Ohio, and was one of seven children born to two fathers.

    Summer first met Willy at a social gathering at his family's church, Faith Tabernacle. It was a small, white church in Nelsonville, Ohio, a bedroom community between Logan and Athens, located on US Route 33 in Athens County, just over the Hocking County line.

    The couple married right after Summer's 2006 high school graduation at her church, First Church Praise and Worship Center, in Logan. Reverend Michael L. Martin performed the ceremony. All agreed Summer was in love and looked forward to a large family and growing old with Willy. Little did they know that Willy's love for his new bride was twisted and would soon reach its boiling point.

    The young woman who was known for her "infectious smile" grew up attending the Pentecostal church with her parents and, after her wedding, was content in being a stay-at-home mom. Alexander, Kaley and Alana soon followed. Summer's life seemed complete to many, but according to family members, she grew tired of being treated as a possession instead of a mutual partner in her marriage.

The fairy tale soon ended when Willy became a possessive and domineering "bully" like his father, forty-seven-year-old William "Bill" Inman. Others realized that the patriarch of this dysfunctional family dominated with an iron fist.

Referred to by peers as "hyper," "controlling," and "scary," he possessed a portly stature barely standing five-foot eight-inches tall with brown eyes and hair, gray at the temples.

Pastor King Kelly married Bill and his wife, forty-six-year-old Sandra, at the church in 1983. Once Bill and Sandra became members, Bill played guitar and piano at Sunday services. The congregation said they found it hard to believe the Inmans were involved with Summer's disappearance, saying, "They seemed such a nice family."

After their wedding, Summer and Willy moved with Bill and Sandra to Florida but returned in 2010 when Bill lost the Florida home through foreclosure. The family rented a house in the small community of Hamden, Ohio, population 871, in Vinton County. The large farmhouse in the country with the huge yard was heaven for the three active children, but it was a hellhole for the intimidated and frightened Summer.

Over time, Summer complained to relatives of being watched like a hawk and that Willy told her he "would kill her" if she ever took the kids from him.

Neighbors observed that Summer and Sandra seldom ventured to town or were seen outdoors. When they did appear, they were "dressed in all black."

According to court records filed in Vinton County, Summer filed for divorce in 2012 on the grounds of domestic violence, verbal abuse, immense fear of bodily harm, and an "almost slavery-like existence" while married and living with Willy and his parents, stating, "My in-laws would gang up on me, to just work things out."

She accused Willy of abandoning or killing two of her cats when she had disagreed with him and that he would "forcibly take her car keys, cell phone and purse" so as to keep her at their marital home. She was granted temporary custody of the children as well as a civil protection order, then she returned to her parents' home in Logan.

She entered counseling and took parenting classes with plans of enrolling in Hocking College's culinary arts program and opening her own restaurant someday.

At the time of her disappearance, police were dumbfounded as to what, if anything, criminal was happening. Some officers theorized that Summer disappeared willingly due to the stress of her pending divorce and her upcoming marriage to her twenty-three-year-old fiancé, Adam Peters. Debra and Mike said Summer leaving on her own was impossible because she loved her children too much to "just abandon them."

Aiding Willy at full speed ahead with the custody battle were his father and mother. They told several people that Summer was "giving them a hard time" about visitation rights to their grandchildren after Summer moved from their home, and they were furious about it.

According to the Inmans' pastor, King Kelly, in early 2012, Bill Inman obtained a minister's license, considering himself a religious leader and conducting Bible classes inside a small building behind the Hamden farmhouse.

In an incorporation document filed with the Ohio

Secretary of State's Office, Bill listed himself as leader of Mercy Tabernacle Church, a nonprofit organization, "to help people who have lost their jobs or been cut back on hours keep their homes."

According to neighbors, he considered the Hamden farmhouse and lands a ranch. They related that Bill often went door to door soliciting donations for what he called "Mercy Ranch," a plan to turn his home into a place for the "wayward and homeless."

The FBI were brought in to help in the disappearance and, after contacting the Bureau of Motor Vehicles, learned Bill Inman had recently purchased a white Crown Victoria and had relatives in the Akron and Cleveland, Ohio, area.

Debra Cook immediately provided Logan Police Chief Aaron Miller with Willy's cell phone number. Numerous attempts to reach Willy were made by the Chief, but Willy did not return the calls until the day after Summer's disappearance.

According to the Chief, during this nineteen-minute call, Willy claimed to not know where Summer was and of being broke down on the Cleveland freeway during the time of Summer's disappearance. Willy's attitude toward having a missing wife was very "unconcerned" and "matter-of-fact," said the Chief. The Logan Police Department then requested Willy's cell phone records from AT&T.

Columbus Police Officer Robert Moledor, a member of the Violent Crimes Task Force, was contacted to assist in the investigation because of his extensive knowledge and training about cell phones and service towers. Based on Moledor's analysis of two phones which were later identified as belonging to William Inman and his son William Inman II, Moledor testified that both cell phones traveled from Northeast Ohio on March 22, 2013, to Logan and then to Nelsonville before returning to Akron the following day.

If Summer's husband and in-laws were unconcerned with finding her, the community of Logan was not. Immediately, Summer's church and other houses of worship held prayer and candlelight vigils for the missing mother.

Summer's friends and family, including fiancé Adam Peters, worked with social networking programs such as Facebook and Twitter in the hope that someone knew her whereabouts.

Friends of the couple said that, even though Summer and Willy were not legally divorced, Summer and Adam were prepared to wed as soon as her signature dried on her divorce papers. Summer had met Adam through her husband when the men became friends while both attended Hocking College.

Also on the case to interview persons of interests and look for suspects was Special Agent McBain of the FBI. She was notified to assist the Logan Police Department with their investigation on March 23, 2013. During the course of her investigation, she interviewed Summer's family and boyfriend.

McBain was trying to find out what Summer was wearing and the habits or problems Summer had with her in-laws – anything that could help locate the missing woman and learn who kidnapped her. McBain was also present at the church when Summer's body was later recovered.

Officer Terry Hudnall of the Akron Police Department and FBI Agent Douglas Porini also conducted surveillance at the Inman home on Faye Road in Akron for a white Ford Crown Victoria that was believed to have been involved in Summer's disappearance from Century National Bank in Logan.

When they arrived at the home, they immediately saw the car in question parked in the driveway. After contacting the legal advisor for the Akron Police

Department, it was determined there was enough evidence to get a search warrant for the home.

The surveillance lasted two hours at which time, around 2:30 p.m., a warrant was obtained. All three Inmans were present.

Once the warrant was signed by a Summit County municipal court judge, the SWAT team entered the home and found the Inman family inside. Willy Inman was located in the kitchen, Bill was in the living room, and Sandra was located in the dining room of the house.

Three vehicles on the property were towed from the home, including the 2005 Ford Crown Victoria, a 1999 Plymouth Voyager, and a 2004 Honda Passport.

Frank Harrah, a detective with the Akron Police Department, described the layout of the Inman home, which included a large walk-in closet on the second floor. Inside the closet, a backpack containing two handguns, a flashlight, two empty magazines, a gold security officer's badge, two walkie-talkies, a fixed-blade knife, and a switchblade knife were located. The guns included a .45 caliber semi-automatic pistol and a 9mm semi-automatic pistol, he noted.

Agent Porini was then tasked with interviewing Willy Inman. During this time, the Akron Police Department conducted a search of the home.

During the interview, Porini noted, Bill Inman yelled from the other room and told his son to stop talking. Porini testified that Bill Inman's tone was "commanding and agitating" when he yelled.

Akron Police Detective Richard Morrison testified that he spoke with neighbors who lived next door to the Inman residence, but nothing peculiar resulted from the questioning. He then walked inside the home and viewed Willy Inman sitting on the couch and approached him.

Morrison stated that Willy asked if law enforcement could determine the age of blood. Morrison replied that they could.

FBI agent Michael Daugherty's job was to decipher the route logged into the GPS that was taken from the Inman home. Daugherty looked at the specific period of March 21 to 23 to see where the GPS had traveled.

According to the GPS, the Inman family arrived at the Lake Logan parking lot at 5:45 p.m. on March 22 -- the night Summer disappeared -- and drove around Logan until 8:07 p.m. when the GPS unit was turned off at the Walmart in Logan. During that period, they stopped at St. John Catholic Church and Oak Grove Cemetery for approximately 20 minutes.

The GPS was turned back on at 11:36 p.m. in Nelsonville, Daugherty noted. They then traveled north through the Wayne National Forest and briefly stopped at a car wash in Dunken Falls before traveling along the Muskingum River, crossing a bridge and traveling north to their home in Akron from there. The vehicle stopped on Interstate 480 around 4 a.m. but also included stops at Pearl Road Auto Parts, Blu Sonic Car Wash, a McDonald's and Speedway.

FBI agent David O'Connor was also present at the Akron home. According to him, he helped perform surveillance on the home and then interviewed Bill Inman, in the kitchen. Willy and Sandra were interviewed in separate rooms.

O'Connor said Bill Inman did not seem overly nervous during the interview. Anytime the FBI interviews someone, they are generally nervous, and Inman did not fit into that category, he said.

During this time, Bill again claimed the family vehicle was broke down on a Cleveland area freeway, and the family slept in the car that night. When O'Connor questioned how no one stopped to assist them, despite being broken down along Interstate 480, a heavily traveled roadway, he said, Bill Inman replied that about eight police cars had passed him. The agent disbelieved the story.

Bill Inman claimed that because of his son's and Summer's separation, their only communication was between their attorneys. Bill also admitted he disliked Adam Peters. There were allegations that Adam had struck one of the grandchildren which angered Bill Inman.

Numerous items were found and seized, including black hoodies, a black backpack, a .45 caliber government firearm, a 9mm Beretta, magazines for both guns, one switchblade, one sheath knife, cell phones, computer and all of its equipment, two vacuum cleaners, a GPS, and miscellaneous receipts. Everything seized was sent to BCI.

A tip hotline was soon established for all information. Residents were asked to search their properties for any strange findings, such as clothing. Civilian search parties were out in force, knocking on doors around the Century National Bank area to see if anyone saw or heard anything strange.

One place the FBI were said to be interested in was Faith Tabernacle since there was a river running behind it.

Soon several helpful but disturbing clues were gathered based on the coordinates of the GPS. The Inmans were seen on videos swapping new tires from the Crown Victoria for used tires at Pearl Road Auto and Salvage in Cleveland, Ohio, two hundred miles from Logan.

Richard Lenz, who had worked at Pearl Road Auto Parts, told Agent Porini that a man fitting Bill Inman's description traded new aluminum wheels and tires from a white Crown Victoria for used tires. He thought it was unusual, but that was exactly what happened.

Agent Porini also visited Pearl Road Auto Parts and the Blu Sonic Car Wash on Orchardview Avenue in Seven Hills, Ohio, because the GPS taken from the home indicated the family had stopped there. There was no sign of Summer Inman in the surveillance video showing the Inman family cleaning their vehicle. The video was retrieved by Porini after he contacted the manager.

According to the car wash video, The Inmans had utilized the car wash at 7:30 a.m. the morning after the kidnapping where they thoroughly cleaned the inside and outside of a Crown Victoria.

Bill Inman was seen removing the police spotlight off the car and transferring the temporary license plate from the rear windshield to the rear bumper. Sandra was seen spraying down the backseat with what appeared to be a cleaning chemical and towel.

A second video from a car wash in McConnelsville, Ohio, showed the Inmans again completely cleaning out the Victoria.

Bill Inman's twisted love for control and power over others, combined with Willy's jealousy over Summer, was their downfall. Believing they had enough evidence to connect the Inmans with Summer's disappearance, all three Inmans were then arrested Thursday, March 24. They again denied any involvement.

They were extradited to Hocking County to face kidnapping and abduction charges. The next day, FBI released footage from inside the Century National Bank. Investigators wanted the public to have a detailed description of Summer's physical appearance and of the clothing she was wearing on the night of her disappearance.

According to Adam Peters, she wore blue jeans and his black T-shirt with white writing on it, saying, "I don't have an anger problem, I have an idiot problem."

Pastor King Kelly told investigators he and the congregation were all shocked by the abduction of Summer and the arrest of the Inmans. He said church members all respected the Inmans and "thought highly" of them. As much as he liked Bill, Pastor Kelly said he had noticed a change in recent years. "One day he got it in his head he was called to preach and simply left."

By March 27, the search had expanded into five counties with police divers searching the nearby Lake Logan and other bodies of water. Police using cadaver dogs scoured the countryside, looking for any signs of Summer. Nothing was discovered.

The next day, another Logan resident told police he saw the Crown Victoria in Logan in the early evening hours of March 22. He said three persons fitting the Inmans' description were inside the vehicle. He also personally knew Summer and knew of her and Willy's ongoing battle over the couple's children.

The afternoon of March 30 found all three Inmans facing individual kidnapping and abduction charges in Hocking County Municipal Court. They appeared before Judge Thomas Gerken, who held a respectable thirty-three years of legal experience under his belt. All three prisoners wore jailhouse orange with their wrists, ankles and mid-sections shackled.

All three pled not guilty, and bail was set at one-hundred-thousand dollars each. Immediately after the hearing, they were transported to Southeastern Ohio Regional Jail, or SEORJ, a five-county holding facility.

Grief-stricken friends and relatives crowded the courtroom that Wednesday to witness the proceedings.

As a teary-eyed Sandra entered the courtroom, she was seen telling Summer's family she was sorry. Many who witnessed the show later told the media they disbelieved the apology, calling Sandra's performance "bad acting."

Described as "relatively mild" by a courtroom reporter during Sandra and Willy Inman's hearing, that was not the case for the father-in-law. During Bill's arraignment, he was seen smirking and mumbling under his breath while the charges against him were read.

Gasps and signs of disgust were heard from spectators, when Bill gave his address as being "the Southeastern Ohio Regional Jail" instead of giving a home address.

Once his arraignment ended, Bill was bombarded with questions from waiting reporters, like "Where's Summer?" "Is Summer dead?" "Did you kill Summer?"

Walking with his head down, Bill adamantly told reporters, "I didn't do a thing to Summer."

Pastor Kelly was present that day, telling reporters Bill helped build parts of the church, transforming a roadhouse called the Scenic Inn when Kelly bought the building in 1978 and turned it into a house of God. Up until a few years earlier, Bill was a member. "They were nice, generous people," Kelly said.

Those turned away stood outside waiting for the results. Some held posters with messages such as "Justice will be served" and "How could you take that mommy from her babies?"

Shouting and cursing at Sandra was heard, directing her attention to the posters. According to some by-standers, the now dubbed "heartless mother-in-law" had the look of fear smeared across her now aged and pale-looking face when she exited the building. After her hearing, she was seen covering her face as she was whisked away by armed guards to the jail van.

It was reported that none of the Inmans would talk with police. A local woman named Sylvia, a habitual drunk driver and cellmate to Sandra, claimed Sandra admitted she and her husband and son kidnapped Summer due to the ongoing custody battle. According to Sylvia, when she asked Sandra why she would do such a thing, Sandra said, "She'll never hurt anyone else again," referring to Summer denying Sandra and Bill visitation rights to their grandchildren.

Although Summer was frightened of her husband, her father-in-law terrified her. In December 2012, Summer brought a deputy to the Hamden residence while she attempted to gather her and her children's belongings. When Adam Peters arrived, Bill Inman threatened to kill him, inciting a physical altercation between the deputy and Bill Inman. The officer tasered Bill before arresting him and transporting him to SEORJ. He was convicted of resisting arrest and disorderly conduct, receiving probation.

Summer's cousin, Kimberly, who lived with Summer and the Inmans in Florida, saw firsthand how dominating the Inmans were. From her observations, the Inman men required their women to abide by their rules with divorce not an option.

She said the Inman men controlled everything the women did, such as what time Summer and Sandra were allowed to eat, what time they could sleep. She said she and her husband moved back to Logan to get away from the Inmans because they could not deal with the way the Inmans mistreated Summer.

Even those unfamiliar to Summer wished for her safe return by starting a "Help Find Summer Cook" Facebook page. Its purpose was to make people aware of Summer's disappearance.

News of the disappearance even made nationally known "Nancy Grace" take notice. She stated that she was appalled by the abduction, broadcasting the disappearance twice.

A big break in the case came on March 28th and 29th, when an SEORJ inmate told Police Chief Miller that Bill Inman confessed to him that police would never find Summer's body as long as "'Willy and Sandra kept quiet.'"

However, staying quiet was not easy for Sandra, and on the afternoon of March 29, Bill received a letter from her stating she was going to make a full confession. After reading the letter, according to jail guards, Inman began sobbing and said, "'I wish we hadn't done it. I wish I hadn't helped my son out. We're all dead now.'"

Deputy Peck conducted the 35-minute interview with Sandra in the presence of Sandra's court-appointed attorney, William Henderson, and Assistant Prosecutor Bill Archer.

Peck later wrote in his report that he believed Sandra was 90 percent truthful in her confession. He claimed she seemed to remember the small details of the crime and was vague about the large details, or made contradictory statements, such as who forced Summer into the Crown Victoria and who drove the car. Peck said he also felt Sandra was trying to minimize the extent of her husband's involvement. She initially said Willy was the only person forcing Summer into the car, but that did not coincide with witness statements.

Sandra stated that her husband and son planned to kidnap Summer to talk to her about the custody of Summer and Willy's children but did not plan to kill her. She said she and her husband and son wanted the grandchildren on the weekends, but Summer would not have it. As far as Sandra was concerned, Summer was being completely irrational about visitation rights.

She said her son Willy was alone in the back seat of the car with Summer from the bank to the church. He continuously told Summer he loved her, but still he placed a zip tie around her neck, causing her death.

Afterward, he panicked, asking for a knife to cut it off. Sandra described the look in her son's eyes afterward. "He had the look of total fear, shock, and 'oh my God, what have I done?'" she said.

Sandra told the group they would find Summer's body in the septic tank behind Faith Tabernacle. She said she originally suggested they place Summer's body in the Hocking River behind the church, but her husband thought it would eventually surface and be discovered.

John Durst, an agent of the Ohio Bureau of Criminal Identification and Investigation, was notified and met fellow investigators and Pastor King Kelly at the crime scene.

Once he arrived at Faith Tabernacle Church, he conducted an investigation of the area. According to him, there was nothing he observed during the process of the scene that a murder had occurred there.

Durst took note of the clothing that Summer was wearing when lifted out of the septic tank, including a shirt, jacket, jeans, belt, socks, and a purse still attached to her arm because of the zip ties wrapped around her wrists.

Durst also noticed that it appeared someone had peeled out from the parking lot of the church in a hurried fashion when they left, based on the tire marks left behind and photographed. The tire tracks were located on the back of the church on the east side and ended approximately 10 to 15 feet from the septic tank in the southwest corner.

The police noticed that there was a slope on the west side of the church where the septic tank was located, yet the individuals driving the vehicle drove on the east side of the church and behind, suggesting familiarity with the location.

Officers reported that they removed several one-inch screws from the septic tank cover in order to reach the body. She was dropped into the tank headfirst. "It was a gruesome and heartbreaking sight," said Durst.

Law enforcement from Hocking and Athens County, along with the FBI, collected evidence. Also present was the Athens county coroner, the York Township Volunteer Fire Department, and an employee of Cardaras Funeral Home.

Durst said he saw a socked foot floating in the septic tank with what appeared to be a zip tie or "quick handcuffs" bound around her ankles.

Scaled photography and castings of tire impressions found at the crime scene were conducted. Shoe impressions were also found near the septic tank, but there was not enough detail for any viable usage.

That area had been scoured just two days earlier, due to the building being on US 33, a logical travel route for the kidnappers.

Summer was positively identified by her driver's license found in her back pocket as well as from several other items within her purse, still attached around her arm. Photographs of the body were then taken. The same zip tie that bound her ankles was used to bind her hands behind her back and was around her neck. "From the ligature around her neck, it was obvious she was killed very quickly," said Agent Durst.

When the find was televised, an outcry of hate was issued throughout networking agencies, with many saying, "Death is not enough for people like the Inmans!"

Deputy Cain said he was not surprised when he learned of Summer's kidnapping and murder. From his experience with the Inmans, he said it was obvious Bill was the leader, like their King, saying, "Sandra and Willy are blinded by loyalty and Bill is blinded by rage."

The county coroner ruled the official cause of death as being "ligature strangulation," the device being a zip tie.

The ME believed Summer was killed about "forty-five minutes" after her abduction, with her being in the septic tank the entire time she was missing. He said her body also showed signs of multiple bruising and abrasions, indicating a "violent struggle."

Kristin Slaper, a forensic scientist with the Ohio Bureau of Criminal Investigation, tested for DNA on several items that were collected as evidence, including the ball cap, the back of a cell phone, the Mountain Dew bottle, a cigarette butt, septic tank lid and screws, and zip ties.

She noted that the only item that contained Bill Inman's DNA was the ball cap, which also contained the DNA of his grandson. One item not tested was the zip tie cut from Summer's neck. Slaper testified that after meeting with her supervisor, technology coordinator, and prosecutors working the case, it was determined that the zip ties should not be tested for DNA because they had been inside a septic tank with sewage from multiple individuals. She claimed testing the zip ties would have yielded DNA results from a myriad of different people.

Those who attended Faith Tabernacle were torn. Many parishioners reportedly knew both families involved. Pastor Kelly said Willy Inman celebrated his sixteenth birthday at the church.

After the discovery of the body, two more witnesses came forward. A Nelsonville Subway Manager said he was on duty the evening of March 22. He told investigators every Tuesday night he had paperwork to submit to headquarters after the computer shut down at 10 p.m. He recalled having problems submitting the report that evening which caused him to be late leaving for his home, which was in Logan.

He recalled speeding down the road toward Logan around 11:30 p.m., when he passed the Faith Tabernacle. He said he noticed what he believed to be a white police car and slowed down. He said he got a good look at the car. He noticed the car was angled toward Logan and was the same model as some police cruisers.

A female Logan resident recalled seeing a white car at Faith Tabernacle around midnight on March 22. The car was backed in "catty-corner" to the church. It being so close to the building was why it caught her eye, she said. "I've never seen a car back up to the church like that," she said in her statement. She looked three or four times, it was parked so strangely.

She recalled the headlights were off, and the front of the vehicle pointed toward Logan. She said she saw the vehicle clearly because the church was well lit and there was a full moon that night. She remembered there were "two dark-haired men" standing by the back door of the church with the doors open, and a "petite blonde-haired woman" sat behind the driver's seat.

On March 31, Debra and Mike Cook were awarded temporary custody of Summer's children. Debra told the judge that living with her and her husband would be in the best interest of her grandchildren.

Willy Inman declined to participate in the hearing but listened to the proceedings by speakerphone. He waived his right to fight for custody and surrendered his parental rights for the very children he killed for.

That same week, Worthington Park held a wake for Summer with over 1,000 in attendance. The event was organized by a past classmate of Summer's. Many were friends, but most never knew the victim. They brought food, money, and clothing for the Inman children.

In Summer's memory, pink and green balloons, her favorite colors, were released by the hundreds at 3 p.m. The releasing of balloons was their way saying Summer is gone but not forgotten.

Later that evening, services at the First Church and Worship Center centered on remembering Summer and her smile, described by some as 'medicine.' The next day, April 5, mournful weather blanketed the skies. The gloomy atmosphere was befitting for the funeral of Summer Dawn Cook Inman.

Several community members attended the Monday afternoon service conducted by Reverend Martin. In attendance were Summer's three young children, her parents, fiancé, friends, strangers and other family members. Summer was interred at New Fairview Memorial Gardens in Rockbridge.

Memorial contributions were being accepted through the Summer Inman Fund at Century National Bank, along with an online guestbook signing available through Cardaras Funeral Home.

April 9th brought another fund raiser for Summer's children, sponsored by the Trinity United Methodist Church, as well as a show of support by many by changing their Facebook profile pictures to candles or pink and green ribbons that read "Justice."

Another mind-blowing incident by Sandra Inman occurred on April 13 when she changed her plea from not guilty to not guilty due to insanity. Her attorneys alleged she was incompetent to stand trial and insane at the time of the murder. A mental evaluation was ordered.

On May 20, 2013, the grand jury indicted Bill and Willy Inman on one count each of aggravated murder and one count each of murder, tampering with evidence and gross abuse of a corpse, along with their original charges of kidnapping and abduction. The case was indicted with capital specifications. Both pled not guilty, and the state sought the death penalty. Their bail was raised to one million dollars each.

Due to Sandra's competency hearing, she was not charged at that time with Summer's murder.

In late May, Doctor Jaime Lai, Psy.D, a clinical and forensic psychologist, found Sandra competent to stand trial. A trial date hearing was ordered, but on June 13, Sandra attempted suicide by jumping from the second level of an indoor common area at the SEORJ. She was treated at the nearby Nelsonville hospital, then released and returned to her cell. A suicide note was discovered in her cell, but the contents were never released.

Attorney Henderson then filed a motion for a second competency evaluation. On June 30, Sandra was moved to the Appalachian Behavior Mental Health Center in Athens. That facility also deemed Sandra competent. Sandra's attorney claimed she was insane at the time of the offense and motioned for Sandra to be examined a third time with a doctor of their choosing. Even though the motion would stall the proceeding of the trial, Judge Gerken granted the motion. Later that same month, Judge Gerken retired, turning the case over to new replacement John T. Wallace.

Judge Wallace was tall, slim, and sported wavy brown hair and blue eyes. He had served as Hocking County Municipal Court judge since 2006. He received his undergraduate degree from the University of South Carolina and his J.D. from Cleveland-Marshall College of Law at Cleveland State University.

On August 16th, Sandra filed a motion requesting Judge Wallace to recuse himself from the case since it was he who signed the search warrants issued on the Akron, Ohio, home owned by the Inmans. The motion was denied.

The month of September brought more legal problems for Sandra. According to Prosecutor Fetherolf, Sandra did not fulfill her part of the agreement in order to have the charges dropped against her by divulging the full details of the crime. Sandra was then charged with murder, tampering with evidence, and gross abuse of a corpse along with the charges of kidnapping and abduction.

Sandra pled not guilty by reason of insanity on those charges also. She was then released from the Appalachian Behavior Mental Health Center, returned to the SEORJ, and bail was raised to a million dollars.

A friend of Sandra's attended her hearing, saying, "If Sandra murdered anyone, she was forced. The Inman men completely control their women."

Little was heard from Bill Inman until September 20 when he motioned that he be allowed sackcloth and ashes for a religious ceremony at SEORJ. He requested a complete set of white garments to wear while praying and fasting as Ecclesiastes 9:8 directs of the devout: "Let they garments always be white, and let thy head lack no ointment." His court-appointed attorneys Andrew Stevenson and K. Robert Toy cited "the denial to freely practice religion is, and will continue to be, a denial of one's right to freely practice his religion."

According to religious leaders, sackcloth and ashes are biblical symbols of mourning or repentance. When asked whether Bill Inman's request for sackcloth and ashes was an admission of guilt, Bill's attorney said "no," claiming Bill was a devoutly religious man engaged in preaching with religion a large part of his life.

The next day, Willy Inman motioned for the exact same religious rights. He also quoted Ecclesiastes 9:8 as the reason.

Willy attended his motion hearing in jailhouse orange and shackles. He had allowed his once well-groomed hair to grow shaggy and now sported a full beard. His request was also granted.

Bill Inman made the front page of *The Logan Daily*

News again on September 29 when he was segregated from other inmates at the jail due to a disciplinary action stemming from his throwing toilet water containing fecal matter and urine on a jailhouse guard. The segregation lasted thirty days, with Bill kept in solitary confinement for twenty-three hours a day. Only minimum items are allowed the inmate such as his blanket, sheet, and Bible. His community items were removed as were his television privileges and phone calls with relatives. He was only permitted to speak and have visits with his clergy and attorneys.

In September, Bill Inman received his change of venue when his defense team learned prospective jurors knew the facts of the case and had decided the question of his guilt. Bill's trial would be held in Ross County, forty miles from Logan, and scheduled for January 10, 2014.

His trial was moved to Chillicothe after attempts to seat an impartial jury in Hocking County in September were unsuccessful. A rumored three-hundred-fifty jurors would visit the Ross County Fairgrounds in three separate shifts to fill out questionnaires about their personal history, opinions about the death penalty, and how much they read or viewed about the case in the media. Jurors who were not dismissed for vacation or medical excuses after completing the questionnaires would return to court for individual questioning by the judge, prosecution and defense on January 15, 2014.

Four jurors would be interviewed each hour until there was a pool of approximately 60 jurors. Following additional questioning, 12 jurors and 4 alternates would be chosen and, once selected, Inman's trial would begin. Hocking County Common Pleas Court Judge John Wallace and his court staff would administer the trial in Ross County, and Wallace explained that once a jury was seated, there would be two parts to the trial.

The first part would determine whether Inman was guilty of a crime, and the second part will take place only if Inman was convicted of aggravated murder with the death penalty specification. If the second part takes place, the trial would enter the mitigation phase, and jurors must then decide if the death penalty was an appropriate sentence based on a number of different factors. Other sentences besides the death penalty could include life in prison without the possibility of parole, life in prison with the possibility of parole after 30 years, and life in prison with the possibility of parole after 25 years.

December 8 brought Doctor Lai attempting to complete her report of Sandra's mental condition at the time of the offense. The evaluation was delayed when Sandra admitted to swallowing 100 pills that morning. She was taken to a nearby hospital to have her stomach pumped. Lai's report was finally completed later that month with her finding Sandra competent at the time of Summer's murder.

In January 2014, when Judge Wallace attempted to set a trial date, Sandra's attorneys asked that the ruling be postponed, allowing them to file a motion to dismiss all charges against her due to a violation of Sandra's speedy trial rights.

Wallace overruled Henderson's motion, stating, "Almost all of Sandra Inman's trial delays are attributed to the many motions and requests for evaluations that Ms. Inman filed." He then scheduled a trial date.

What some believed to be another stall was granted on April 9. In a handwritten motion, filed by Sandra Inman from her cell, she asked for new court-appointed counsel citing her attorneys had not supplied her with requested information about her case and she did not trust them.

According to Sandra's attorneys, Sandra was uncooperative.

On the one-year anniversary of Summer's murder, friends and family gathered for a candlelight vigil at 7:30 p.m. at Worthington Park to honor her memory. This event was so far the largest turnout connected to this heinous crime. In May, Hocking County Commissioners earmarked $100,000 out of a contingency fund containing $200,000 to cover the costs of the first two trials. The money was originally allocated for the trial of Bill Inman; however, his trial would now require much more than originally estimated.

June 6, 2013, was the first day of Willy Inman's week-long trial. The state presented nearly thirty witnesses and more than one-hundred-ninety pieces of evidence.

Doctor Brian Douglas Casto, a forensic scientist with the Montgomery County Coroner's Office, testified to the condition of Summer's body. He stated that the zip tie pulled around her neck was so tight that a pair of wire cutters was needed to remove it. He held up the zip ties that had been logged into evidence and identified them as the ones he removed from Summer's body.

Concerning the backpack found in the Akron home, Detective Frank Harrah admitted on cross-examination by the defense that there were no identifying marks on the outside of the backpack, and no forensic analysis was conducted to determine the owner. Harrah also admitted that a stun gun was not found inside the home or in any of the vehicles searched.

Special Agent Mark Koller, a member of the Special Investigation Unit of the Ohio Bureau of Criminal Investigation, testified. That department assists local law enforcement with major crimes. He was asked to process three vehicles which were parked in the driveway of the Inman home.

After describing the process used to collect forensic evidence from the vehicles, Koller noted that the Ford Crown Victoria was of particular interest because the inside of it was particularly clean while the outside of it was dirty in comparison.

He said muddy handprints on the exterior of the car indicated that the car may have become stuck in the mud, and it appeared people pushed on the vehicle in an effort to free it. Despite the muddy handprints located on the exterior of the car, though, there were no fingerprints located inside. Koller said, "This is the only one where I can recall off-hand that was too clean to obtain fingerprints on the interior." He claimed that during his career, he had collected evidence from approximately 100 vehicles.

The exterior of the vehicle was a different story, he said, as 25 areas of fingerprints were located, which was an unusual amount.

Evidence collected from the interior of the car included drinking cups from various gas stations and fast food restaurants, a cigarette butt, a black belt, a black nylon case similar to those used to hold stun guns, and a red cap. Also found was a prescription pill bottle with Willy Inman's name on it. The prescription was for Phentermine HCL, an appetite suppressant.

Jurors were shown on a large projection screen photographs of Summer taken shortly after her body was retrieved from the septic tank, including close-ups of the zip ties that were on her arms and around her neck.

The day of jubilation for Summer's friends and relatives came when Willy Inman was found guilty on all six counts. The jury of six men and six women took only three-and-a-half hours to unanimously reach the guilty verdict. The jury found him guilty of specifications that make him eligible for the death penalty, including the act being committed with "prior calculation and design."

Summer's family momentarily cheered when the first guilty verdict was read for aggravated murder, then the guilty verdicts kept coming. Next would be the mitigation phase.

The defense never called any witnesses, and Willy did not take the stand in his own defense. Willy's paternal grandmother was present throughout the trial and wept openly and often. She was one who was very angry of the guilty verdict and vented her hostility toward the defense's "sloppy and amateurish job" once outside the courtroom.

One of Summer's aunts spoke on behalf of her family. She said they were all very relieved that Willy was found guilty. "It doesn't bring Summer back, but I feel such relief," she told reporters. She described Willy's relationship with Summer as "scary," although Summer gave him "several chances" to mend their crumbling marriage.

During the mitigation phase on June 14, Willy's only witness was forensic psychologist William Stinson, who told the court, "Willy never became his own person. He was never his own thinker, or had his own plans."

According to Willy, as long as he and Sandra obeyed his father's choices, everything was fine. The doctor claimed Willy spent his life in the grip of a "controlling father and an indulgent mother."

He described Willy as having an arrested development. He said Willy stopped maturing emotionally and developmentally "so that he was very much a child" in that regard.

What Doctor Stinson said made little difference to the jury, for they unanimously decided Willy Inman deserved life in prison without parole. The jurors claimed mitigating factors outweighed aggravated circumstances as the reason they dismissed the death sentence.

One juror said the decision to forgo the death penalty was "hard." She said the photographs of Summer's body when removed from the septic tank was "horrific." The factor that brought it to a head, she said, were the GPS coordinates, Willy's lies to police, and his cell phone that placed him in Logan during the time of the abduction. "The majority of us felt like he took someone's life from them, so why should he have any part of his life," she said.

Believing one part of the Inman trial was over and residents could find closure, they found they were mistaken. On June 27, Willy filed a motion for a new trial alleging prosecutors failed to disclose information about a witness's prior felony conviction of sexual gross imposition from 1999. This new finding contended the defense might have cast doubt on the reliability of the witness. Two weeks later, the motion was denied.

Then just days after her only child was sentenced to spend the rest of his natural life behind bars, Sandra pled guilty to all charges relating to her involvement in Summer's death.

She sat beside her new court-appointed attorney, and wept as her counsel spoke for her. Kristen Burkett told the court Sandra helped kidnap Summer because her three grandchildren accused Summer and Adam Peters of abusing them. "Sandra honestly believed she was helping her grandchildren when Summer was kidnapped," said Burkett to the court. Sandra was then sentenced to 15 years to life in prison. Summer's family accepted the plea deal.

On August 16, Bill Inman was involved in a physical fight over a television with a much younger inmate and sustained minor facial injuries. No charges were filed against either man.

On August 21, he was back in court, asking for the state to remove the death penalty as a possible punishment if he were convicted. His attorney, Andrew Stevenson, contended that a plea deal prosecutors made with Sandra Inman prevented the state from pursuing the death penalty against him. Their main witnesses at that hearing were Attorney William Henderson and Kristen Burkett.

Both Henderson and Burkett testified that Sandra upheld her end of the original plea agreement, providing both details of Summer's murder and the location of the body, as well as pleading guilty to murder and kidnapping.

Prosecutor Laina Fetherolf, Paul Scarsella, and the Hocking County deputy Sandra confessed to disagree. They alleged Sandra reneged on her deal by withholding evidence and did not fully disclose the details of the murder.

According to Andrew Stevenson, Sandra told authorities 151 case facts they had not previously known about, including that Summer was murdered, the location of her body, who was responsible for her death and where the crime took place. The Judge ruled in favor of the State and upheld the death penalty stipulation. According to court records, the trials of Sandra and Willy Inman cost Hocking County taxpayers $154,065.

On December 10, 2013, Bill Inman sat with his attorneys in Ross County Common Pleas Court. It was the last scheduled omnibus hearing prior to the start of his trial.

After a thirty-minute conference with Prosecutor Fetherolf, Paul Scarsella, and the defense attorneys in judge's chambers, Judge Wallace called the issues being discussed on the record "rather mundane."

Discussed during the ten minutes of the hearing included both sides agreeing for potential jurors to fill out their questionnaires at the Ross County Fairgrounds to accommodate the large number of potential jurors.

When January rolled around, there were still no plea deals offered for Bill Inman. The prosecution said they were eager for trial. Unlike his wife, Bill had no problems with his counsel, telling Judge Wallace he was receiving adequate representation.

Hocking County was responsible for the mileage for the court staff traveling to Ross County each day. The juror fee in Ross County was twenty dollars per day during trial, which was less than the forty dollars Hocking County pays.

In terms of security, Bill Inman stayed in the Ross County jail facility throughout the duration of the trial. That arrangement made it more feasible for Hocking County than if he were transported daily from one county to the other.

January 28th opened with the now forty-eight-year-old Bill Inman's trial. Dressed in a grey suit and red tie, the defendant was now described by one reporter as "the quiet rabbit." He no longer jeered or snickered at the judge or prosecutor as he did during his past court appearances. He obviously now understood the seriousness of it all.

When defense attorney Andrew Stevenson delivered an opening statement, he agreed with the majority of evidence against him. The defense now admitted that although Bill Inman made the foolish decision of helping his son kidnap Summer, her murder was not Bill's intention but a horrible mistake.

The defense reminded the jury that it was Willy who actually placed the zip tie around Summer's neck, causing her death, a fact that ended with the incarceration of Willy and Sandra months earlier.

Attorney Stevenson informed the jury that he was not going to debate to whether or not his client was at the scene of the murder. According to Stevenson, the issue was, did Bill Inman want Summer Inman killed, and did he help plan the murder? He told the jury his client's intent that day was to talk with Summer about the upcoming divorce, saying, "That's what your focus should be on." He adamantly denied his client wanted or participated in the murder.

Stevenson contended that the prosecution wanted the jury to conclude that "they," the Inman family, killed Summer, but that was not the case, he said. Only Bill Inman was on trial now. Sandra and Willy were convicted for their part of the crime. He asked the jury to focus on the evidence that would prove Bill Inman did not kill Summer. The prosecution contended that Bill Inman "helped place the zip tie around Summer's neck" to restrain her while in the car.

As with the previous trial, Debra and Mike Cook, along with Adam Peters, attended daily. During the testimony of Debra Cook and Adam Peters, Bill was seen shaking his head several times. That was said to be the only indication of emotion he displayed.

The witnesses in Bill Inman's trial were the same as in the first two. Numerous expert and civilian testimony was heard.

Jurors also viewed surveillance footage taken from the Blu Sonic Car Wash where the Inmans stopped to clean their vehicle before returning to their Akron home.

Defense attorneys argued that the Phillips screwdriver needed to remove the lid from the septic tank of Faith Tabernacle Church did not match the flat-head screwdriver that was recovered from William Inman's vehicle. That statement was intended to indicate reasonable doubt and to minimize Bill Inman's part in the crime. Officer Cluely admitted that no screwdriver fitting the septic tank lid was found on any of the Inmans or confiscated during any search and seizure.

On cross examination by the prosecution, the state argued that just like the missing screwdriver, Summer's shoes also were never recovered. However, it was known from the bank surveillance tape that she was wearing shoes when she left work.

When questioned by Paul Scarsella, Cluely indicated that it would be impossible to scour every inch of ground along the route the Inmans took from Nelsonville back to their home in Akron the following day to determine if shoes or a Phillips screwdriver was tossed out the window.

When asked if police searched different areas for the screwdriver, Cluely said "no," indicating the police would have no idea where to search. When asked to describe the clothing Summer was wearing when she was recovered from the septic tank, Cluely said she had on the exact same clothing she was seen wearing in the bank surveillance tape, being a jacket, a shirt that said 'I don't have an anger problem,' blue jeans, purse, underwear and bra. He said he did not know about her socks, but her shoes were missing, and she had her purse still on her arm.

When Kristin Slaper testified to her testing the various evidence, Stevenson commented that zip ties are interesting because they have little ridges. He said that if a person took someone's hand and ran it against those ridges, there was the possibility those skin cells would come off on the zip tie. He said that would explain that the DNA of the person who pulled the zip tie might have been embedded on the ridges.

Slaper said, from her knowledge of DNA, that would not be the case since the zip ties were in the septic tank. Stevenson than pointed out that it was not her job to "assume" but to analyze.

Under cross examination by Paul Scarsella, Slaper claimed it would be impossible to guarantee the accuracy of any DNA profile taken from any evidence collected from septic tank fluid.

Stevenson then pointed out that Slaper should have completed a DNA analysis just to view the results in case her belief was wrong. He pointed out that while DNA from multiple individuals may have been detected, it still could have warranted results.

Again, on redirect from Paul Scarsella, Slaper explained that if Stevenson had asked for the zip tie to be analyzed, she would have done so. That statement struck a nerve with Stevenson, who objected before Slaper had a chance to answer. When both sets of attorneys approached the bench, Stevenson was visibly upset and pointed his finger at Scarsella in an angry manner.

Defense attorney K. Robert Toy attempted to punch holes through one witness's claims of seeing the Inmans at the Faith Tabernacle Church the night Summer disappeared. Toy pointed out that the woman waited nine days after her "alleged" sighting to report her claims to police.

She admitted that she did not write down the time when she drove past the church and that she made a statement to police based on her memory several days later.

On Wednesday, January 30, the judge overruled a motion filed by the defense to allow a former Chief deputy of the Hocking County Sheriff's Office to testify about his and Sandra Inman's conversation when she directed authorities to Summer's body.

Sandra told the deputy it was her son who pulled the zip tie around Summer's neck causing her death. She adamantly claimed from the beginning that she and her husband did not kill or assist her son with the killing. The defense insisted that the deputy was a witness to Sandra's confession and should be allowed to testify.

In the final hour of court proceedings, the defense team filed several motions in a final effort to prove their client was not the individual responsible for pulling the zip tie that strangled Summer.

Wallace overruled the motion following

approximately 20 minutes of deliberation in judge's chambers. He did, however, allow the prosecution to argue that the defendant helped place the zip tie around Summer's neck but he must refrain from arguing that Bill Inman "pulled the zip tie."

Attorney Toy became enraged and, within seconds of the judge's ruling, filed a motion declaring that his client was denied access to a fair trial under the Sixth Amendment to the Constitution. The judge overruled that motion as well.

Stevenson then filed a motion for a mistrial because the state had not met its burden of proof to show the defendant was guilty of the aggravated murder and murder charges. Again, the motion was denied. Five minutes later, Stevenson appealed the judge's decision, and that, too, was denied.

The defense then rested its case after presenting 80 pieces of evidence and no witnesses.

The jurors were then instructed to pack a suitcase, as it was likely they would be sequestered at a hotel until a verdict was reached.

The State rested its case on January 31 after presenting 180 pieces of evidence and providing testimony from 25 witnesses.

Closing arguments on February 4 were as dramatic in Bill Inman's trial as were the trials of his wife and son.

Again, as in his opening statement, defense attorney Stevenson argued there was no prior calculation and design in Summer's death because it was horribly planned and poorly executed. According to Stevenson, Summer was killed by accident, and the decision to dump her body head first into the septic tank of Faith Tabernacle Church was poorly planned. The Inmans simply panicked once they realized Summer was dead.

Stevenson insisted there was no evidence that the

murder and septic tank were predetermined. There were never any witnesses who came forward with testimony that any of the Inmans discussed the septic tank, he said.

He insisted his client merely wanted to talk with Summer about the grandkids, accusing Adam Peters of abusing them. He described the killing of Summer as stupid, moronic, reckless, but accidental also, saying Willy Inman did something terrible, tragically wrong, and in ten seconds, Summer was dead. Now the family was in a panic. They had a dead body with them. It was dark, and the adrenaline was pumping. Everyone was screaming at one another. Willy was freaking out.

He described the Inmans that evening as driving away from Logan scared and frightened. Then they saw the church they once attended, and where does someone feel safe at, Stevenson asked. He insisted that if the Inmans had planned the murder ahead of time, they would have gotten away with it. Their mistakes and being caught proves there was no premeditation on Bill Inman's part and, therefore, he was innocent of murder.

Paul Scarsella delivered the closing argument in the trial that ended as quickly as the previous two trials did. He claimed there was no doubt that Bill Inman was one of two men who forced Summer Inman into a vehicle, which ultimately led to her death. He called the killing "premeditated and with prior calculation."

He reminded the jury that the law and its definition of aggravated murder states that it does not matter which of the three put the zip tie around Summer's neck. He insisted that all three had that purpose, and all three helped in that purpose, therefore, all three are guilty. He claimed Bill Inman had murder on his mind that evening when he helped force Summer into the back seat of that car to the point that she screamed so loudly that a witness said it sounded like "someone was being murdered in the parking lot." Also, he helped pepper spray Richard Leake.

Scarsella told the jury that Summer went unwillingly, as attested by her own screams, with her estranged husband and in-laws. He reminded the jury of the female joggers who heard Summer scream so loud, the screams echoed off one of the buildings as if "someone was being killed."

He reminded the jury that Summer was so concerned about her safety and so feared her husband and his parents that she insisted on texting either her mother or her boyfriend when she arrived at work, and then again as soon as she was ready to leave her workplace. She monitored herself because she feared what her husband and his parents would do to her, and her fears became reality.

Scarsella questioned claims made by the defense that the Inman family had only attempted to speak with Summer and not kill her. The jury heard about the abduction kit the Inmans had with them when they went to "just speak" with Summer: zip ties, Tasers, they were dressed in all black and described by one witness as "looking like Ninjas, or bank robbers." Scarsella said Bill Inman's claims of just wanting to speak with his daughter-in-law, whom he loathed, made no sense and was a lie.

Then at approximately 5:20 p.m., the jury returned with a guilty verdict on all six counts: two counts of aggravated murder, murder, kidnapping, tampering with evidence and abuse of a corpse.

While Judge Wallace read the verdicts, Bill Inman sat silently, consoled briefly by Andrew Stevenson placing his arm around him. That was only the second emotion Bill Inman showed throughout his trial.

According to Debra Cook, the family was very

"satisfied and relieved." She described the past two years of attending trials as "long."

Mike Cook told reporters that Bill Inman's sentence would not matter since they were simply pleased that he was found guilty. Many on Facebook replied that they also were content with the guilty verdict and that Bill Inman did not find a loophole and weasel his way out of a guilty verdict.

Few had doubts that Bill would get life without parole, and that was his sentence, handed down on February 6. During this time, the defense brought in three character witnesses.

Bill's sister, Tammy, detailed the gruesome and often torturous beatings that she and Bill endured at the hand of their father. She claimed no family member escaped unscathed, testifying to being beaten with their father's preferred weapon, a leather belt.

She recalled being struck three hundred times with the belt for sneaking out of her home once. Later she received an additional two hundred for the same offense. She recalled the latter incident due to the fact that her father suffered a heart attack during the second round of lashings.

On cross examination, Paul Scarsella called into question Tammy's credibility as a witness. Her arrest record for a prior heroin conviction and the fact that she had battled addiction for years made her testimony less believable. She admitted to her past indiscretions. She claimed Bill never relinquished his faith in her and prayed for her to overcome her addiction.

Larry McKinnes, Bill's stepfather, testified that Bill moved into his home with Sandra when he was eighteen, after high school graduation.

Larry described Bill as initially being very defensive

and guarded because of his abusive childhood. Only after Bill began attending church regularly did he grow into someone deeply rooted who cared for his family and church community.

He explained that shortly after moving in, Bill discovered he enjoyed working with his hands and became a self-taught carpenter who learned the trade by helping individuals construct new additions to their homes, built garages, and completed any construction task when asked.

Doctor James P. Reardon, a psychologist who completed multiple mental examinations on all three Inmans, described Bill Inman as having a strong faith and a strong belief in helping his family overcome all odds. This belief eventually caused him to snap and led to his murderous choices, said Reardon.

Reardon stated that Bill Inman felt the need to over-compensate for his own childhood by providing a better life for his son. That better life included providing for not only his son, Willy, but his grandchildren. Because of that deep-seated need to protect, when allegations of child abuse and neglect on the part of Summer's boyfriend were made, Bill felt powerless -- just as he did when he was an abused child being neglected by his father.

Bill did not want his grandchildren to experience the same mistreatment he had as a boy. So when authorities determined after their investigation that allegations against the boyfriend were unfounded, Bill made the devastating choice to take matters into his own hands.

Doctor Reardon said Bill admitted to having an overwhelming sense of powerlessness that awakened old memories from his own torturous childhood, which were too powerful to ignore. Bill had fought for so long to overcome the feelings he felt while living with his father that when he believed his grandchildren were in danger and being abused, he was compelled to act. In addition, when the allegations were determined to be unfounded, that was when the plan to kidnap Summer was hatched, the doctor testified.

Doctor Reardon's testimony, combined with attorney Toy's impassioned plea to spare Bill Inman's life, was enough for jurors to warrant Inman receiving a life sentence without the possibility of parole rather than the death penalty. The jury took just two hours to reach that decision. The entire trial was concluded.

During sentencing, Paul Scarsella and Laina Fetherolf read prepared statements from Debra Cook and Mike Cook Jr., Summer's brother, and her sister, Courtney Williams.

In Mike Cooks Jr.'s statement, he called Bill Inman a bully and a coward who terrorized and abused others who were either physically or emotionally weaker than he was. He said Bill looked to himself as big and strong, but all he did was destroy another person's life. He told Bill he was a "weak and pathetic excuse" for a human.

Mike Jr. then talked of Bill's supposed love and devotion to God, saying no man of God would ever inflict the amount of pain on so many lives as he had. He said a man of God showed love, compassion, and understanding, with a voice of reason. None of those virtues are ones Bill ever possessed, he said, telling Bill he dishonored and disrespected those who do possess such qualities.

He then described Summer as a butterfly, claiming her life around him was her caterpillar stage, breaking free from him and her cocoon, to find love again and become the butterfly she was meant to be.

Judge Wallace then sentenced Bill Inman to a prison term of ten years on the charge of kidnapping, three years for tampering with evidence and one year for abuse of a corpse. Those years will be served first, Judge Wallace noted, prior to the life without parole sentence on the two counts of aggravated murder and additional count of murder. According to *The Logan Daily News*, if future changes to Ohio law warrant sentencing structure reform, Bill's sentence would be difficult to change.

After sentencing, the Judge thanked the jurors for their time and efforts, telling them they did an admirable job. He then described the trial proceedings as a "long, unpleasant road" for the residents of Ohio, and especially for those living in Hocking County.

He went on to remind the court that Logan was one of the smallest counties in Ohio. With only four or five counties in Ohio smaller than Hocking County, he said that when one lives in a place like Logan, Ohio, one believed kidnapping or murders happened in large towns and one felt immune. However, "obviously we are not immune," he said, since it happened in Logan, Ohio. Whenever a sad event like this occurs, just like in a pond, it ripples out to everyone, he said. He named the many lives that were affected by the murder, saying he felt only sorrow concerning the entire matter.

In the courtroom hallway after the hearing, Summer's brother-in-law said the family was glad the trial was over, but at the same time, there was no way to find closure from the situation. He said family members were still very saddened by Summer's murder, but glad the trials were concluded so they can now move forward with their lives.

The jurors spoke with the prosecution and defense for forty minutes afterwards about why they chose life without parole. Both defense attorneys said they were grateful the sentence was not death. They believed Bill Inman would adjust to prison life and be a respectful prisoner at the Noble Correctional Institute in Caldwell.

Prosecutor Fetherolf told waiting reporters afterward that she does and has always felt that the death penalty was an appropriate option in this case. She called the jury conscientious and attentive and said she respected their decision. She said she was pleased that parole for Bill Inman was not an option so that the Cook family can move forward without that specter hanging over them.

According to *The Logan Daily News,* trouble seemed to follow Willy Inman to prison. Found inside the window sill of his cell during a routine inspection was a "shank." He shared a cell with several inmates but admitted the weapon was his when asked by one of the officers inspecting. Willy offered no explanation for the weapon but received a fifteen-day segregation, although there was one other prisoner inside the same cell.

Inmate #665-992 was found guilty of violating Rule 36 of the Prisoner Code of Conduct, which prohibited possessing any and all weapons.

Shortly after the violations hearing was concluded, rumors circulated that Willy was somehow sending his father, Bill Inman, a secret coded message. That rumor was squashed when the prison spokesperson explained that Bill Inman was not even in that prison.

Upon his release on February 16, Willy was placed in a close-security housing unit, which was one level higher than minimum security and one less than maximum.

The Death of Innocence

Home to Ohio University and Hocking College, Athens County, Ohio, was formed in 1805 and held a population of 64,753. Nestled deep in the Appalachian foothills of Southeast Ohio, its lively arts and music scene entertained locals and visitors alike all year round. The eclectic shopping and dining scene was a result of the presence of a large university and rich Appalachian heritage. Hunting, kayaking, bouldering, hiking, cycling, and mountain biking are some of the most popular outdoor activities.

Boasting more activities then ticks on a dog, the rare action the county was not proudly known for was cold-blooded murder. Monday, May 23rd, 2011, changed all that when the Athens County Emergency Medical Service received a call.

When the paramedics arrived at the three-bedroom trailer in the small community of The Plains, they were shocked at what they found. Four-year-old blue-eyed Kaylen Young was unresponsive with "suspicious marks" on her body and neck indicating physical abuse. The child's head and face were saturated with blood, making her long blonde hair almost unrecognizable.

She was rushed to the local O'Bleness Memorial Hospital, a private, not-for-profit hospital established in 1921. Even though O'Bleness Hospital was an acute-care facility offering the latest technologies and services with highly skilled, trained, and experienced healthcare professionals, it was not prepared for Kaylen's life-threatening injuries.

According to Athens County Sheriff, Pat Kelly, deputies were called to the hospital along with the Athens

County Children's Services.

Sheriff Kelly's biography on the Athens County Sheriff's Office website depicts the tall, stout, white-haired man with the receding hairline. Kelly was born in Nelsonville, Ohio, December 14, 1950. He and his wife raised five children. He came from a long line of peacekeepers and was on the board of numerous charities.

Once hospital staff realized the seriousness of Kaylen's injuries, she was flown to Nationwide Children's Hospital in Columbus, a 12-story, state-of-the-art hospital.

The only other persons known to be at the trailer during the apparent assault were twenty-five-year-old Ashley Young, Kaylen's stepmother, and Ashley's five-week-old daughter Allyza. Information gathered from neighbors indicated family friend, thirty-six-year-old Brandi Taylor arrived during the commotion. Brandi drove Ashley and her infant to the hospital as they followed the ambulance.

Moments after Kaylen left for the Columbus hospital, search warrants were executed for the Young home. Due to Kaylen's injuries, Ashley was taken into custody. She was transported to Southeastern Ohio Regional Jail, or SEORJ, and her infant was handed over to a Children's Services caseworker.

When Detective Sedgwick and other Investigators arrived, they easily located Ashley's cell phone she said she misplaced, the reason she gave for not calling 911.

According to 911, they received two calls about the Young residence that day from neighbors. Twenty-nine-year-old Sandy Kinnison told police she heard Ashley yelling for help, screaming, "She had a seizure. She had a seizure."

According to Sandy, when she entered the Young trailer, she saw Kaylen lying on the floor "like a broken angel." Her eyes were open but blank, and there was an apparent bruise on the side of her head. She described the trailer as "neat" with most of the family's belongings packed away. Ashley and Craig were in the process of moving, having been recently evicted for not paying rent, she said.

According to paramedics and investigators, the physical evidence told a very different and horrifying tale. Bits of Kaylen's hair scattered around the residence and the multiple injuries to her body suggested a violent altercation. Ashley told them Allyza was lying on the sofa in the living room when Kaylen fell and hit her head and suddenly began having seizures involving tremors. Young's husband, forty-two-year-old Craig Young, Kaylen's biological father, was at work.

Immediately Craig hired Columbus attorney Dennis W. McNamara to represent Ashley and to help him regain custody of his infant. Ashley refused to talk with Investigators.

Two days later proved to be the worst day for Kaylen and Ashley. According to a Nationwide Children's Hospital spokesperson, the child died without ever regaining consciousness. A brain scan was conducted and no brain activity was detected. Kaylen's biological mother, Crystal Westerviller, and father were present along with both sets of grandparents and other relatives.

Kaylen's parents made the devastating choice of removing their child from life support. She was pronounced dead at 12:50 p.m. on May 25, just three days before her fifth birthday. The child's body was removed to the Franklin County Coroner's Office. That medical examiner discovered several areas of the head, brain and skull which suffered damage.

Kaylen's paternal grandfather addressed the reporters before leaving the hospital. He explained that his son had lost almost everything -- his wife, his home and his first born. "Countless other lives are affected as well," he said. He said none of them would ever get to hear Kaylen say she loved them again or hear her wonderful giggle.

Her obituary stated that Kaylen Michelle Young was born May 30, 2008, in Athens. She attended The Plains Preschool, enjoyed the outdoors and spending time with family and friends. Kaylen's death, though tragic, was not without its own sliver of light. Her last gift was donating life to others as an organ donor.

Crystal Westerviller stated that a two-year-old boy in Arizona received Kaylen's heart. She said the boy's family contacted her to thank them. "I'm glad Kaylen's death was not completely useless," Crystal said. She said Kaylen lived on, and she would be happy knowing her organ gave life.

Crystal told the local news media that each year before Kaylen's birthday and Christmas, the two cleaned out Kaylen's toy box with Kaylen perfectly willing to donate the old toys to other kids. Crystal said Kaylen loved helping others. "She was very special. No doubt about it."

To add insult to injury, when Crystal Westerviller asked the public for help in paying for funeral expenses, she said money poured in, but some who offered to collect contributions kept the money.

In checking with Kaylen's relatives, Sheriff Kelly discovered very little of the money collected reached Craig Young who was in charge of funeral arrangements. To help with expenses, a charity softball game was held in Athens, and the money raised went to affray Kaylen's funeral expenses. Sheriff Kelly meanwhile announced to the *Athens Messenger* that he issued a public warning for anyone who would exploit a child's death for profit. He explained that type of behavior was considered theft by deception, saying if those responsible are located, there would be charges filed.

Services were held at Hughes-Moquin Funeral Home

with burial in New Marshfield Cemetery. Contributions were collected at the funeral home for expenses.

Besides her parents, her sisters, Allyza Young and Kearston and Kelsey Shiller survived Kaylen.

Kaylen's preschool teacher said she still pictured Kaylen walking down the hallways of The Plains Elementary. "Kaylen loved school," she said. She claimed if Kaylen had made it to the sixth grade, she would have run that school, describing the girl as an "alpha female."

Even persons who never met the cheerful, rambunctious girl attended the service. Some said they were shocked to read of Kaylen's death and could not fathom how it happened. Others said no matter what, there was nothing a child could do that would lead to a severe beating ending in death.

Detective Steve Sedwick was also present at the funeral. He talked further with Sandy Kinnison, who admitted she did not know Ashley Young well but recalled that weeks before Kaylen's death, Ashley began making the girl stay inside the trailer when she arrived home from preschool. She noted that Kaylen was forbidden to play outside anymore. She said she surmised that Ashley was a strict parent, but she did believe it odd that Kaylen was not allowed outside at all.

After talking with hospital personnel and residents at the trailer court, investigators immediately released an (APB) or All-Points Bulletin for Brandi. The Athens County Sheriff's Office believed she held answers about Kaylen's death. Authorities asked for the public's help by broadcasting the woman's photograph they received from the Ohio Bureau of Motor Vehicles as well as physical characteristics.

Detective Sedwick announced during a press conference that authorities believed Brandi frequented The

Plains, Athens, Nelsonville and Glouster areas. By June 2, the mystery woman was found when she came forward after learning of Kaylen's death. Brandi testified before the Athens Grand Jury, who handed down a superseding indictment against Ashley Young.

Brandi told the Grand Jury that Kaylen was a good child who loved to ride her motorcycle, or play dress up, or paint her fingernails and play with her Barbies. "She loved her Barbies," said Brandi. Nobody was allowed to touch the Barbie playhouse because Kaylen had the Barbies "just always a certain way."

On June 7, Ashley was arraigned in Athens County Common Pleas Court. She entered the courtroom in tears and wearing jailhouse orange. She pled not guilty to aggravated murder and child endangerment.

Assigned to the case was Assistant Prosecutor, thirty-one-year-old Keller Blackburn. The stout, dark-eyed and dark-haired man was running for re-election. He hailed from Nelsonville, Ohio, population 5,392, graduating from the Cleveland Marshall College of Law in 2006.

Ashley's attorney spoke for her, telling the court the same story Ashley gave to authorities and paramedics. Kaylen had a normal day on May 23. However, after returning home from preschool, she fell to the floor from a distance of no more than the height of a four-year-old. She suddenly appeared to undergo some type of seizure involving tremors.

Ashley Young said the child had gotten off the school bus around noon. Ashley picked her up from the bus stop and brought her back to the trailer as usual. Then around 4 p.m., Kaylen "didn't feel well and just collapsed and appeared to be having a seizure."

Attorney McNamara said, to his knowledge, the child had never experienced seizures before and recently was examined by a pediatrician.

When asked by Assistant Prosecutor Blackburn how Kaylen received the bruises around her neck and face area, neither Ashley nor her attorney had an answer.

According to Assistant Prosecutor Blackburn, Ashley Young "purposely caused the death of Kaylen Young by blunt force trauma to the head." He said the evidence would prove Ashley choked Kaylen and slammed her head onto the floor of their home with such force that an "imprint of Kaylen's head" was found in the carpet of the home.

According to the Ohio Revised Code, aggravated murder was a special felony and, if convicted at trial, Ashley faced life in prison, life in prison without parole, or death. Endangering children was a second-degree felony with a penalty of eight years in prison and a $15,000 fine.

Whether or not the home was in disarray did not matter to the prosecution, because a struggle was never determined. Sandra Kinnison told authorities that the home was neat and clean except for the family packing to move. Paramedics and investigators said differently.

After the indictment, Blackburn told waiting reporters he could have sought the death penalty since the victim was under the age of thirteen. He said the sheriff was in agreement to not seek the death penalty.

Blackburn said if he had credible evidence proving Ashley had a long history of abusing Kaylen, he might have sought the death penalty. Ashley was put under a million-dollar bail. According to the media, many in the local community expressed outrage over Kaylen's death.

Blackburn said he was aware of the public outcry to "burn" Ashley Young, but he said a prosecutor's job was to seek appropriate justice and to "take rage away from the decision-making process."

He said this case was the most heinous crime against

a child in the county's history, comparing it to *State v. Nguyen, 2013-Ohio-3170,* a violent rape case in 2010 that resulted in a man being sentenced to thirty years in prison.

When reporters canvassed the Young neighborhood, one neighbor commented about Kaylen recently getting a new baby sibling. He said it was terrible that Kaylen was ripped from her life at this point.

According to one mother whose daughter attended Kaylen's preschool, Kaylen had the biggest, most beautiful blue eyes. The woman claimed Kaylen could make one smile in no time. "She was always smiling. She was always laughing," the woman said.

When questioned by an Athens reporter, Kaylen's paternal grandmother said Kaylen was proud to be a big sister. From her home, which sat just blocks from Ashley and Craig's trailer, the woman said, "There are no words to describe the heartbreak, pain, and loss that we are experiencing."

On July 12, more charges were filed against Ashley. The new charges included felony murder, two counts of child endangering, one count of tampering with evidence, and one count of attempted aggravated possession of drugs.

The tampering with evidence charge stemmed from Ashley allegedly concealing the shirt worn by Kaylen the day of the assault. The drug charge was from Ashley's attempt to purchase Percocets.

According to Brandi Taylor, while following the EMS ambulance to the hospital, Ashley instructed her to a home to allow her to purchase the drug.

The day after Ashley's murder charge, Craig filed for divorce. The grounds were established as being Ashley's imprisonment and extreme cruelty. Craig also refused to continue paying for private counsel, and public defender fifty-seven-year-old Herman Carson took over the case. A tall, sturdy man, Attorney Carson wore glasses and sported a receding hairline.

Court records indicate one witness for the prosecution was Vickie Whitley, Kaylen's sometime babysitter. She told the media Kaylen was not much for television. She said the child sat only for a few minutes during a cartoon before she would be running around and playing.

When it came to her favorite foods, Vickie claimed Kaylen was not fussy but said Kaylen's father forbid her to have pop. It was funny, she said, because when Kaylen was at her house, she would share pop with her, and the minute Craig walked through the door, Kaylen gave her up and said, "Daddy, Vickie give me pop."

On September 8, Ashley and Craig's divorce was finalized. Craig was granted permanent custody of the couple's then four-month-old daughter.

The court ordered that, for Allyza's best interests, Ashley not allowed to have any kind of interaction with her once she was released from prison, including access to school records. Ashley was ordered to pay child support for each month once released from prison.

Due to the severity of the charges against Ashley, she was transferred to Appalachian Behavioral Healthcare in Athens on September 22 for a court-ordered evaluation by psychologist Jolie Brams.

Doctor Brams reported Ashley had an "immediate need for inpatient hospitalization." The only information released to the media was that Ashley would be returned to the Southeastern Ohio Regional Jail "when and if the staff of ABH determines her condition was stabilized." Ashley stayed less than a week at the mental facility and was returned to SEORJ. Doctor Brams deemed Ashley competent to stand trial.

On October 13, 2011, Attorney Carson filed a motion asking Judge Ward to find Ashley non-competent for trial.

According to the Athens *Messenger*, the Prosecutor agreed with Attorney Carson, saying sending Ashley to The Timothy B. Moritz Center in Columbus was essentially "like getting a second opinion on her competence." Attorney Carson then asked that her medical records be sealed.

When asked by reporters his opinion, Assistant Prosecutor Blackburn said he was confident that Ashley Young would stand trial once her competency was restored.

As the case against Ashley was under way, most returned to their mundane lives. Christmas 2012 was especially hard for Craig Young and his family. Craig's sister said each holiday brought back the realization that Kaylen was gone forever. For her, the tough part of Kaylen being gone was waking and realizing Kaylen was not around anymore, and never would be again.

She described how she and Craig gathered Kaylen's belongings and gave them to a local church. "All her little clothes. Her favorite toys. Bags and bags of things, we gave away," she said.

After approximately seven months of treatment at the Moritz Center, Ashley was ruled mentally competent for trial and returned to SEORJ on May 28, 2012. She then filed a plea of not guilty due to insanity.

According to court records, Attorney Carson hired private psychologist Doctor Richard Reardon for another opinion on Ashley's competency. The doctor met with her at SEORJ June 18, 2012. Doctor Reardon was a physician used by many held on felony charges.

Ashley told Doctor Reardon that after she left the Moritz Center and returned to SEORJ, she was removed from most of the medication she was prescribed while in the Moritz Center.

From that day's observation, Reardon believed Ashley's depression had significantly worsened. He described her as "very somber," saying she did not smile at any point during the time that the two talked.

Ashley told Doctor Reardon she felt as if she were in a box and could not show emotion. She felt she could not talk to anyone and was slipping downhill; she felt herself becoming more depressed. She said she felt as if she were going insane.

She claimed that while at the Moritz Center, she could work on things, saying at SEORJ there was nothing. "No good medical treatment."

The doctor reported that Ashley "was extremely upset and cried throughout the session." He noticed she had lost a significant amount of weight while at SEORJ. He considered it very likely that if her condition continued to deteriorate, it would reach a point where she could no longer assist her attorneys in her defense or participate meaningfully in her trial – the criteria for competence.

Just days later, they were in court again. Attorney Carson filed a motion asking the court to send Ashley back to the Moritz Center "so that her competency to stand trial can be maintained."

Called to testify about Young's competency was Doctor Reardon. He told the court of his examination of Ashley on June 18. He stressed the fact that Ashley was only ruled competent to stand trial after receiving approximately seven months of treatment for numerous disorders at Moritz Center. These treatments included post-traumatic stress disorder, poly-substance dependence, and adjustment disorder with depression. Her treatment included taking three psychotropic medications and regular counseling sessions from psychologists.

He told the court that at this time he believed Ashley

to be competent. He also believed her overall psychological condition had a bearing on her competence and had deteriorated significantly since the last time he talked with her, which was at the Moritz Center, and somewhat since his June 18 session with her.

When Judge Ward questioned Doctor Reardon about Ashley's mental capacity if she continued to stay at SEORJ or transferred to a mental facility such as Appalachian Behavioral Healthcare, Doctor Reardon said the Moritz Center would be the best location because Ashley was able to connect with the psychologists there.

The doctor stated his opinion to return Ashley to the Moritz Center was not a matter of her being comfortable. "I understand she's facing some serious charges, and to be honest, her comfort shouldn't be a primary concern," he said.

He said the Moritz Center had a remarkably competent staff who knew Ashley, and they could begin the stabilization process almost immediately. He said whether she was sent to Tri-Valley Mental Health or Appalachian Behavioral Health, there was going to be a lot more of a process involved.

On Wednesday, August 22, Judge Ward ruled Ashley was competent and would not be returned to any mental facility. Court reporters observed that Ashley sat motionless beside her attorney. A trial date was then set.

On October 2, after conversing with her attorney, Ashley withdrew her not guilty by reason of insanity plea and entered an Alford plea.

According to Wikipedia, in an Alford Plea, the defendant does not admit the act, but admits that the State has sufficient evidence to convince a reasonable juror of their guilt. The Court then found Ashley guilty.

Through trembling lips and tears, Ashley answered

"yes" each time she was individually asked by Judge Ward if she was pleading guilty to the charges of aggravated murder, murder, child endangering, tampering with evidence and attempted aggravated possession of drugs. The Young family attended and struggled with their emotions throughout the hearing.

Eight days later, Ashley was sentenced. Friends and family of Kaylen Young gathered in front of the Athens County Courthouse. This was an opportunity to show support for Kaylen and to remember the girl whose life was tragically cut short.

According to one neighbor, every person who had contact with Kaylen felt the same way. "She was a rambunctious little child that was just full of love." Rebecca, like many that day, held a sign that read "Justice 4 Kaylen."

Another said Kaylen loved to play with her My Little Ponies. She liked fishing. She was just a typical little girl but she was also a little bit of a tomboy. She liked racing and four-wheeling with her dad. She liked that kind of stuff.

The Richardson family attended the sentencing in memory of Kaylen. They also said they knew of Kaylen's bubbling personality, calling her a little princess and a diva at times. They said Kaylen loved life and brought smiles to everyone's faces. They told the reporter they were angry and disgusted by Kaylen's death.

In front of a packed courtroom with members of her family and Craig Young's family. Ashley, now twenty-six years old, was sentenced to life in prison without the possibility of parole until twenty years was served. Craig was unable to raise his head to look at his ex-wife throughout most of the proceedings.

Prior to her sentencing, victim impact statements were read. Kaylen's maternal grandmother described Kaylen as a beautiful child inside and out. She was our daughter, our granddaughter, our niece, our cousin, and our friend. There was now a huge hole in their lives that would never be filled. She said family would not have the pleasure of watching Kaylen grow up, lose her first tooth, receive her driver's license or go on her first date.

Craig Young then spoke. He said his dreams of what Kaylen may have grown up to be were shattered because she was taken from them. It was not God's will for her to leave them, he said. It was not God's plan for her to die so soon. She was taken from us because of a "stupid, selfish, cruel act." He could not continue and returned to his seat.

During Craig's statement, Ashley broke down and sobbed. Tears also ran down the faces of other members of each family in the court.

Before he sentenced Ashley, Judge Ward said his piece, claiming Kaylen did not deserve to die at the hand of someone she loved and trusted and called "Mom." She was only four years old and could not fight back, he said.

He then ordered Ashley to stand before the court and receive her sentence. When asked if she had anything to say to the court, she whispered "no". To the shock of onlookers, Ashley never said she was sorry.

Attorney Carson asked the court to accept the plea bargain and reiterated that his client was well aware that there was no guarantee that parole will be granted in twenty years. Upon leaving the courtroom, Attorney Carson told reporters, "There are no winners in this courtroom today."

In a press conference afterward, Assistant Prosecutor Blackburn said he would oppose any attempt of parole until she served twenty years.

As of the writing of this book, Ashley was serving her sentence in the Dayton Correctional Institute in Dayton, Ohio. Craig Young said his family remember Kaylen not by going to her gravesite, but more so through stories. He claimed he and his family are now at the point where they can tell stories about her and laugh.

He said it was very hard in the beginning because he and relatives would tell the stories and end up in tears. He said they all remember Kaylen by getting together and talking about the fun times. He said they are a very close-knit family and have many pleasant stories to remember her by.

Deadly Rival

What was reported on Tuesday, October 23, 2012, in the small glass industrial town of Lancaster, Ohio, population 38,780, was in debate. Police contended a love triangle turned deadly.

As 911 dispatchers desperately tried to get an address, the tall, slim Stephanie Adams screamed and begged her ex-husband, Kevin Adams, to stop pointing a gun at her. "Kevin, no, Kevin, no, Kevin, no," she said. "Please don't do this."

The brawny, tattooed Lancaster native did not listen. He responded by repeatedly calling the woman he vowed before God to love and honor obscene names. The last moments of their lives was recorded at 1:20 a.m. on Stephanie's cell phone.

The recently divorced couple, who were married for twenty years, was heard screaming and cursing at one another before a series of gunshots disrupted their argument. The line stayed open while the dispatcher yelled, "Hello, hello, hello? Ma'am?" According to call logs, Stephanie provided the street address but not the house number.

The Lancaster Police Chief, when dispatchers were unable to pinpoint an exact location, sent several units to the 100 block of Cleveland Avenue around 1:20 a.m. The first officer to arrive reported hearing a possible gunshot at 1:29 a.m. Another officer reported two more shots fired at 1:30 a.m., just as they entered the home. They were too late.

Inside the modest well-kept home, officers found a decorated off-duty Lancaster police officer, fifty-six-year-old

Randy Bartow of Logan, Ohio, dead. Stoutly built and sporting glasses and mustache, Bartow was identified as Stephanie's boyfriend and a twenty-year veteran of the Lancaster Police Department.

According to Randy's "Remember Me" Facebook account, within two hours of his learned death, over four-hundred people shared their memories of him.

Found beside one another in the next room was a deceased Stephanie with Kevin clinging to life. He was transported to Fairfield Medical Center where he died at 2:24 a.m.

A neighbor and family friend claimed Kevin typically carried a gun with him. The murder weapon, according to one officer at the scene, was a pistol, still in its owner's hand.

The neighbor proceeded to tell authorities Kevin had received a call from his daughter who was worried after not hearing from her mother after work. Kevin went to Stephanie's home to check on her, but when he arrived, he found her with Bartow. The couple also had a grown son. They divorced in May 2012 but had been spending time together as a family.

According to court records, Kevin was previously convicted of illegally carrying a concealed weapon, inducing panic and resisting arrest in 2007. He was sentenced to three years of probation starting in August 2007.

Several neighbors recalled to police of hearing the disturbance. "We heard a scream and then I heard the sirens come out," a second neighbor said. Reportedly, numerous police officers arrived at the shocking scene.

One woman who lived next door to where the Adamses used to live when they were married, described Kevin as a good boy, hard worker, and that he would do anything for a friend.

She said she was floored when they filed for divorce but said the split was not ugly. She recalled Kevin helping Stephanie move into her new home with the pair parting on friendly terms.

She claimed Kevin and Stephanie continued to do things as a family for their granddaughter's sake. Other friends said they celebrated Kevin's birthday together just days before the shootings. However, something disturbing must have changed in 24 hours.

She described the news of the murders-suicide as devastating, saying, "I just thought so much of Kevin."

One friend of Randy's commented on his "Remember Me" page. She still had the miniature dollar shirt Randy made her. It hung on her fridge, she said, and she would always have that memory of his kind and gentle way. "Rest in Peace my Friend," she wrote.

Neighbors noted that Stephanie had recently moved to the neighborhood. She and Kevin were married in 1991 and were known as doting grandparents to their only grandchild. Some who knew Stephanie told police she and Randy had recently begun dating.

According to the couple's daughter, Stephanie and Randy were through and were not even on speaking terms. Some who posted comments about Stephanie and Randy's relationship on social networks rebuffed that statement.

Using Facebook, some who followed the murders said unkind things about Stephanie and Randy's alleged "romance," which greatly infuriated Stephanie's daughter to the point of her cursing them out.

Stephanie's boss and friend, a sales manager at Darfus Realty where Stephanie had worked as a real-estate agent for eight years, stated, "Stephanie was always bright and cheery, no matter what was going on in her life."

He said he knew Kevin Adams, and the man

possessed a sinister personality and his "crazy" behavior toward Stephanie had once gotten him kicked out of a popular sports bar in Lancaster called Roosters, where Stephanie served part-time. He described Kevin as very possessive and unable to deal with the divorce.

A couple who lived next door to Stephanie said Kevin and Stephanie planned to accompany their granddaughter trick or treating in the neighborhood just three days away.

The couple claimed seeing Kevin arrive at Stephanie's house late that evening. When Kevin saw Randy on the front porch, an argument ensued. "It started outside, but eventually they went inside."

The couple then went to bed but were woke by hearing voices bickering and a woman screaming. At first, they thought the noise came from Paul's Nite Club just down the street, but then they heard "popping" noises like a gun.

Twenty minutes later, they heard squad cars coming up the street. After hearing the sirens stop close to their home, they went outside to investigate. They were shocked to see several ambulances and officers in front of Stephanie's home. "Initially, I didn't put two and two together," the woman said.

The Lancaster Police Chief said Randy was on the verge of retirement, and his premature death left an unfillable void at the station. "Randy's first asset was his ability to interact sincerely," said the Chief. He described Randy as having a gift at putting people at ease and defusing conflicts. He said Randy's death was "difficult to deal with."

When interviewed, the Hocking County Sheriff said Randy had a great outlook on life and personality and was willing to help anyone, an all-around good person. "He'll be greatly missed," he said.

The cold rainy day of October 28, 2012, was the date of Randy's funeral. *The Lancaster Eagle Gazette* covered the service. What started as a 9 a.m. briefing at the Lancaster Police Department turned into an 11 a.m. service at the Logan Church of the Nazarene, then to the burial at Greenlawn Cemetery in Nelsonville.

Many used the drive to the cemetery to reflect on their lost friend. Randy's former partner said he chuckled when driving to the cemetery which was located in an isolated area. "That's just the way Randy was, he was a prankster," he said.

He reminisced on his and Randy's good times together as he drove along. He was glad people in mourning were able to find humor during the service, and he thought Randy would have appreciated it. "He was laughing at us, trust me," he said. He said Randy found humor in everything.

Another who spoke at Randy's service said Randy was known for carrying a supply of fresh dollar bills that he would take from his pocket and make into tiny, origami shirts and pants for the children he encountered. She recalled saving many a folded dollar as a child. More recently, the officer had given her five-year-old daughter one of the tiny keepsakes. "He always made you laugh and smile," she said. She believed The Lancaster Police Department needed more officers like Officer Randy.

Lancaster was not the only law enforcement agency represented at the funeral. Officers from Lithopolis, Baltimore, Columbus, Logan, Pickerington and Hocking County, among others, attended.

Most of those officers stood at attention in spitting rain as Randy's casket was transported to the hearse and again at the gravesite while the remaining members of the force served as pallbearers. The police officers stood six rows deep at Greenlawn Cemetery below an American flag lowered to half-staff with a black bow affixed to its corner.

An eighteen-year veteran of the Lancaster Police Department was among the law enforcement clothed in dress uniforms standing at attention while five bagpipers and three drummers commemorated Randy Bartow with "Amazing Grace."

He described Randy as unlike most people -- very sincere. "Randy really would give a person the shirt off his back," he said. He spoke at the service, focusing on many of the pranks that he and Randy shared in their time in the narcotics unit. He recalled that the always well-mannered Randy was the only man he knew who ended undercover drug deals by saying, "Thank you, sir. Have a nice day."

A Communication Technician who worked alongside the fallen officer described Randy as "the brother I never had." She also spoke of Randy's practical jokes and playful fibs while the two worked together. She spoke of Randy telling her and other co-workers of his being an ordained minister and blind in one eye -- all lies! "He really had some of us believing his jokes," she said. The woman laughed at her own gullibility and tendency to fall victim to Randy's pranks as the nearly 400 people at the church laughed with her.

Another said he believed, with Randy's humble nature and ability to find joy in all aspects of life, the hour-long service in Logan and final ceremony in Nelsonville probably was more than enough in Randy's mind. He described Randy as an individual who did not want "glory" or to be "fussed over". He said Randy was not the type who dwelled on sorrow. "It's like, 'Get yourself up, brush yourself off and get on with life. You've got a life to live, so live it.'"

The Lancaster Police Department did some folding of their own to conclude the funeral. The flag that lay on Randy's casket throughout the service was folded according to protocol, and then Chief Bailey presented it to the deceased officer's family.

The Logan Police Chief said he was not surprised that so many people in the law enforcement community felt compelled to pay their respects.

He said Randy was equally as highly thought of with the Logan Police Department as he was with the Lancaster Department. He described Randy as having a wonderful community spirit and touching everyone.

According to Randy's obituary, he was born in Columbus, Ohio, and survived by one daughter and three brothers. Before spending twenty years at the Lancaster Police Department, he had served with the Nelsonville Police Department and Logan Police Department.

An adjunct faculty member at Hocking College teaching Law Science, Randy had formerly worked for the Ohio Department of Natural Resources in the Oil and Reclamation Department.

A Logan High School graduate from the class of 1974, Randy was a member of the Fraternal Order of Police, honored as Officer of the Year in 1999 and 2002.

Another achievement arrived in 2002 when he received the Ohio House of Representatives Brett Markwood Award. A true American, Randy had served in the United States Marine Reserves and the Ohio National Guard.

For those wanting to contribute to his memory, the family suggested contributions be made to Special Friends of Hocking County, a non-profit after-school program for children. Many attending Randy's service remembered him as the ideal neighborhood cop.

When a dear friend of Stephanie's, a student and member of The Human Services Student Association (HSSA) located in Lancaster, Ohio, learned of Stephanie's murder, she said she dedicated the upcoming event "walk in their shoes" to raise awareness of domestic violence.

According to the HSSA website, it was an organization geared to promoting professional and ethical development of its members and to recognize high achievement in the pursuit of academic excellence. The organization had planned the walk several weeks earlier to mark National Domestic Violence Prevention Month.

The woman stated she had no idea the walk she and her classmates coordinated would be dedicated to Stephanie. When she learned of Stephanie's abrupt death, she said she immediately wanted to do something to honor her friend, saying, "Stephanie was one of those people who, if you needed anything, no matter what, she would do everything in her power to do it for you. She had the hugest heart."

She said all money raised during the walk was donated to the Lighthouse, a domestic violence shelter in Lancaster. She and Stephanie's co-workers from Roosters carried pictures of Stephanie during the walk. They told reporters they dealt with Stephanie's death by remembering the good times they shared.

They also hung handmade posters inside the restaurant and, after hours, retreated outside to light candles on the patio and share funny stories and memories of Stephanie.

She explained Stephanie was a good listener and gave helpful advice, someone who did not complain about personal problems.

At the same time Stephanie was being immortalized, across town, Randy Barstow's co-workers at the Lancaster Police Department grieved for him. The chief of police told the *Lancaster Eagle Gazette* reporter Randy was well liked amongst community members and co-workers and was off-duty the morning he was killed.

The atmosphere inside the police station that day was described as "very solemn." The Chief said employees went through the motions to complete their jobs, saying everyone was affected by the murders-suicide.

The Chief recalled how much of an influence Randy had on others when he received a Facebook message Tuesday from a former Turkish exchange student who met Randy during his stay in Lancaster. He said Randy was one officer who acted as tour guide and participated in a tour of the police building for international exchange students. Up to twenty-five kids would tour the station. The Chief said Randy had the ability to engage those children so well that the foreign student still remembered him and, when he learned of the news, knew exactly who Randy was.

Fellow officers said Randy was humble about winning several awards within the police department. In Randy's personnel file, one found small notes, cards and letters on official stationary, saying the same thing -- how he went out of his way to help somebody.

When interviewed, a Lancaster Municipal Court Judge spoke of Randy's ability to make a positive impression on everyone he met. He said he met Randy when the officer worked on the court security unit, calling him an "absolute pleasure."

"He was a generous individual," said the judge. He recalled how Randy became personally involved in helping drug addicts, often having deep conversations with people struggling with drugs, and backed it up with a great smile.

The Commander of the Fairfield-Hocking Major Crimes Unit described Randy as a compassionate person good at his job. He said Randy cared for others and actually did help many.

Kevin and Stephanie's niece said she believed Kevin snapped that night. She believed when Kevin saw Randy at

Stephanie's home early that morning, he became heartbroken.

She said her uncle and aunt were in the process of working things out, even though they had divorced. She said Stephanie and Kevin were high school sweethearts and, even when things were rough, always showed a united front. "He was the happiest I've seen him in years," she said. She described Kevin as a loving grandfather. She said she had hoped Stephanie and Kevin might be buried together. They were not.

She said the entire family was distraught by the shootings. Many did not understand how such a violent action could happen in their family. Most, she said, had many unanswered questions. She remembered Kevin as a loving person, which nobody realized.

She explained how Kevin served as a special forces Army Ranger in Desert Storm and had been retired from the Army for nearly ten years. She said Kevin had a tough exterior, but he had a good, gentle heart. She recalled how she and the other family children looked up to Kevin growing up, and continue to. "He was amazing and will be missed," she said.

The couple's daughter, on her Facebook account, wrote of her childhood filled with love and devoted parents. She spoke of sleeping in the middle of her parents and of Stephanie bringing her a glass of milk and a slice of cheese at bedtime, of Stephanie tickling her back and feet, and the many cats the family had who shared her bed.

On October 27, 2012, Kevin J. Adams was laid to rest in the Elm Wood Cemetery. His obituary indicated he was born October 21, 1972, and hailed from Hilliard, Ohio. He was a 1991 graduate of Lancaster High School. Besides his children and grandchild, five brothers survived Kevin.

Like his victims, Kevin was remembered by many,

loved much, and greatly missed, with the Chase family remembering him as 'Big Brutus.'

Mr. Chase related that Kevin was childhood friends to his two sons. They remember Kevin Adams as a smiling young man who loved life.

After several weeks of interviews, the FBI ruled the deaths as a double murder-suicide and closed the case. From all evidence gathered, Kevin Adams was determined to be the only shooter that cool morning on a quiet street in Lancaster, Ohio.

The Possession

New York City (2007)

When a frantic 9-1-1 call came in to the police station at 8:30 p.m. on July 28, 2007, a sobbing twenty-nine-year-old Brigitte Harris told the dispatcher she wanted desperately to save the life of her bleeding father, Eric Goodrich.

She gave the operator her apartment address. She would later tell authorities, she did not want to kill her sexually abusive father, but only to disable his weapon of abuse -- his penis.

She informed the operator she was walking in the direction of the police station and then hung up. She recalled walking to the nearby Hudson River and tossing the penis into the ocean. She never arrived at the police station.

Instead, she called her big sister Carleen and confessed to her what she had just done to their Liberian-born father. Carleen recalled being in total shock at her baby sister's gruesome confession. She begged Brigitte not to discard the appendage, saying doctors had the medical technology to reattach such things.

Brigitte, her hair adorned with cornrows, cried into the telephone. "It was the evil in our father. Now the evil is gone. He can hurt no more!"

Carleen advised Brigitte to come to her home, and when she arrived, her sister called an ambulance. After seeing Brigitte, her face stained with tears and splattered with blood, with the scalpel in hand and in a "zombie-like state of mind", they decided to check her into the Richmond University Medical Center psychiatric ward.

Meanwhile, back at Brigitte's apartment, two responding beat cops arrived. What the officers found, they said they never forgot, and neither did the two million five hundred thousand other citizens.

Initially the officers thought the man lying in a pool of blood was shot or stabbed to death. Not until they turned him over onto his back did they realize the sadistic nature of his wounds. Little did everyone involved realize that the crime would turn relative against relative, divide a city, and be known as New York City's most bizarre murder. The actions of the scalpel-wielding Brigitte, inside her Brownstone apartment that warm summer evening, rocked the nation and gave revenge a new meaning.

Born Brigitte Harris on June 6, 1981, in the back seat of a cab outside a Staten Island hospital — an emergency delivery to mother Lucy-Anna Harris, she was one of four children born out of wedlock. Little did the soft-spoken woman realize that by the time she was thirty-one, she would be an inmate at Riker's Island.

She discovered her now frail father was in town when she received a telephone call from Carleen one early afternoon in 2007. Carleen told Brigitte their father wished to speak with them. Neither sister had seen or spoken with Eric for eight years.

Brigitte described how she took a two-hour subway-and-ferry ride from her apartment to Carleen's house. Carleen recalled Brigitte acting anxious when she arrived, noticing the meeting between Brigitte and Eric was uneasy from the start.

Carleen would tell police she watched Brigitte leave her living room for the kitchen where she followed. She said Brigitte was upset and she tried to calm her by suggesting she converse with Eric and perhaps he would feel remorse for the years of abuse and apologize.

Although Eric suffered from reoccurring kidney stones, by all accounts the 200-pound man was still robust. Brigitte said she was unprepared for what she saw. Her father was not the arrogant, verbally abusive person she remembered from her childhood. He spoke to her as an adult, not the child she once was.

Brigitte recalled accepting Eric's business card and telephone number. They spoke standing in the living room with Eric showing respect toward her, a quality she said Eric had for few.

Eric then asked her to buy him a V8 Splash. She walked to a nearby store to make the purchase and returned. What she saw upon re-entering Carleen's home, according to Brigitte, put her deadly plan in motion.

Sitting on the couch was Eric holding his eight-year-old granddaughter on his lap as he had done with Brigitte and Carleen all those years ago. The child was playing and laughing, she said, as innocent and happy children do, but Brigitte said she knew what Eric's intentions were. He was truly the wolf in sheep's clothing.

Carleen remembered Brigitte becoming irate, and the sisters argued over Eric's actions and of his plans to stay overnight in the home. Brigitte claimed she told her sister that she, of all people, knew Eric was dangerous around children. Carleen told her baby sister to forget about the abuse saying, "You just move on. You just do it."

Within minutes, Eric had joined them. He informed Brigitte of his plans to return to Africa with both of Carleen's daughters, a decision Eric would not live to see. When Brigitte returned to her apartment, she admitted to scouring the Internet on the statute of limitations, learning they had expired concerning her sexual assaults. Since Eric had not actually assaulted her niece, she knew police would not do anything. He had no record in New York of assaulting any other person. Her search for the Lorena Bobbitt case revealed doctors had medical technology for reattaching a penis.

She read of cases in China and in Europe and learned a penis could be severed without killing the man. She then purchased a package of 50 scalpels on eBay for $6.83, including shipping in June.

She purchased a camcorder and, after turning it on, aimed it at herself and began talking. *Okay, so, testing right now. My name is Brigitte Harris, and this is the story of my life. Well, not the whole thing, obviously. It'll take way too long. Just the summary reasons — why I'm doing what I'm about to do, why I feel I have to do it, why it must be done, why I've waited this long to do it. Therefore, you can judge me. However, before you do, get the whole story. That's all I ask.*

Brigitte admitted to inviting her father over to confront him about his long-term sexual abuse against her. She wanted her father to understand how much he hurt her, not only physically, but also emotionally and psychologically. She said she hated Eric and will never speak to him again after this day, saying, and "He will forever be dead to me." She described her pain as consuming her life, making it impossible for her to maintain a relationship with a man, and "made me hate myself."

On July 28, just three days after first talking with Eric, Brigitte called her father at the phone number he gave her, asking that they speak alone in her Rockaway apartment, and Eric agreed. She told police she only wanted to reason with him and to change his mind about leaving the country with her nieces.

Carleen told police that when Eric told her Brigitte invited him to her apartment, she assumed everything between daughter and father was fine. Boy, was she wrong.

In her confession to police, Brigitte admitted to meeting Eric at Carleen's home the morning of July 28. He seemed even weaker than he had been a month earlier, she recalled. She was unaware, but Eric had spent much of July in and out of the hospital, passing the kidney stone. They traveled back to her apartment together and, on the train, she saw him eyeing some young girls, each no older than ten. She held her tongue, she said.

Once at her apartment in Queens, she poured him a glass of water. Brigitte claimed she asked Eric to seek professional help, but he denied having serious problems. She then tried showing Eric documentation from off the Internet about what rape and incest does to children, continuing into adulthood. He again denied raping her. He refused to look at the documentation.

When she told him she remembered the first time he tried to rape her, she claimed he told her she was too young to remember such things. He said it calmly, she recalled. No shock at her vulgar accusation. Not denial, just a casual dismissal. She then talked about the oral sex he forced her to do at the age of four. He completely denied that act.

With the pornography he made her watch with him, he justified that by saying he was merely teaching her to clean herself, teaching her to be a woman. Then he made the comment she had waited for so long. He said he never penetrated her, so he did nothing wrong.

Then he said he was sorry if she thought he hurt her. She said that was Eric's way of apologizing to her -- trying to make her think she imagined the years of abuse.

He then justified the rapes by telling her it was customary in African cultures for a father to take his daughter's virginity right before marriage. He said what happened with her and Carleen was a normal thing for fathers to do with their daughters. She admitted Eric's

78

constant denials angered her.

He was no longer denying the assaults. She now felt vindicated. She asked about the last time he tried raping her when she was seventeen. That was when Eric changed the subject completely, she said. He now wanted to talk about Brigitte's eighteen-year-old sister Lovette.

He claimed the girl was gang raped when she was a child in Liberia, during the time Brigitte was living there. He blamed Brigitte for the fact that no one in the family learned of Lovette's rapes earlier.

Brigitte admitted she called him a liar, saying she had nothing to do with Lovette's rapes. He was playing on her guilt in case Lovette ever claimed Eric raped her, and Brigitte believed he already had. All the emotions Brigitte felt during her assaults rushed out -- self-loathing, guilt, rage, and hate.

That was when things turned verbal, then physical, she said, but she was determined to stop him from raping children. She recalled yelling at him. She said he stood and stepped toward her, and she removed the pepper spray she carried on her belt clip. She sprayed him several times while struggling to free herself from his grasp. They fell to the floor and the coffee table broke.

She said emotions raced through her mind at that moment. She did and did not understand that her actions were wrong. All she thought of, she said, were her nieces. She had to keep Eric from hurting them, and the penis was the tool that did the hurting. "It was the evil in Eric," she said.

She remembered her security-guard training and quickly got the upper hand. She recalled how he passed out. She then retrieved the handcuffs, a novelty she had bought after her friends teased her about her job as a rent-a-cop. After placing them on Eric, she tied his legs together with a curtain cord. He woke and began screaming. She grabbed a towel from a nearby chair, stuffing it into his mouth and tying it around his neck. She then noticed he was having trouble breathing.

She panicked, she said, then scrambled to revive him. First, she splashed him with water and called his name. He regained consciousness and began screaming for help. She gagged him with a towel, stuffing part of it into his mouth. Using duct tape, she secured it, leaving small holes for air. She pulled down his trousers, ready with a pair of scissors. They failed to do the job. She then remembered the scalpels and went in search of them.

On her return, to keep him quiet, she pressed her knee onto his windpipe as she crouched over him. One cut was enough. There was only a minimal amount of blood, she said. She was not through yet. She turned on the stove and laid the organ on the flame. Only the smell of burning flesh made what she had done seem real to her, she said. Her stomach turned. She felt nauseous. She turned the flame off and placed the now burned organ inside a paper towel and left. She eventually threw the penis under the boardwalk.

She remembered calling 9-1-1 several times to report the incident and to see if Eric was alive. However, by the time the police arrived, there was no saving Eric.

The prosecution later maintained Brigitte planned killing Eric from the beginning; her researching the internet for scalpels before killing Eric proved premeditation. Burning the penis on the stove, before throwing it off the pier, was to cover up what she did. Searching the Internet for the Lorena Bobbitt case -- that all proved she planned this attack. "Eric dying was just a misfortune for Eric," said the Prosecutor.

According to Brigitte, she endured parental abandonment and abuses her entire life. She recalled being two years old when Lucy-Anne left her and three other siblings with a neighbor woman who also lived in their Park Hill, New York, apartments. They were placed into the foster-care system.

In 1984, they were living with their father on Long Island. In one of her earliest childhood memories, Eric ordered her, at the age of three, to undress and lie naked on a bed in a guest room. She remembers him getting on top of her. She remembered the telephone ringing and pleading with him to answer the phone—and him telling her, "Don't worry about it." She remembered him getting off her and her holding her doll and being in pain.

The abuse by Eric stopped only when he returned to Liberia, leaving Brigitte and Carleen with numerous abusive relatives. The sisters claimed their maternal grandmother physically abused them, forcing the small girls into doing all the housework, including scrubbing floors and washing an endless supply of dirty dishes. In that home, which should have been filled love and safety, Brigitte claimed their grandmother used them as slaves and routinely hit them with a stick if they disobeyed.

The torture, according to Brigitte, did not stop there. In that home, she claimed an older cousin forced her to perform oral sex on him each Sunday after church services. She said she told her grandmother, but the woman did nothing to stop the assaults.

She told police that during a family trip to Liberia to visit Eric, she informed her mother and her pastor of the abuse. They confronted Eric, who adamantly denied all the abuse allegations, calling Brigitte "crazy and a liar." Either she informed other family members who disbelieved her, or, as one aunt said, "No matter what Eric did, he is still your father."

Once, in 2002, while she was watching her niece and nephew at Carleen's home, Eric called her cell phone and refused to tell her how he retrieved her number. She told him to lose the number and never call again.

He then arrived at Carleen's home. Brigitte was terrified. She recalled that when Eric approached the front door, she panicked and locked it before calling Carleen who came home and found Brigitte and the children locked in the bathroom.

The next time she and Eric spoke was at Carleen's house. She said she believed her father wanted to be friends because he was sick and old and for no other reason.

Once she was on American soil, Brigitte tried building a new life for herself. She stayed with family between stints at women's shelters. She finished high school and went to college for a year, then got work as a $17-an-hour security guard in a freight section of Kennedy Airport. She made some friends on Myspace and started dressing Goth with spiked collars and multicolored hair extensions.

Brigitte never spoke kindly of her father, according to the shelter manager. He said she punished herself over the years by living a destructive lifestyle and bottling up the hate. He said Brigitte refused counseling, claiming she was too angry and ashamed to talk to a stranger, so the manager listened when Brigitte needed her to. He believed her years of abuse caused her to "snap."

Slowly, the front she had created started coming apart. She moved to an apartment in Rockaway Park in 2006 -- only two blocks from the beach she wrote about on Myspace. "Sweet beach parties, makin S'mores, bonfires, gettin drunk and watch'n the sunrise," she wrote. "It does not get any better than that." However, she found she could not hold a relationship and had to be drunk when around others.

She said she tried talking about the abuse with her family but claimed the Goodridge family was a different culture, saying that in Africa, skeletons stay in the closet. She said the family knew what Eric was, but for some reason they decided to protect him. She believed it was his wealth.

In April 2007, she swallowed an overdose of pills at work. When an ambulance arrived, she went home, refusing to talk about why she did it. A few weeks later, she learned from a family friend that her father was coming back to America and staying in her sister's house — with her sister's daughters.

After being discharged from the psychiatric ward on August 16, 2007, Brigitte was charged with second-degree murder and first-degree manslaughter. She was held at Riker's Island, a 413.7-acre ten-jail facility located on the East River between Queens and The Bronx.

On her Myspace page, Brigitte referred to herself as "Lady Vengeance" and "The Original Dark Angel." She continuously claimed throughout her ordeal that she had not intended to kill her father, saying, "I felt I had to stop him," to "take away his weapon."

Carleen hired defense lawyer Arthur L. Aidala to represent Brigitte. He met with her inside the sanitarium. Through tears, she revealed her terrible secret. She gave her attorney a detailed account of her abused home life, sexually, verbally and physically with Eric and other relatives.

She claimed that Eric had told her that in some African cultures, fathers take their daughter's virginity in a show of love. Carleen also broke her silence, admitting she also was sexually abused by their father but was too afraid to speak up. She set up a website called savebridget.com to raise money for Brigitte's legal defense.

The case went national. Due to her abuse allegations, Brigitte received an outpouring of supporters, including U.S. Senator Chuck Schumer and New York State Senators Diane Savino and Eric Adams.

Numerous reporters interviewed her. She claimed she was unsure of what she would tell the court but said she hoped her case would shed more light on sex abuse in the home. Reporters quoted her as saying, "People need to start talking about parental sexual assaults because people don't want to believe it happens. It's too gruesome."

An avalanche of supporters wrote to newspaper companies saying they were glad Eric was dead. Many said they believed pedophilia was difficult or impossible to cure. Death was the only cure, aside from castration, many said.

One jailhouse interview was with the *Daily News*. The soft-spoken, now crucifix-wearing woman was now wearing short hair in cornrows, sporting glasses and weighing a whopping three-hundred pounds, the result of a combination of junk food at Riker's Island and the antidepressants she was prescribed.

She maintained her original story: she never intended to murder her father. She claimed that thinking back, she would have found another avenue in dealing with the abuse, but she believed at the time no one would believe her. She said people do not want to believe parental sexual abuse exists, that no parent could be so cruel to their child, "But it happens."

After Brigitte's arrest, her siblings were interviewed; all of them confirmed her allegations against Eric were true. She also admitted her father was the closest stable person in her childhood.

Eric Goodridge was well known in the Staten Island African community. After leaving Liberia as a young man, he became a financial success in the U.S. His businesses included a taxi-service, records, and imports and exports.

Lucy-Anna had nothing good to say about the father of her children, calling Eric a philanderer with an interest in young girls.

Brigitte claimed she was around four years old when Eric forced her to perform oral sex on him for the first time. She remembered how Eric laid her naked on a bed and after shedding his trousers, removed his penis from his underwear and instructed her to "'suck on it.'"

She recalled she must have done it wrong, because she said Eric told her to "'suck on it like a bottle.'" She said he began to laugh and said, "'Don't worry. I'll teach you.'"

At the age of twelve, Brigitte said she returned to Liberia to live with her mother, a visit she hoped would bond mother and daughter. The tearful reunion soon turned violent. She claimed Lucy-Anna was as abusive as Eric was towards her. She described a beating by her mother with a rattan to the point of leaving her with permanent scars. The abuse, both verbal and physical, became so unbearable, she returned to her father's home and endured further sexual assaults.

She claimed that when she told her mother she wanted to live with Eric, she said Lucy-Anna refused to allow that because of the rapes Brigitte had accused Eric of committing. Brigitte said she then denied Eric ever raped her, saying she made the whole story up. She had convinced herself the abuse never happened, as if it were "a nightmare, not reality," she said.

When Brigitte returned to Liberia with Eric, he was living with two women she described as distant cousins -- with whom Eric often had threesomes. Brigitte said her father performed oral sex on her and then made her watch adult films.

She recalled that on New Year's Eve 1997, Eric attempted an unsuccessful sexual attack. Later she fell asleep, only to awake in the middle of the night as he was performing oral sex on her. She said before she was fully awake, she experienced some sort of pleasure. When she realized it was Eric, she began crying and fighting him off, and he gave up.

She was seventeen when she finally got away from Eric for good and returned to Lucy-Anne, also in Liberia. Eric allowed Brigitte to leave, tossing her passport at her rudely and letting her know he disapproved of her abandoning her friends. She stayed with her mother until her eighteenth birthday when she could qualify for a repatriation loan.

What still bothered Brigitte, she said, was the fact that when she left Liberia for the last time, she had promised Lovette she would be back for her. A decade later, that promise still weighed on her.

At her apartment, the photographer snapped pictures of each room of Brigitte's apartment and various shots of the victim from different angles. Two homicide detectives interviewed fellow tenants.

The detectives reported that most would not answer their doors. The one person who talked with them was a senior citizen living across the hall from Brigitte's apartment.

He claimed Brigitte often gave elaborate costume parties into the wee hours of the morning, but she kept the noise down because she "didn't want trouble with the boys in blue." He had nothing but praise for the melancholy single woman.

After the Medical Examiner did his initial examination, he had the body removed to the city morgue. The apartment was searched with a fine-tooth comb. Within minutes, the detectives found Brigitte's taped confession and the scalpels.

The tape became an important part of the State's prosecution case. Upon entering the "rose-scented master bedroom, lit by black lights," as described by one detective, two large boxes atop a dresser held blonde and red-shaded wigs of different lengths. The closet held ironed clothes with creased jeans. Neatly placed on the closet floor side by side were shoes. Photographs of Brigitte Harris adorned that room, as did the living room.

The computer revealed more bizarre evidence, bringing horrifying details to light. A medical website indicated Brigitte had ordered a scalpel six weeks earlier and paid with a Visa card. That, to the detectives, proved intent.

Further surfing provided the officers with more damaging news. Located on an erotic website was Brigitte's pen name, "The Dark Angel." It was clear to the investigators -- their prime suspect liked the wild side of life. The computer and its wires were confiscated.

After checking in at headquarters, the officers discovered Brigitte's whereabouts. Minutes later, the building's proprietor arrived. The condition of the deceased was now spreading through the dominantly black community.

One neighbor claimed not knowing the deceased, but he, too, had only noteworthy words for Brigitte. He told the detectives that "having a Lorena Bobbitt done on a person ain't something police can hide."

He described Brigitte as a brooder -- as if she had the whole weight of the world on her. She was a loner and always carried a flask of whiskey in her pocket. She always paid her rent on time, and with cash, never food stamps, "like some tenants do," and she seemed sad all the time.

He claimed he never had complaints about Brigitte from the other tenants. When asked if Brigitte had male friends over, he said when she did bring a fella home, she never let him stay overnight. It's like "after they did their thing, she wanted him gone so she could be alone." He said she seemed to need a lot of space.

The detectives reportedly speculated Brigitte was bi-polar. Another call to headquarters verified she never arrived. Believing she was on the run, investigators notified area hospitals, thinking perhaps she injured herself during the struggle.

One co-worker described Brigitte as "reliable and honest." However, he, like the property owner, saw the emptiness and inner pain Brigitte harbored. He recalled she seemed angry all the time. She smiled a lot, he said, but it was only on the surface.

Another co-worker told investigators she and Brigitte buddied around in the beginning, but Brigitte was too "hum drum for my taste," describing Brigitte as the "museum type."

Some would say old-fashioned never goes out of style, and Brigitte simply played it safe. Others found the stout loner boring and avoided her, believing that one day she would erupt.

Investigators were curious to what caused the brick wall in front of their suspect and knew they could be looking for a serial killer. They knew severing a penis was uncommon, fearing Eric Goodridge was not the last.

When investigators received news from headquarters of a woman fitting Brigitte's description recently transported to the local psych ward, they rushed to get her statement. Unfortunately, what officers faced was the legal system.

Hoping to interview Brigitte while her memory was still fresh, the officers were rudely disappointed. According to the attending physician, not only was Brigitte heavily sedated but soon after her admittance had tried committing suicide by hanging herself from her room's overhead light. Her weight caused the light to break free from the ceiling, alerting personnel. "It was a close call," said the doctor.

The investigators knew most suicide attempts were a cry for help. With Brigitte being under psychiatric care and prescribed anti-depressants, they would now need a court order to interrogate her.

According to the coroner who performed the autopsy, a severed penis does not cause enough blood loss to cause death. The compiled autopsy report stated the cause of death was officially asphyxiation due to a towel forced down the victim's throat. The coroner reported that death might have been a heart attack brought on by the shock of having "his manhood removed."

Carleen told authorities that, even though Eric raised them, he never treated them as a father should. She said he never wanted either girl and passed them off from relative to relative.

She talked of Lucy-Anne arriving in the U.S. in the 1970s. Eric lived in the U.S. for several years and was an entrepreneur. She described her father as "a man who always found ways to get other people to do the work for him."

She admitted that she at times resented her father's financial success, as did the majority of Eric's family, except Brigitte. She claimed Brigitte despised the man and his money, only wanting his acceptance that she was his biological daughter. He died before acknowledging her.

Carleen claimed she and Brigitte loved their mother and was the happiest when around her, even though the woman was often gone. She talked of her mother abandoning her and Brigitte with a neighbor woman on the ruse of going to the grocery store. According to Carleen, her mother told her and Brigitte she would return soon but boarded a plane to Liberia without them.

Carleen claimed she handled their mother's rejection better than Brigitte, who wore her heart on her sleeve. She recalled Brigitte crying herself to sleep for weeks, and the fact that their parents did not want them affected Brigitte into her adulthood.

When Lucy-Anne failed to return by nightfall, the neighbor called CPS who took custody of them before placing them in separate foster homes.

She remembered calling Brigitte the morning Eric arrived on her doorstep asking to see Brigitte. She said her father never announced in advance of his arrival, saying, "He'd just knock on the door, and ya knew he was in town."

Carleen recalled Brigitte being anxious when she learned of their father's arrival. She assumed Brigitte was glad to see him.

She said the visit was uncomfortable for them all. She claimed Brigitte told Eric she "needed to lay things to rest once and for all." Carleen would later tell investigators she was unsure as to what Brigitte meant by that statement, but it would be used against Brigitte later.

Carleen insisted Brigitte did not invite their father into her home to kill him, saying, "She ain't got it in her to kill in cold blood."

The authorities failed in keeping the details of the crime from reporters. Four days after the barbaric incident, the case made local front-page news. "DAUGHTER SEVERS FATHER'S PENIS" highlighted the morning paper.

Living in the city established in 1683, with over 2,300,000 residents, and named after the Queen consort, Portuguese Princess Catherine of Braganza, reporters clamped their teeth to the city's most meaty and sadistic crime in decades. They immediately staked out Brigitte's neighborhood, interviewing anyone who would talk.

Some interviewed called the crime "revenge" due to Brigitte's alleged rape charge against her father. Others thought Brigitte "insane" and "a man hater," calling her pure evil. Many believed the mutilation a payback for something deep-rooted, or a burglary or drug deal gone wrong.

Since her arrest, reporters, curiosity seekers, Brigitte haters, and other various social whack jobs flocked to Brigitte's apartment house. The yellow crime scene tape that once bordered the front door was dislodged and the apartment ransacked.

The strangest sensation coming from the crime was the invention of the "Eric sandwich," consisting of sausage balls in tomato sauce minus the hot dog. Vendors sold the concoction on corners and in front of businesses.

One tenant in Brigitte's apartment told authorities Brigitte did not "take crap" from anyone. She claimed Brigitte accused her of stealing her satin nightgown from the washer in the basement Laundromat. Heated words were exchanged, but nothing to call the police about.

This woman recalled an older dark man enter the apartment the day Eric died. She did not see his face, but she heard what sounded like an argument soon after the man entered. She said the argument lasted only a short time. Authorities surmised Brigitte silenced Eric's screams by shoving the shirt into his mouth. She was another who knew Brigitte needed to be inebriated when socializing.

Another neighbor, a bald, skinny, middle-aged man, came forward accusing Brigitte of throwing loud parties which often led to police being called. Just before the murder, he recalled Brigitte began dressing in all black "like it was Halloween 24/7." A religious woman from the third floor recalled Brigitte referring to herself as "The Dark Angel" who righted wrong.

Brigitte supporters gathered daily outside the clinic that housed her, chanting, "Set Brigitte free. Set Brigitte free," while holding homemade signs condemning rape and incest.

Inside the sanitarium was not much better. Brigitte's doctor had made it clear to investigators that there would be no interrogation without a court order.

When interviewed, Brigitte said she did not expect many to understand about that horrible day. Each person had very different views about the penis removal. Some surmised bad parents raise many children and they do not grow up and seek revenge. Others believed her hysterical call to 9-1-1 was an act -- deforming the man, then acting as savior to try to save him.

Many said she should have told Eric to go to hell and informed CPS of his lewd intentions, insisting there were many other routes she could have taken besides murder.

According to Attorney Aidala, he spent three weeks with Brigitte inside the sanitarium probing into his very emotionally disturbed client's mind. He said he beseeched her to open up if she wanted him to save her from prison or, worse, the electric chair.

Brigitte said she could not talk about the murder or abuse, saying she could not believe Eric was actually dead. She claimed she only wanted to stop him from taking her nieces to Liberia with him. He would have raped them, too, she claimed, calling him a monster. She believed he needed to be stopped, but not by murder, saying, "I can never forgive myself."

Her attorney described Brigitte as like a turtle, wanting to crawl inside her shell, thinking everything will disappear. He said he needed to know the entire life story that would make her do such a horrendous thing to another.

The attorney recalled Brigitte's discussions filled with anger, shame, self-loathing, and buckets of tears into her pillow. He said he treated her as if she were his child, putting his arm around her as she cried on his shoulder at times. He said he could help her, but only if she allowed him to, meaning he needed her absolute honesty and trust as she took him step by step through that morning inside her apartment.

Brigitte recalled pouring out her heart to her attorney. She was prescribed anti-depressants and counseling with a sexual abuse counselor twice a day inside the hospital.

With every area business televising the case, everyone was watching for the outcome, with most hating Brigitte, dubbed the "scalpel-wielding lunatic." Everyone knew Brigitte's face and address.

Her apartment windows were broken out from neighborhood children throwing rocks. The only persons on Brigitte's side at this point were her attorney, her sister and mother, sexual assault survivors and their advocates.

Eric's family turned against Brigitte and adamantly denied the sexual abuse allegations against him. Eric's elderly mother, through a thick African accent, tearfully told reporters stationed outside her home that her son was a good man, saying, "He respected businessman. He helps people. Not hurt them."

Held throughout the city were awareness rallies in Brigitte's honor to inform the public of her plight. Everyone in her neighborhood seemed to know Brigitte for one reason or another. Several interviewed claimed she was an alcoholic for some time, that she drowned her sorrows in self-pity until finding a close circle of friends who helped her sober up and "get her act together." Those groups of individuals were rumored to be of the Gothic crowd.

The appearance of dozens of black-dressed persons with matching nail polish and lipstick was a welcome sight, some said. Each held signs containing slogans such as "We love you Brigitte" and "Free Brigitte," written in red bold letters.

Brigitte's attorney was always available for interviews and talk shows also. He claimed his young client suffered for years from Post-Traumatic Stress Disorder, saying, "Brigitte Harris was a long-time victim of her father's insatiable and twisted appetite for incestuous sex in the name of love."

He claimed there was ample evidence of long-term systematic sexual abuse and rape by the deceased. He referred to Brigitte as the victim in this case, with the Prosecutor now wanting to "rape her all over again" by filing ridiculous and unwarranted charges against her when she was clearly defending herself and her young relatives.

Evidence of Brigitte's supporters was everywhere. If not on television or in newspapers, the evidence was nailed to trees and telephone poles. The flyers asked for public support and understanding -- and for an acquittal.

Carleen insisted the case against Brigitte was not whether to approve or disapprove, claiming "Monsters need dealt with in extreme ways." She claimed Brigitte did not kill Eric when she mutilated him; she killed the evil part of him. His dying was an accident, and the jury will see that, calling Brigitte a "good person."

Carleen called herself an introvert and claimed that was how she coped with the abuse. She claimed she kept the abuse hidden safely inside for many years until discovering God, saying Brigitte had not found God.

She said her husband was supportive, calling him her salvation. Brigitte was emotionally weaker and should have sought professional counseling, but she was too full of anger and hurt to seek outside help.

Supporters for Eric contend that "good people" seek legal help instead of taking matters into their own hands.

Carleen's response to the overwhelming negative reactions against Brigitte was that she was too weak to say "no" to Eric and the abuse, but Brigitte said "no" in her own way. She claimed what happened to Eric was her fault also, saying she should never have agreed to allow Eric to take her children to Liberia.

During Brigitte's many incarcerated interviews, reporters described her as calm. Some believed her attitude stemmed from her prescribed anti-depressants. Others believed her new outlook on life and her actions came from her now getting the psychiatric help she desperately needed. Her attorney was present for each interview. That helped ease her state of mind, she said. During many interviews, she was photographed smiling, saying she was relieved she could tell her side of the story.

Brigitte said for years, Eric and his relatives talked disrespectfully about Lucy-Anna, claiming the woman never wanted them and chose not to visit. She claimed to not care what others said of her mother, for she loved the woman anyway. She told herself something horrible must have happened to Lucy-Anna sometime in her life, forcing her to abandon her daughters.

She claimed she and Carleen lived with their mother for three months. After contracting malaria, she was hospitalized for two weeks. Her mother never came to visit, claiming her church was having a revival.

When Eric discovered Brigitte was at the hospital, she said he signed her out and returned to the States with her and Carleen where the assaults immediately resumed.

She recalled accidentally breaking a plate while washing dishes. Her grandmother beat her with a wooden spoon over her entire body. She said she screamed and begged her to stop, but she did not. She limped in pain for days. Brigitte and Carleen were home schooled. She said Eric was clever in keeping her and her sister from the outside world, preventing others of discovering his monstrous acts.

According to police reports, Lucy-Anna was staying in a New York motel when interviewed by police. She denied knowing anything about the murder. She described Eric as a monster, saying she wished she had tried harder to get custody of her daughters. She blamed herself for what happened. She claimed no one could stand against Eric. "It was like his word was holy. No one disbelieved what he said," she replied.

She believed Eric's relatives turned a blind eye to the rapes because of the man's wealth -- because he found the American dream. She described Eric as a success, a financial genius -- and a devil, treating everyone outside his family with respect and warmth, but terrorizing his babies.

In the medical examiner's report, he stated he felt Brigitte did not intentionally kill her father, but accidentally asphyxiated him when she tied the towel around his neck, stuffing part of it into his mouth.

Along with a sexual abuse survivor hot-line and television appearances by Carleen, supporters rented entire billboards to inform the public of her plight. Public opinions were rampant. Investigators feared that if Brigitte did not receive prison time, there would be an open range for this type of vengeance. Women everywhere might believe they can mutilate their husband or boyfriend if abused. City officials feared the entire justice system would be on trial.

Psychiatrists stated the severing of an alleged abuser's penis was very uncommon. Brigitte's hate festered for years, they claimed. Some called the crime premeditated, saying the jury would see through her pathetic "poor me" act, finding her guilty.

Each time Brigitte appeared in court, numerous armed police officers were on hand for security support. Political supporters for Brigitte gave public speeches and voiced her innocence and pled for her rightful acquittal. City officials, appalled at her choice of revenge, vowed "justice will be served" and "Eric will not be forgotten."

On her first appearance inside a courtroom, her

attorney was aghast at the shoddy appearance of his client. He scolded the arresting officers for not allowing Brigitte to dress properly, saying, "She's in her pajamas, for goodness sake." He then requested and was granted the removal of Brigitte's handcuffs. He described her that day as being in a daze, as if she knew not where she was.

Brigitte later said she was in a daze during her first court appearance, saying she could not believe what she was going through was real.

Several members of Eric's family traveled from Rhode Island and Colorado for the short hearing. They each hugged the Prosecutor and ignored Brigitte's relatives. Carleen, though, did not appear. In her place was an advocate from a domestic violence non-profit group supporting those retaliating against their abuser.

Brigitte pled not guilty due to mental defect. She was devastated when denied bail, but her attorney claimed that ruling was normal for such charges. He also claimed she was safer behind bars than outside with Eric supporters.

She stayed incarcerated for nearly two years. On September 30, 2009, Brigitte sat beside her attorney. Her rainbow-colored hair extensions were gone, her Goth gear replaced by a demure black sweater and purple shawl. Her two years behind bars waiting for her trial had seen a drastic change in the once wild-child-dressed father killer.

When testifying, Brigitte admitted to buying the scalpel over the internet while researching the 1993 castration case of Lorena Bobbitt, along with other similar cases, discovering that organs can be reattached. Thus she cooked the evidence before discarding it under a bridge.

In their opening statement, prosecutors maintained that Brigitte intentionally lured her father to her apartment with the sole purpose of murdering him, that she made the entire abuse story up as an excuse to kill her father, a wealthy man she resented. After handcuffing Eric to a chair, she wrapped a long-sleeved shirt around his neck. She stuffed one sleeve down his throat, before removing his penis with the scalpel, causing him to choke to death.

 Brigitte argued that her motive for the killing was not revenge but an act to prevent Eric from taking her young nieces to Liberia and molesting them.

 Eric's relatives continued to deny the allegations that he was a rapist. According to Eric's mother, who attended each day dressed in mourning black, "the allegations came from the fantasies of Brigitte's twisted mind." The woman sobbed quietly as if on cue, remarked one reporter.

 The state therapists assigned to her case had diagnosed Brigitte as being mentally fit for trial. She, in the beginning of her incarceration, was declared depressed and disassociated emotionally, but never delusional. The facts of her case were never in dispute.

 The physical evidence found at the crime scene -- her apartment -- showed how she did it; the confession video explained why. As for what may have driven her to do it, the Prosecutor argued in her opening statement that whatever horrors Harris had endured at the hands of her father should have little bearing on the crime itself. She told the court she was not here to debate whether or not the abuse Brigitte alleged occurred or not. What she did want the jury to understand was the fact Brigitte never reported the abuse to the police, to child services, or even to members of her own family -- the relatives who were now denying Brigitte ever complained that Eric raped her. Instead, said Ross, the defendant chose to take the law into her own hands. She made a deliberate choice to make a plan, to execute that plan, to put that plan into action.

 Arthur Aidala, alongside co-counsel Michael Cibella, offered the jury the same set of facts with a completely different interpretation. He admitted a crime occurred and that Brigitte was somewhat responsible.

However, he told the jury they should consider not just what his client did to her father, but everything her father had done to her. He said that if the Prosecutor wants to talk of vengeance, you must therefore keep in mind, revenge only existed because of Eric Goodridge's long-term brutality. A deep-rooted "sin," he called it.

Then, for one hour, Attorney Aidala went through every known detail of the abuse, sparing no details. He claimed the legal system was not there to help Brigitte because of her "learned abuse." Her abuser, Eric Goodridge, conditioned her to the point of her being too terrified to call police or the children's services. She did, however, tell numerous relatives, but they refused to help her -- maybe because of Eric's wealth, and perhaps because of his being a relative with a high standing within the community. Brigitte could not stop Eric because he would not stop, so she stopped him in the only way she knew how, to take away his weapon of mass destruction.

The jury was given the option of first- and second-degree manslaughter along with the second-degree murder charge. A conviction of second-degree murder can also be lowered to first-degree manslaughter on the grounds of "extreme emotional disturbance," a mitigating defense that argues that the perpetrator was somehow driven to act by what he or she perceived as a legitimate threat. Brigitte's case depended not just on whether the jury believed her guilty, but whether she had been, in some way, provoked into an act of self-defense.

She took the stand in her own defense with her attorney spending most of his time with her discussing Eric's actions front and center. Later on, Carleen also took the stand. She was not asked directly about the abuse, since much of it allegedly happened when she was not living with Brigitte, but she displayed sympathy toward her younger sister, bringing many jurors to tears.

It was over with within one day. Even Brigitte was shocked. She had never thought that her story would inspire so much sympathy. The jury did, however, believe Brigitte was guilty of some type of crime, even though they knew she did not want Eric to die.

The jury dismissed the murder charge and found her guilty of second-degree manslaughter. Juror George Tsourakis told the court, "None of us felt that she deserved to get any murder charges. So we decided on second-degree manslaughter."

However, he and fellow jurors felt since Brigitte's actions did contribute to his death, the second-degree manslaughter charge fit. "We gave her what she deserved."

To settle on second-degree-manslaughter, the jury was convinced Brigitte's actions demonstrated a reckless disregard for human life but were not meant to kill. Some of the jurors felt the heinous act of killing Eric was his gagging to death, not the removal of his penis.

Tsourakis told waiting reporters that he felt Brigitte did not seem reckless by using the towel to silence her father because that kind of behavior was routinely portrayed on television. "I wouldn't have thought he'd die from that, either," he said.

Brigitte recalled watching the jurors as they reentered the courtroom, saying, "The jurors had their poker faces on." She said she could not tell how they voted, only hoping they understood what she endured all those years, and that she truly did what she felt she must do. One reporter described Brigitte's testimony as heartbreaking. Another said Brigitte lived a life of "pure hell".

Eleven of the twelve jurors wrote letters to the judge

asking that Brigitte's sentence be time served. He ignored the letters.

According to Brigitte's defense attorney, who represented her pro bono, seven jurors wrote Judge Cooperman asking him to sentence Brigitte to time served to allow her to seek the psychiatric help she needed. According to Attorney Aidala, he had spoken with many judges, prosecutors and defense attorneys with none ever hearing of jurors doing this.

Despite jury letters, Judge Cooperman threw the book at the woman who made New York history by sentencing Brigitte to the maximum of five to fifteen years. That punishment by New York law was harsh, thought many, saying no one would forget Brigitte for her crime with many never forgiving her.

Seven of the jurors were so supportive of Brigitte that in the days leading up to her sentencing, they wrote the judge asking him to give her no more jail time at all. "Brigitte was sentenced on the day her father molested her," wrote Blanche O'Donnell. "She deserves a life full of love and support, not prison."

One juror sent Brigitte a book as a gift. Still another sent her a Whitney Houston CD. Several social workers from Riker's pledged to find her a job and give her free counseling if the judge would set her free.

Judge Arthur Cooperman was unmoved. He claimed the jury demonstrated leniency that only the court should have exercised.

She served five years before being paroled on August 13, 2012. Upon her release, Brigitte told waiting reporters that she now understood that killing Eric was not the answer, saying, "I can't believe I actually did it." She maintained that that her goal that dreadful day was to stop the abuse. She said she hoped to work for STEPS, an advocacy group whose goal was to End Family Violence.

The case caused much controversy among the relatives and the courts with some psychiatrists saying she did not deserve jail, she had suffered enough. Her relatives claimed she had years to handle the situation by reporting to the proper authorities and chose to do nothing.

While incarcerated in maximum security, Brigitte's case was profiled on television networks including Investigative Discovery program Deadly Women and the Oxygen Network series Snapped. Armed guards were nearby during each interview Brigitte gave. Reporters said her story never changed. She mutilated her father to stop the cycle of abuse.

According to Brigitte, as soon as she began serving her time, she began planning her future. She made the best of prison life. She took cooking class and spent her time reading mysteries and vampire-inspired novels. She now claimed she wished she had told someone outside her family, a schoolmate or neighbor. She blamed her anti-social behavior on the abuse. She received much support while in prison from other women claiming parental sexual abuse. She said she will not allow what happened to stop her from living a productive and happy life.

Once she entered Bedford Hills, Brigitte said she received the therapy and support she never had before. She said it would be wonderful to be one of the shiny, happy people, not just pretending to be happy and not having to have memories or flashbacks. She knew that was not to be, though, for her psychologists told her she would never get over her abuse but would need to learn to deal with it. She said learning how to deal with her abuse and the flashbacks was her biggest issue now.

However, she missed her sister's daughters, the very children she thought she was saving by attacking her father.

She also longed to hear from Lovette, she said, who still lives in Liberia in the reach of her father's family.

At night, she dreamed of being in Africa and not being able to help protect Lovette. She said that even when Eric came to her home to converse with her, she was unsure if she could face him about the attacks. However, he mentioned Lovette being raped and blaming it on her. All her anger poured out.

During one interview, she revealed that she had just one dream about Eric Goodridge. She said they were in Africa. The weird part was he was protecting her from somebody else who had abused her. "He ran the guy over with his Jeep," she said.

The reporter suggested that the dream could be about the life that she wanted -- a life where she had a father who helped her.

She now believed what she did was wrong, and she should have found a legal way to stop Eric. Her advice for other victims of physical or sexual abuse was to inform others until someone listened. Do not take matters into your own hands as she did. Nothing was worth going to prison over or taking someone's life. "In some way, I will always pay a price for killing Eric," she said.

Brigitte returned to Queens after her release from prison. She claimed to be happy and enjoying her freedom and her sister and nieces. She became a counselor for sexually abused women.

Home Town Hero

Solving the Deaf School Murders

According to Craig Plunkett, Joseph Mesa will never realize the amount of pain he caused his victims' families. The tall father with the receding hairline and glasses said there was no amount of Joseph's apologizing that will fill the emptiness in their hearts. He was exactly where his kind belongs.

At a time when young persons are a step closer to their future, and parents look forward to being empty nesters, a parent's worst nightmare took place in a small college town in Washington, D.C.

Using sign language, forty-two-year-old Kathleen said good-bye to her eighteen-year-old son and youngest child, Eric, as he excitedly exited her vehicle in front of the prestigious Gallaudet School for the Deaf. "Call me every night," the slender, freckled-faced mother said in sign.

"Don't worry," signed the scrawny red-haired boy who suffered from Cerebral Palsy as he smiled and walked into the four-story brick building.

Forty-seven-year-old Craig recalled how thrilled the family was upon learning of Eric's acceptance into the Gallaudet College for the Deaf. "It was his first choice of college," he said.

The energetic and always smiling student shared his west wing dorm with mutually knowledge-craving and elated students, many far from home like Eric.

Nineteen-year-old Minch, a slender, dark-haired, dark-eyed drama student, who dreamed of being the next

Steven Spielberg, recalled how Eric religiously kept his room door open. He said the two became "fast friends."

Everyone seemed to like the outgoing Eric with his infectious smile. He talked to everyone. No matter how late it was, if one had a problem to talk out, Eric's shoulder was readily available.

A female student recalled Eric having two older sisters and discussing girl stuff; issues such as boys or weight or jealousy matters did not embarrass him. He always gave good advice, she said. His advice was what she said she would miss the most about him -- their talks.

Everyone at school missed Eric that early morning just one short month after the start of the semester. Minch, who had the room two doors down, reported him missing from math class. When leaving his room that morning, he noticed Eric's door was closed. He thought that strange because Eric's door was always open. "He liked watching people walk down the hall and would wave at all of us," he said.

Therefore, when the sixty-two-year-old Dean went to Eric's room, he received the shock of his life. Lying face down in a pool of blood was the bludgeoned, stabbed and choked body of Eric Plunkett.

Immediately the entire college went on lockdown. Staff counselor Candace, a blonde with green eyes, recalled how police swarmed the campus while yellow crime scene tape surrounded the entire building. Students were instructed to remain in their rooms, and all classes were canceled for the rest of the week. "Everyone was terrified."

For twenty-eight-year-old Detective Luanne Morrison, Eric's murder became her first homicide case. The brunette with large blue eyes recalled the sight of the young man's room, describing it as something "only seen in horror films." Blood was everywhere. On the ceilings, under the bed, in the corners. It was shocking, she said. When she first noticed the metal chair near the body, she thought perhaps Eric had tried to commit suicide by hanging himself from his ceiling light.

Her partner, veteran detective thirty-seven-year-old Ralph Marker, saw the crime scene very differently. The stout father of two with small green eyes said that with the amount of blood present, he immediately ruled out suicide. It was obvious to him; this murder was a crime of passion. That meant the authorities could be looking for a female, as well as a male, meaning the entire college body were suspects.

The detectives had the painstaking task of finding the young man's killer, but even worse for the Dean was his duty to notify Eric's parents. He said Eric's parents lived in Minnesota. He then checked Eric's school records and discovered his parents were active in their neighborhood church. After locating the telephone number of the family's minister, he notified him of Eric's demise. The minister agreed to go to the Plunkett residence and comfort the parents while the Dean spoke with the parents from his office.

Kathleen and Craig recalled being abruptly woke by the ringing of the doorbell that morning just as their bedside telephone simultaneously rang. After instructing her drowsy husband to answer the telephone, Kathleen dragged herself from the bed and down the stairs to the front door.

To her surprise, her minister and two local police officers stood at attention. She recalled hearing Craig talking on the bedroom phone.

She said she was in total shock and disbelief when told the devastating news of Eric being beaten to death inside the dorm room he had decorated with shades of earth tones, his favorite colors. She remembered everything becoming eerily quiet at that moment as if time had stopped. She saw the minister's mouth moving but could not hear what he was saying once she heard the words "Eric is dead."

Craig recalled a similar and horrifying feeling when realizing the caller was the College Dean. When told about the murder, he said he immediately blamed himself since it was his idea for Eric to go to an out-of-state college. He said allowing Eric to go to college was the hardest thing to forgive himself for.

Both parents immediately drove to the deserted campus. They recalled not seeing anyone in sight. It was obvious to them; Eric's murder was no ordinary crime. Craig compared the campus to a graveyard. "The entire campus looked dead," he said.

Police dogs were everywhere, sniffing around and inside each building. Officers checked trashcans. All the license plate numbers from every vehicle on the campus parking lot were written down and put into a database for later use if need be.

Once the couple checked into a nearby hotel, they were asked to accompany Detective Marker to the police station for questioning. Once there, they were separated and asked to provide a written statement concerning their whereabouts for the timeline of Eric's attack.

Kathleen recalled being angry that the detectives suggested she and Craig had killed their own son. She said she felt like slapping the detective. Both were asked separately if they knew of anyone who wanted Eric dead.

They said "no." Both claimed that as far as they knew, Eric had no enemies and no romantic relationships that had soured recently.

As the investigation progressed, the detectives discovered Eric was gay and had recently come out of the closet. Now the worry of the murder being a hate crime had risen, which lengthened the suspect and motive list.

Kathleen said she and Craig considered the possibility of Eric being gay as the reason he was killed. She admitted Eric exhibited feminine features and mannerisms and loved reading romance novels, but she insisted his sexual preference did not matter to the rest of the family. "We just loved him," she said.

At the college, the Dean explained to the detectives that the Gallaudet staff were tolerant of others. He also knew many others were intolerable of such lifestyles, saying, "Hate is a powerful anger tool."

Kathleen said the thought of her son, her baby, being savagely murdered for being a homosexual was like killing Eric twice. She and Craig said they could not fathom anyone killing another human being for their sexual orientation. The police were clearly looking for a monster.

That evening, the campus held a candlelight vigil for Eric. Kathleen and Craig attended and met many of their son's classmates. Sign language poetry readings were held, and deaf students through interpreters recalled their time with Eric. One student described Eric as being easy to like, saying she never saw him unhappy.

Minch said during his speech that the entire campus would miss Eric. He recalled his short friendship with Eric as something he will never forget. He said Eric never spoke unkindly to anyone and claimed Eric loved everyone he met.

Kathleen and Craig wept throughout the vigil, thanking everyone for the large turnout of not just deaf students, but ordinary citizens also. She recalled how they all seemed so caring and hugged her and Craig, telling them Eric had changed their lives for the better. The couple said knowing that "really helped them through the mourning process."

The officers worked around the clock for Eric's killer. At all times, at least fifteen officers were assigned to the case. While some looked for suspects and interviewed students, others concentrated on gathering evidence from the crime scene. They reported they hoped that during the struggle, the killer had cut himself and his blood was at the crime scene, but no such luck.

A press statement from Detective Marker indicated the person responsible either wore gloves or did not harm himself during the attack.

Later revealed by forensic evidence was the fact that the attack was quick and from behind. It was clearly overkill. Besides being deaf, Eric was born with cerebral palsy. Kathleen and Craig claimed their son never allowed his disabilities to hold him back from anything, saying it was his idea to go to college and become a Deaf Ed teacher. "He wanted to help others like himself," recalled Kathleen.

The police believed, with his limited strength, Eric was unable to defend himself and therefore was easily overpowered and brought to the floor. Forensic Scientist Fred Waits explained that the evidence indicated once Eric was down, his killer kicked him several times. The evidence indicated that while Eric was still alive, the assailant then used a knife he probably brought with him, since no weapon was found, and stabbed the victim with multiple blows. When that form of murder also failed, the assailant used a nearby metal chair to finish him off.

Intense violence was used in this killing, reported Detective Morrison. That and the fact that Eric was a member of a gay fraternity also led authorities to believe Eric was romantically involved with another man, either a student, a stranger, or even one of the instructors. For some time, detectives said they had few clues but many theories.

After contacting some of the members of the gay

fraternity, Detectives Marker and Morrison discovered it was Eric's idea to start a gay fraternity. Deaf student Richie recalled that the five of them met at the café down the street with Eric coming up with the club's name, "The Wild Wild West Club."

Soon after talking with Richie, the detectives received an anonymous phone call concerning Minch, one member of the gay fraternity. This young classmate and supposedly good friend of Eric's was one of many students who hugged Eric's parents during the vigil and who stayed in contact with them through letters once they returned home.

Detective Marker recalled as Minch sat in the interrogation room of the police department, he was visibly nervous. According to the detective, Minch "bit his nails and drank an abundance of water" offered to him by the officers. Through an interpreter, officers interrogated Minch concerning Eric's attraction to the heterosexual man which he kept secret from police when first questioned.

According to the detectives, he did not answer right away. The detectives viewed this gesture as a stalling motion. Then slowly, choosing his words carefully, he began to sign.

He told the officers, he kept the proposition secret because he did not want police believing him gay or that he killed Eric. He cited the college's rule of no "trouble" of any kind, or it's expulsion. The college does not allow second chances. Reportedly, the waiting list for enrollment was long.

When asked by Detective Marker why he felt Eric was sexually attracted to him, Minch explained that the two watched a movie together in Eric's room one evening. "Just hang'n out," he said. Then Eric made a pass at him, which shocked him, he said. He claimed he immediately made it clear he was not a homosexual and was not interested in

Eric in that manner. He said Eric would not take "no" for an answer, saying "'just give it a try.'" Minch claimed Eric grew angry.

When the detective insinuated the two then fought, Minch denied it, but the detectives did not believe him.

Smiling like the spider that ate the fly, Detective Marker insisted that if a man came on to him like he said Eric did, he would "pound his face in." The detective claimed Minch again denied he and Eric fought.

Sweating like a horse, Minch insisted it was nothing like the officers insinuated, but again the officers felt Minch was lying. They pressed for an answer. Detective Marker told Minch they could easily find the truth by interviewing other students to see if any of them saw anything or if Eric told someone of the fight.

Buckling under the pressure, Minch reluctantly admitted he "touched Eric with his fist," but adamantly denied killing the young man.

Minch covered his face with his hands insisting he was defending himself. The interview was curtailed and Minch was then placed under arrest for second-degree murder. Detective Morrison slapped the cuffs on the now sobbing man before reading him his rights.

Afterward, officers escorted Minch down a flight of stairs into the basement of the century-old building where he was fingerprinted before being placed on suicide watch.

That evening, all television stations within the campus area reported Detective Marker's press announcement that a suspect was in custody. He announced that police believed that after Eric made sexual advances to Minch, a fight escalated into murder. The entire community breathed a sigh of relief.

The son of two deaf parents, Minch came to the college from New Hampshire and quickly befriended Eric.

His younger brother and five cousins were also deaf. Many students would later say they witnessed Minch grieving when he learned of his friend's murder.

The entire police department celebrated with champagne. Their high-profile case was solved -- case closed. Detective Marker immediately called Eric's family with the news.

Kathleen said she was beside herself when she learned of the arrest but was shocked to find out whom it was the police had in custody.

The Dean said he and other staff members were also stunned to learn Minch was accused of being the killer. He recalled attending the vigil for Eric and watched Minch hug the parents. Minch even posted a dedication to Eric on his Web page. It was all quite baffling, he said.

Craig said he and Kathleen never dreamed the killer was Minch. He recalled how kind and thoughtful Minch was to them at the candlelight vigil. He even helped organize it. He said it must be true; looks are deceiving.

The campus was elated with the news of the incarceration. Gallaudet was now safe again, many felt. No longer would the students need to travel in groups or be escorted by campus security to their classes. Many students were shocked to discover whom the police had in custody. Most disbelieved the killer was Minch.

One said Minch could not kill anyone. He claimed Minch refused to kill spiders when he found them inside his room. "He picks them up and carries them outside," he said.

Another who claimed knowing Minch for years said Minch never said an unkind word about Eric, calling the two "best friends."

Some began to wonder if the police had the right person in custody, or had law enforcement made an arrest too soon? One week later, the grand jury summoned Minch. With many students still reeling from Eric's murder, Minch's friends rallied to his defense and attended the hearing. His incredulous parents also attended.

Through their interpreter, the couple told the press that Minch was no murderer, and they did not believe he confessed as was reported. They claimed Minch encouraged persons with normal hearing to study sign language, saying, "It is an art form."

Unfortunately, for Detectives Marker and Morrison, at the Grand Jury arraignment, the U.S. Attorney's Office dropped the charges against Minch, citing insufficient evidence. According to the Attorney General, since Minch did not actually confess to the murder, his office did not feel a release from custody was the right choice, but Minch was still a suspect and the only suspect authorities had at that time.

What the public did not know was that Detective Marker possessed a mixed performance record. Nearly half of his cases within six years on the force remained unsolved, and many arrests were dismissed for lack of evidence. He was an "arrest now and find evidence later" kind of cop, which did not set well with his superiors.

The case detectives were sure Minch was the killer and kept him under strict surveillance. They followed him everywhere, hoping he would slip up and reveal he was the guilty one. According to Detective Marker, the police merely had to apply more hard work and get evidence to nail Minch. He believed Minch had motive and opportunity to commit this crime.

Even with Minch's release from custody and the charges against him dropped, that did not satisfy the college concerning his innocence. He was suspended from campus immediately. He was devastated. According to Minch's father, all his son cared about was getting a college education, saying, "Eric dying has destroyed my son also." His suspension was then announced through the provost to an assembly of students with many of them protesting that Minch's rights were violated. The provost, though, stood his ground and deemed the suspension necessary for the safety of the remaining students and faculty and for Minch.

According to the Gallaudet spokesperson, Minch received numerous threats against his life after his arrest. The school felt suspending him was the right choice for all concerned parties.

The campus was fearful again. With Eric's killer still on the loose, the students felt safe only when traveling in groups and relying on campus security for protection. Many carried pepper spray while others bought handguns small enough to conceal under clothing or inside purses. Women took free self-defense classes the college offered.

Without Gallaudet, and between the death threats and his face being as popular as the President's, Mitch returned to his home state of Michigan. He told a local reporter that his dreams of becoming a filmmaker were over. His leaving campus, he said, was the hardest thing for him, next to losing Eric.

Eric's parents were furious when told of Minch's release. Kathleen demanded to know why the authorities did not have their T's crossed before arresting someone and announcing it to the public? "Don't they realize how foolish that makes the department look?" she said.

The detectives were also devastated by Minch's release, according to Detective Morrison. Only two months after the murder, the case went cold but not forgotten. She was determined to find the culprit, she said, but they had no new suspects. She understood how frightened the community was and how aggravated the parents must feel, but law enforcement's hands were tied.

By fall, all leads had dried up and the investigation was placed on the back burner. The college threw a Thanksgiving party for students and faculty. Catered food and an open bar were furnished.

All became quiet with nothing unusual happening on campus after Minch left. Some felt he was Eric's murderer and should have been prosecuted. Some students left directly after the murder and never returned. Gallaudet felt a financial blow with the absent students and with the decrease in new enrollment since the case went national.

For the students that chose to stay, there were signs of getting back into the swing of things. They again enjoyed dorm parties and staying out late, as long as they were in groups.

While Eric's parents tried to cope with their loss and the idea that their son's killer may never be caught, Kathleen continued to give interviews whenever asked. She did not want the public to forget about her son. "The depths of my grief are indescribable," she said. She told the media she needed to be strong for her family and believed the public looked down on her for not showing her grief publicly.

According to Craig, Kathleen never showed public pain. She cried for Eric in privacy, but he believed showing public sorrow was expected of a murder victim's parent. By Christmas, the police got a break in the case, and it came from outside sources. As Kathleen sorted through Eric's mail one morning, she said she noticed his Visa card had recently been used. She immediately notified Detectives Marker and Morrison.

After talking with Kathleen about the possibility of the killer using Eric's credit cards, Detective Marker admitted law enforcement dropped the ball. No officer conducted an inventory of Eric's property inside his room, which was customary on any murder or burglary case. "We messed up," he said.

According to the Dean, when the public discovered proper channels were ignored when searching Eric's room, they let the police know about it. Parents and students picketed the police headquarters, demanding answers. The police almost had a riot on their hands.

Once Candace learned the police were tracking down Eric's credit cards, she notified the Dean, and together they did a search of records for the college cafeteria. They discovered Eric's credit card was used several times after his murder to purchase meals.

The detectives traced the purchases of the credit cards. They discovered the purchaser had used the cards to buy alcohol from a local store that had a reputation for selling alcohol to underage people. Detective Morrison said she asked to see the security cameras at some of these stores the cards were used at, but unfortunately, too much time had elapsed and the videos were erased or taped over.

Kathleen immediately canceled all of Eric's credit cards, but the credit card companies were notified of the murder, and they agreed to keep tabs on the cards in case someone tried to use them again.

Soon the police got a bite. Someone tried using one of the cards three times after it was canceled. The credit card company immediately notified police, and the detectives went to the store where the card was presented and viewed the video.

However, the police hit a brick wall. The video was too grainy and out of focus for any positive identification to be made. The person using the card appeared to be a short male, but other than that, nothing. That was the last time the killer tried using Eric's credit cards. The leads dried up again.

According to a Gallaudet spokesperson, that winter, the school bought eight new security cameras, but none was installed and no explanation or reason was given. Minch found what work he could in his home state, but police were still surveying him; at one time he was photographed kicking a trashcan into the street.

According to Detective Marker, once he reviewed the surveillance footage, he believed Minch had a large amount of pent-up rage. He said the biggest break came when the brown hairs found on Eric were used to summon Minch to another grand jury hearing.

When subpoenaed to the grand jury hearing, Minch said he thought his nightmare was over when he returned home. He believed police would harass him until they found sufficient evidence to pin Eric's murder on him, and he believed they did not care if he was innocent.

Minch showed up at the hearing alone and was supplied with an interpreter. After two hours of questions and answers, the jury concluded their investigation. He was told the court would notify him later and for him not to leave the state without notifying the Attorney General's Office. He said he felt like a fly under a microscope.

Detective Marker admitted his office put the heat on Minch, saying, "We believed he was a murderer, and it was just a matter of time before we got the evidence we needed to prosecute him." He said the case was not going to go away, and he refused to allow Eric's murder to become an unsolved mystery.

When Kathleen learned of the second grand jury hearing, she said she did not know what to think. She and Craig were grateful the police wanted to find their son's killer, but they did not want to see an innocent man go to prison. They wanted justice, not revenge. They said the case was very difficult for a long time.

Minch was due to fly home right after the grand jury hearing, but did he? Records showed he stayed another night in town. Was he there to commit another crime? some wondered. Was he staying over just to spend time with friends he left behind and had not seen for months?

Then at 4:15 a.m., the fire alarm was triggered. The place went crazy. Students woke from the noise terrified someone had broken into their building. Room lights turned on one after another as frenzied students and secret lovers, some dressed, others not, rallied into the halls to watch and add to the confusion. Police swarmed the area with the canine unit, hoping to catch the person or persons who activated the alarm. The Dean instructed all students to the dining hall for roll call.

Candace recalled watching the Dean sign an alphabetical roll call of the entire student enrollment. Each time a student was accounted for, heard were welcomed sighs and cries of relief for that person's safety. She said they all hoped everyone was accounted for and the tripping of the alarm was accidental or a prank.

She recalled that by the time the Dean was into the T's of the alphabet, the students were smiling and hugging one another, believing that all the students were accounted for. Then the Dean came to a person who was absent. This was another morning everyone remembered. When Benjamin Varner did not answer, they knew he was dead. Everyone felt sick.

A former student recalled girls screaming and crying believing Benjamin was dead. They believed the killer had struck again -- and perhaps was still inside the dorm or on campus somewhere. It was the most terrifying night of everyone's life. "I left at daybreak and never went back," she said.

Indeed, the killer had struck again. Nineteen-year-old

Benjamin Varner lay dead on his floor with numerous stab wounds to his chest and neck area. The crime scene was eerily similar to that of victim Eric Plunkett. Once again, the campus swarmed with police officers and forensic specialists.

Forensic Scientist Fred Langley surmised after the second murder that the killer was a student. Surrounding the campus was a nine-foot wrought iron fence; all doors, windows and front gate were automatically locked at 6 p.m. A security guard guarded the front gate nightly. To get inside the buildings, one must have a key-card.

When rumors circulated that the killer might be a student because of the easy access into the locked buildings, the school prayed they were wrong. Having a killer emerge from a community more like family than what most campuses offer seemed especially wounding. "It's hard to believe one of us students has it in them to kill in that fashion," a female student wrote on a reporter's pad.

"The killer being a student would have been the worst possible news for the college," said the Dean. When the killer was captured, he hoped the person was a drifter or an escaped lunatic with a stolen key-card. "Students are always misplacing their key-cards," he said.

When Benjamin's body was discovered, Detective Marker wanted to talk with Minch immediately. As the police knew, he was still in town. Some of the officers thought it just a coincidence that Minch was around at the same time a second victim was found at the same campus, but Marker did not.

By the time Detectives Marker and Morrison left the second crime scene, Minch was on a plane for home. They immediately made arrangements through headquarters to fly to Detroit. As far as they were concerned, the young man had a lot of explaining to do.

When Kathleen learned of the second murder, she said she also felt Minch was involved in Benjamin's death. How could one person have so much bad luck? she thought, and she did not believe in coincidences.

According to the forensic evidence, Benjamin's crime scene had many similarities to the first crime. His room door was closed. He was savagely beaten with different forms of weaponry, and the room was covered with blood splatter. His broken glasses lay next to his body.

Benjamin, unlike Eric, had numerous defense wounds on his hands and arms, according to Fred Langley. It was obvious he put up a tremendous fight for his life. The cause of death for Benjamin was fifteen stab wounds.

The Dean, as with Eric's murder, removed all students from the hall and placed them in the adjoining Westbrook Hall. No one wanted to sleep in the hall that two students were murdered in, and the Dean did not blame them.

Craig believed there was a serial killer stalking the campus. Now another family was going through what his family was still trying to cope with. His heart went out to the family, he said.

When Detectives Morrison and Marker came to Minch's house to inform him of Benjamin's murder, and the M.O. was the same as Eric's murder, he knew the officers believed he killed both men. He said he thought his nightmare had ended, but soon realized it had just begun.

Through an interpreter, the detectives interviewed Minch in his family home with his parents present for four hours. He adamantly denied having anything to do with either murder.

He claimed to be in a hotel room miles away packing to return home when Benjamin was killed. He knew the detectives thought him a liar, but he knew he was innocent.

He just wished someone other than relatives believed him. They would soon have to believe the shaggy-haired man when he presented receipts from his hotel room.

During the evidence recovery of Benjamin's room, Fred Langley and his team used luminol to find trace blood and other body fluids. They reportedly discovered a bloody shoe print left behind by the killer. It was a big break in the second case. Langley said shoe prints were as accurate as fingerprints in identifying a suspect. "All the lab rats were very excited," he said.

The shoe print was identified as belonging to an Air Max Cross Trainer of a Nike brand, size 9, and Benjamin wore a size 11. Authorities knew it belonged to the killer.

According to Benjamin's mother, it was her idea for Benjamin to attend the deaf school. She said he did not want to leave his hometown and be so far away, but she assured him he would be okay. She said she would never forgive herself. She recalled how he cried when she dropped him off at the front doors, saying, "He was my whole life."

Detective Morrison was sure they were close to solving the murders. With the finding of the shoe print, she said they finally knew something solid about the murderer. Then when officers discovered, in one of the dumpsters behind the campus, a black-and-yellow jacket covered in blood, she knew they were closing in on the suspect.

Kathleen recalled that the weeks it took to analyze the evidence found at Benjamin's crime scene seemed more like months. However, the detectives kept her and Craig clued to all new evidence, including keeping Minch under surveillance, since he wore size 9 shoes and might be the killer.

It was discovered that the murder weapon used on Eric was a paring knife. The killer left it behind. When Candace learned that the knife was used to kill Benjamin, she said it really bothered her because it was a gift from his parents. They apparently had sent it to him from Wisconsin to cut his apples with. They were his favorite fruit. "He ate one each night before going to bed," she said. "I still think about that."

According to Detective Marker, with the second murder, the killer left behind incriminating evidence. It was obvious to authorities that the killer was either in a hurry, interrupted by something or someone, or injured during the fight. Benjamin weighed over two hundred pounds and was a formidable opponent.

With the shoe size being a small size for a male, the detectives surmised the killer was a small man but relatively strong. Perhaps he was an athlete, jogger or weight lifter. Many of the male students did have physically enhancing hobbies, which would allow them to overpower a man Benjamin's size, especially since this attack was from behind like Eric's murder.

There were now two victims within a six-month period. A black cloud hung over Gallaudet. Everyone walked on pins and needles. Even staff members discussed their fears with one another. Some even talked about leaving. The Dean had put his whole life into this campus. It was the place he wanted to retire from, receive tenure from.

Each murder had consisted of a great amount of violence -- kicking, choking, stabbing, and bludgeoning. The investigators knew that only an inexperienced killer uses multiple techniques on his victim. It was obvious the killer was young.

When authorities realized that the killer might be a student, they suggested gathering DNA samples of each male. The Dean absolutely refused that idea, citing invasion of privacy and the fear of inducing another panic, not to mention losing more students.

However, according to Candace, students were already panicky and terrified. After Benjamin's death, students left Gallaudet in droves, she said. This was clearly the worst time in the college's history for enrollment.

Kathleen and Craig watched the news nightly; the students were simply terrified that they would be next, and the parents did not blame them.

After the detectives came to see Minch after Benjamin's murder, he claimed he began having nightmares and bouts of crying. He said he would break down and start crying for no apparent reason. He said he felt helpless that many outside his family believed he killed the students. He said his nerves became so bad that he could not work anymore. His profile was now in the Michigan newspapers as a person of interest.

Candace had stayed in touch with Minch after he left the campus. She knew he was having a hard time of things. Reporters were stationed outside of his parents' home after Benjamin's death. She knew he was a virtual prisoner in his own home.

Craig and Kathleen also knew of Minch's family plight. They watched the case religiously with each new lead. They knew that cars belonging to Minch's parents were vandalized. Their windows were broken out. People were frightened of the possibility of a two-time murderer living in their neighborhood. They wanted the family gone.

Once detectives discovered that the blood on the jacket and shoe print belonged to Benjamin, they went looking for the owner. Detective Marker said he had his fingers crossed that someone inside Gallaudet would recognize that jacket. "This was where good old-fashioned legwork paid off," he said.

Detective Morrison was put in charge of keeping track of Benjamin's credit card activity. She said they did not want to make the same mistake with Benjamin as they did with Eric concerning Eric's credit card activity. She immediately got an inventory of Benjamin's belongings and soon discovered what was missing from his dorm room.

When Kathleen heard the detectives were closing in on a suspect, she said she was beside herself. She knew Eric's murder would have a closure. She believed no parent should go through what this senseless, cold-hearted killer put her family and the Varners through.

Missing from Benjamin's room were credit cards and blank bank checks. When police learned one of the checks had been cashed, they acted quickly. When the detectives viewed the bank video, Morrison said she suspected the killer was a homeless person or a drug addict. What they saw was mind blowing.

The last person the detectives said they suspected and had eliminated early in the Eric Plunkett murder case was right there on the video. He wore no disguise. He did not act nervous. He was as cool as a cucumber when cashing that stolen check. His completely calm and collected attitude enraged investigators. Detective Marker said if he could have reached into that video and wrung his neck, he would have done so.

The detectives knew the man. He was the student who lived across the hall from Eric. He hugged Eric's parents at the candlelight vigil. He told police Eric was an inspiration to all deaf people. The son-of-a-bitch fooled everyone.

Armed with a search warrant, Detectives Marker and Morrison with officer back-up stormed the dorm room of Joseph Mesa. He was not present. An immediate A.P.B. was issued for his arrest. Found inside the room were brown hairs from Joseph's hairbrush which were bagged for evidence. In the closet, they discovered every shirt was a size medium except one. It was a 2X, many sizes too big for

Joseph, but not for Benjamin. They bagged that also.

Minch's DNA already cleared him of being the donor of the brown hairs found in Benjamin's hand; still he was kept under surveillance, being he was the only suspect at that time.

Prime evidence found inside that room were Benjamin's wallet and identification card and the Nike Air Max shoes located in the bottom of the closet, said Detective Marker.

In the late hour of February 27, after Joseph discovered police wanted him, he turned himself in to campus security. Case detectives immediately took him into custody and interrogated him at the police station.

Kathleen still believed that if police had taken an inventory of Eric's room and known what valuables were missing, they would have caught Joseph sooner, and maybe Benjamin Varner would be alive.

When Craig and Kathleen learned they had a new suspect in custody, Craig said they could not believe who it was. They never dreamed it was Joseph. The small, quiet-spoken man from Guam was very comforting to them at the vigil, said Craig. He even wept during his eulogy for Eric. "The man was truly a chameleon -- and that was the worst kind of killer," Craig said.

Twenty-year-old Joseph Mesa came to Gallaudet by scholarship. He was his hometown hero and looked upon as an inspiration to other handicapped and poor Asian children. "Don't let being deaf hold you back," he told the village children.

His community, upon learning of his arrest, was shocked and devastated, not only for the deaths of the two American students, but because Joseph destroyed his life and his good standing in the Guam community.

Minch recalled that not until Joseph was charged

with the murders did the cops clear him. He described the feeling as like a three-hundred-pound weight lifted from him. From then on, he said he never lost another night's sleep. The Dean called him and offered to re-instate him, but he declined. He said with everything he had been through, too many bad feelings stayed with him and he had no desire to belong to that college again.

Through an interpreter, the detectives confronted Joseph about cashing one of Benjamin's checks for $600. He immediately went on the defense, stating Benjamin wrote that check to him before he died, but detectives proved that statement false. The department's handwriting expert easily proved the check was written in Joseph's handwriting, not Benjamin's.

Once detectives had Joseph in the interrogation room, they confronted him with the evidence concerning the Benjamin Varner case. Joseph denied the jacket found in the dumpster was his.

That statement was also false. A photograph of the jacket circulated around campus, and two students came forward and identified the item as being worn by Joseph. After learning that news, Joseph knew the jig was up.

The Dean recalled that when the murder details were released, they were bone chilling. He said the murders were the worst crimes Gallaudet ever experienced in its history. "I don't believe any of us will be the same again," he said.

According to Detective Marker, Joseph confessed everything that evening. He rattled on and on like a music box. Once the suspect began speaking, he told the officers everything they needed to know.

Through an interpreter, and for three hours, Joseph relived the murder of Benjamin Varner. His excuse for taking a human life and destroying the victims' families was "I couldn't help myself. This urge came over me to kill. I tried to fight it, but I couldn't."

He then told detectives that when he saw the checkbook on a table, he just had to have it. He said Benjamin was alone and it just happened. He then saw the knife by the microwave and stabbed him in the neck from behind. He screamed and said he was going to report Joseph and have him arrested. Joseph became scared, he said, and started stabbing Benjamin repeatedly.

According to Joseph, his victim, who outweighed him by almost seventy-five pounds, fought back, but in the process of losing large amounts of blood, he was unable to continue fighting off his attacker and eventually fell to the floor. At that time, Joseph admitted to kicking him in the head a few times, then he grabbed a wooden statue and beat Benjamin in the face until he stopped moving.

Detective Morrison recalled how Joseph showed no emotion when talking about killing Benjamin. She described Joseph's no-care attitude as if he was reciting his address or telephone number. "Taking a human life was as easy as baking a pie to him," she said.

Joseph admitted he went to Benjamin's dorm room for the sole purpose of robbing the fellow student. After Benjamin was dead, Joseph explained how he washed his hands off in Benjamin's dorm room sink and put on one of Benjamin's T-shirts to conceal his bloody clothes. He then said he ransacked the room and found credit cards in a dresser drawer, which he also stole.

The over-sized T-shirt was used as evidence against Joseph at trial. After confessing to the heinous murder of Benjamin, the police wanted to see if he would cop to Eric's murder as well. The detectives had suspected Joseph of both murders but needed him to say it for the record.

Detective Marker then asked the young murderer if

he wished to tell them anything else, and he should clear his conscience if there was anything else he wanted to tell the officers, saying, "You should clear your conscience." That was when Joseph admitted to killing Eric Plunkett also. He then asked for a glass of water, and one was provided.

After drinking a full glass of the liquid, again and in grisly detail, Joseph told detectives how the murder of Eric Plunkett happened. Joseph admitted he had planned the murder for two days, even though he claimed to respect the small geeky-looking man. He tried to diminish his involvement with the murder by saying, "I don't know why I killed him, it just happened."

Joseph stared straight ahead, his large dark eyes fixed on Detective Marker, and explained without emotion how he entered Eric's room that day asking for money. He claimed Eric denied having any money to loan. Joseph said he disbelieved that, since Eric's parents routinely bought him gifts or sent him money from home.

He believed Eric was lying and he became angry, he said. That was when Joseph made the conscious decision to kill. Joseph said when Eric, who was sixty pounds lighter, turned his back to him, he grabbed him around the neck and choked him to the floor. He was aware Eric had cerebral palsy and knew he would be easy to overpower.

Joseph said he thought he could strangle Eric, but he tried to yell for help, which frightened Joseph, so he began kicking him in the head and face, but that did not kill him either. He then recalled using his knife to stab his victim several times. He explained how Eric gasped for air before dying. That, according to Joseph, was when he bludgeoned him over the head with the metal chair.

When asked by Detective Morrison where the knife was, Joseph admitted he left the knife in Eric's room but retrieved it later. He said he remembered not leaving fingerprints which would identify him. He then threw the weapon into the local river which ran directly behind the campus.

Joseph's confessions filled in the blanks for the investigators. His motive for the murders was old-fashioned greed. He needed money but said he did not realize how "messy" the actual killing would be. He said he believed the victims would die quickly because of the amount of force he used on them or, in Eric's case, since he was sickly.

After learning of Joseph's confession, local reporters bombarded the police station wanting to know why so much evidence was overlooked. Morrison, Marker, and their captain took a lot of heat from reporters at the *Washington Post*.

Reporters had tracked the records back to the arrest of Minch, to try to learn why the police had never considered Joseph a suspect. It turned out that the detectives had missed some key evidence that could have prevented the murder of Benjamin Varner.

Among the problems was the fact that Eric Plunkett's wallet had been missing from his room, which would point toward robbery as a motive and alert police to look for financial transactions.

In fact, Eric's debit card had been used on the day he died, yet no one followed up on that obvious clue. In addition, Mesa already had a record of debit card thefts, and he was the one who had alerted the RA to the supposed odor. A basic rule of police work, apparently not followed, was to check out the first person at the scene.

The mistakes began almost immediately. The police had interviewed Mesa since he lived across the hall but had not requested a background check on him which would have revealed the suspension for theft. They also did not investigate the fact that Mesa's account differed from that of others; no one else had smelled an odor. His behavior had been indicative of a person who wanted the body to be found.

Once it was found, there was no routine inventory of items in Eric's room, which would have turned up the missing items. The detectives also failed to follow up on purchases made with the card, which meant that no one requested videotapes from the stores where the purchases were made until after the tapes had been erased.

Then there was the Minch interrogation. There was never any confession, but records indicate that Marker told his superiors he had extracted a confession. No one asked for corroborating evidence, and a newly promoted commander had failed to question the detective closely.

A new team of detectives was assigned after Minch was released, but they had accepted Minch as the suspect, failing to look for new clues or consider other angles. It was a classic case of tunnel vision: they all were thinking inside the box that the first detective had built, despite his obvious errors. No one established a timeline leading up to the murder, another routine investigative activity. In short, there were many inexcusable errors.

Once Joseph was charged with two counts of first-degree murder, he was sent for psychological observation to Doctor Rufus Long. Doctor Long often worked with law enforcement and had thirty years' experience in criminal psychology.

According to the doctor, when first meeting Joseph, he described both murders in joyful detail, with no remorse for what he put his two victims through. In one counseling session, he admitted that after washing Benjamin's blood off his hands and face, he stayed with the corpse for two hours, so he could admire his handiwork. "He often smiled during his reenactments of the crimes," Long said.

Defense attorney Ferris R. Bond was tall and handsome with sandy-colored hair and brown eyes. He said he accepted Joseph's case because he honestly believed Joseph suffered from schizophrenia and uncontrollable rage. It was obvious to Bond that Joseph was unaware of the impact of what the murders would do to the families, saying, "He was completely matter-of-fact about everything he did."

When Kathleen learned of Joseph's defense, she admitted, after reading Joseph's confession, she believed he was sorry he was caught but not for committing the murders. She said her family had only fond memories of Joseph after Eric died. Finding out later that Joseph was their son's killer crushed their hearts again.

During Joseph's counseling sessions, Doctor Long explained how Joseph enjoyed reminiscing about his violent past. During one session, he confessed that at a young age, he put kittens into a sack and stomped them to death -- much like when he kicked Eric and Benjamin before actually killing them.

The doctor later testified that Joseph stood and demonstrated the stomping of the kittens with his feet. "His eyes twinkled. It really made him happy reliving what he had done to those helpless cats," he said.

With most psychopaths, said Doctor Long, they have little or no empathy for others. They look at any life, whether animal or human life, as insignificant, like stepping on a bug. It was no big deal to kill, they believed, and they always found a way to justify their crimes.

Joseph admitted to Doctor Long that once the attack started on Eric, he did not think twice about killing him. Since Eric suffered from cerebral palsy, Joseph looked upon him as being inferior, useless. By the time he decided to kill Benjamin, Joseph said he had lost his fear of killing. The fear of discovery was still very much present, but doing the physical attack, and the blood and violence that go with murder, had faded from Joseph's mind. "Joseph told me that he was perfecting his skill and looked forward to more victims," he said.

When reports of Joseph's counseling sessions were revealed, Candace said she believed that Joseph, if not caught, would have continued preying on campus students. "There's no doubt in my mind. It was in his blood to kill," she said.

Like many psychopaths, Joseph kept souvenirs of his crimes. He kept Benjamin's T-shirt and hung it in his closet, which clearly shows Joseph enjoyed the kill and wanted to relive it repeatedly. The T-shirt was a constant reminder to Joseph of what he had done, and he was proud of his work.

Kathleen said when she and Craig learned officers discovered credit cards belonging to Eric and Benjamin while searching Joseph's room, they knew that Joseph was a black-hearted and soulless monster. They believed he cared nothing about the families' pain. Kathleen said even after the cards were canceled by the families, Joseph held on to them, "like a prize...or a favorite toy...and that's frightening."

According to Minch, when he learned Joseph reported the fight between him and Eric to frame him for the murder, he hated him. He claimed that accusation turned his life upside down. He was unsure if he would ever completely recover from the accusations of being labeled a murderer.

According to Doctor Long, there are always signs of a violent person's nature. However, with Joseph, as with most killers or violent offenders, the "red flags" are overlooked for many reasons. No parent wants to think their child is "bad" or "crazy" or a danger to others, he said. Parents often make excuses for their children when the child does something wrong. All down through history, there have been parents who hid their child's demonic behavior to protect the child and to shield them from public ridicule.

As far as Attorney Bond was concerned, Joseph suffered from years of mental problems caused by a father who had beaten him because of his inability to communicate. The result induced him to fly into uncontrollable fits of rage and commit destructive actions.

Joseph claimed he felt unwanted and unloved by his family. His father told reporters that he had not understood the effect of his behavior on his son, saying, "It is the way children are raised in Guam." He claimed to not know any better.

Attorney Bond described his client as delusional since childhood, and as Joseph matured, he suffered from reoccurring nightmares where a black-gloved wrestling star called the Undertaker told him to do heinous things. He claimed a pair of black leather-gloved hands had signed to him, ordering him to kill, saying, "I felt as if they were more powerful than I am."

He claimed those hands had been signing to him since childhood. He blamed the gloved hands for his bludgeoning the family cat with a baseball bat. The hands had shown him in dreams how to kill his victims.

Detective Marker, who worked Homicide for over twenty years, said the Joseph Mesa case was the worst he had seen, describing the man as "pure evil." He felt proud realizing he helped stop Joseph when he was still a young man, saying, "Some killers never get caught, and that really angers me."

It would be another two years before Joseph entered a courtroom to stand trial for his insidious murders. His attorney argued that Joseph was unfit to stand trial, claiming Joseph had suffered from hallucinations since childhood, and saying, "He needs a hospital, not prison."

The case investigators agreed with the defense in that Joseph does suffer from mental problems; however, he knew exactly what he was doing when he killed those young men. He had already admitted he killed for money, saying he "was after easy money."

Doctor Long disagreed that Joseph's main goal for committing murder was for monetary gain. He believed Joseph was a thrill killer, saying, "He got off on the adrenalin rush." Doctor Long said the money was secondary to the kill. He said Joseph staying with the corpse of Benjamin Varner proves that.

Candace thought Joseph claiming incompetence was ridiculous. She claimed his college IQ scores, his being on the Dean's list, and his overall productivity while enrolled at Gallaudet proved he was intelligent. She recalled how he always showed up for class prepared. She believed his attempt to portray himself a "dummy" was his way of lying to save himself from prison or the electric chair. "He became a pathetic person in the end," she said.

According to the reporters covering the trial, the defense claimed everything under the stars was wrong with Joseph Mesa. If Joseph and his attorney could come up with excuses for Joseph's twisted and barbaric behavior, they did.

The three psychiatrists that had examined Joseph for the prosecution found him to be depressed and antisocial, but sane. All said he was faking a mental illness, but defense experts said that Mesa suffered from a rare condition known as Intermittent Explosive Disorder, and thus he could not control his actions.

Intermittent Explosive Disorder: an impulse control disorder in which a person fails to resist aggressive impulses that are out of proportion to the provoking situation. The person often describes the episode as being precipitated by significant tension or rage; their thoughts race, their body tingles or tightens, they feel overwhelmed by the need to act out. Once they do, the episode results in a sharp decline in arousal and a feeling of relief.

The defense and their psychiatrists introduced Joseph Mesa's childhood abuse history. Craig and Kathleen attended the entire three-week trial. Kathleen recalled that what the defense counsel tried to get the jury to believe was laughable, describing the trial as "a circus." She said the jurors themselves would have to be schizophrenic to believe the defense's version of the facts. She and many others called the defense tactics ridiculous.

Discovered is the fact that Joseph had his own defense plans. Halfway through the trial of March and April 2002, Joseph wrote his girlfriend, who was also a deaf student, asking her to lie for him and to testify that she knew him to be mentally unstable. In one letter, he admitted to her he was faking his insanity defense, saying, "It isn't true, but I hope it will work, anyway."

He also sent a letter to his brother-in-law in Guam to persuade him to destroy evidence. Investigators who learned about these communications confiscated a series of letters, and defense attorney Ferris R. Bond moved to have them suppressed.

Joseph's girlfriend stood behind her man until she realized he had played her. Once she received his confession about the insanity pleas being a cynical con, her eyes opened and she saw Joseph Mesa, the man she had loved all this time, for the monster he really was. She turned the letter over to authorities who, in turn, used it against him, sealing his fate.

The federal prosecution team was Assistant U. S. Attorney Jeb Richards and Assistant U. S. Attorney Jennifer M. Collins. Their argument was simple: Mesa had methodically selected specific individuals to rob and kill.

The defense's argument was more surprising. A lifetime of frustration over his inability to communicate had triggered Joseph's bad behavior. He had directions to kill in his head, not from voices, as hearing people might, but in sign language. Thus, at the time of both murders, Joseph had been legally insane, even though the defense had no apparent explanation for Joseph's lack of remorse after the murders or even after his confession. He never apologized to the victims' parents.

The trial required an interpreter for Joseph, which meant the procedure would be much longer than normal because all comments had to be relayed to him. The courtroom windows were covered, and Joseph was given a partition for private conferences with his attorney, which had to be conducted in sign language. Once everything was in place, the trial commenced.

With an above average I.Q. and being a conman all his life, Joseph honestly believed he could fake his way out of two murders. He had more tricks up his sleeve, which took many by surprise and left everyone laughing. He insisted on taking the stand in his own defense.

Testifying via an interpreter, Joseph went into an almost trance-like state on the stand. He claimed he confessed out of guilt and to allow the school community some peace of mind. Some felt he thought his "generous" impulse would count in his favor. It did not. According to one reporter, throughout the confession, Joseph alternated between being disturbed by his committing the murders and being indifferent.

Joseph insisted he had no control over his actions, as if he were someone's puppet. He had Lucifer on one shoulder during the murders urging him to get money, and on the other shoulder was his angel, his normal side, pleading with him to do no wrong. This animated rendition of "voices in my head" might have fooled a dumb few; however, theft was a long way from murder, and so if the "devil" was urging him to steal, what was his reasoning for the murders? He had no viable explanations.

He claimed that to fight the evil hands so he would be caught and prevented from killing again, he intentionally used a bank, which had a surveillance camera, to cash Benjamin's check. The last on Joseph's hit list, he said, were the lead prosecutor and himself. If his attempt at talking of suicide was for sympathy, he received none. Juries quietly snickered at his outlandish and unsuccessful attempt to be found innocent. After his testimony, the court broke for lunch, and Joseph then placed a fast-food order.

In the end, his "devil's hands" defense did not prevail. Neither did the diagnosis of Intermittent Explosive Disorder. The jury deliberated only three hours and found him guilty of two counts of first-degree murder. The boy once named by classmates "Most likely to be rich" was going to spend the rest of his life in prison. He showed no expression as he heard his fate via an interpreter.

His family was absent, having received notification too late to get to the courtroom. In July, Joseph was sentenced to life without parole. His attorney said he would appeal because Joseph had not understood his rights when he gave the confession. In addition, it was not clear that police interpreters had accurately communicated their questions to Joseph. Since then, all appeals have been exercised.

After the trial, Craig Plunkett commented that it was the "right verdict," and Benjamin's mother acknowledged that she was happy with the verdict, however little it did to erase her pain.

Minch filed a lawsuit for false arrest and defamation

of character and settled out of court for an undisclosed amount of money.

Doctor Long said, as with most psychopaths, they believe they can manipulate those that care about them even from behind bars.

It took the jury less than three hours to convict Joseph of two counts of first-degree murder, for both Eric and Benjamin. He received two life sentences without parole.

Kathleen spoke with waiting reporters immediately after the trial. She told them that not until after the trial was she able to think about beginning life without Eric. All this time, she said, she felt no sense of peace, saying, "Eric was the light of our lives."

Craig told reporters he and Kathleen were going to live their lives the way Eric lived, saying their son had love for other people and made them proud to be his parents. He believed Joseph would never realize the amount of pain he caused his victims' families. He said there is no amount of his saying he is sorry that would fill the emptiness in his and Kathleen's hearts. "He's exactly where his kind belongs," he said.

Kathleen still considers the one thing about Eric she missed the most was his coming through the front door saying, "Mom, I'm home," something he did every day when coming home after school.

Joseph Mesa's twisted love for monetary gain outweighed his compassion for his fellow man, plain and simple.

The families of Eric Plunkett and Benjamin Varner filed a wrongful death suit against Mesa and received an undisclosed amount. Both families donated a portion of the money in memory of their sons.

Cogswell Hall was converted from a dorm into a

general use building with a memorial set up to honor the victims.

The Girl Not Forgotten

When a frantic thirty-six-year-old Ed Zarzycka drove to the police station to report his thirteen-year-old daughter missing, little did the father of three realize she was already dead and buried.

The brown-haired man with the thick mustache, built like a lumberjack, recalled how the middle-aged and pleasantly plump dispatcher looked up at him with a blank look and quietly said, "Has your daughter been missing for at least twenty-four hours?"

He told her "no," and she nonchalantly told him the girl was probably hanging out with friends and would return home shortly. She then returned to her snack. When he told her that he and his older daughter and ex-wife had contacted everyone the young girl knew, the dispatcher shrugged her shoulders while washing her sandwich down with a soda.

Ed felt his antipathy turning to anger at this arrogant, non-caring person who took his dilemma with a grain of salt. He again asked her to allow him to make an official report. She said, "no exceptions," then closed the window. The desperate father turned and left.

Ed returned after the required amount of time expired. The dispatcher turned the report over to a missing persons detective, fifty-three-year-old Don Roberts, a stout seasoned cop with twenty-eight years under his belt. Happily married to his wife of twenty-six years, the dark-eyed poker player was familiar with frantic parents. He also knew most children Cindy Zarzycka's age were rebellious and probably hiding at a friend's house. He believed she would return home as soon as she thought her parents understood her or bought her that new album by Madonna or Cindy Lauper so many youngsters Cindy's age were crazy over.

Don's helper and sidekick was the twenty-seven-year-old tall, handsome Derek McLaughlin. He was fresh from police academy and eager to sink his teeth into a meaty case. He eagerly accepted his minor role in this game of cat and mouse he called law enforcement.

Within minutes, the men were at the front door of the Zarzycka residence. Once inside they sat with the anxious family. Thirty-five-year-old ex-wife Linda was also present. She and Ed, a construction worker, had been divorced for two years. It was an amicable severing of the marriage with Ed getting custody of the couple's three children. Linda lived only a few blocks away and saw her kids frequently.

After the detectives sat, Don got to the point. The detectives' first question was when each last saw Cindy. The man of the home started. He cleared his throat and began. He claimed he last saw his youngest daughter on Sunday morning, around eight, while he was pulling out of his driveway and headed toward his brother's farm to help cut wood for the upcoming winter, a seasonal favor Ed routinely did.

He said Cindy had just arrived home from spending the night with her friend Mary Dooley, who lived four doors down. She said she was going to take a shower. That was the last time he spoke with her. He said he returned home around four that evening, and then by dinnertime at 6 p.m., when Cindy was not home, he called Linda and told her to send Cindy home. He said he figured Cindy was at her house since Linda only lived three blocks away.

However, Linda told the group Cindy had not been at

her home since late Saturday afternoon when she dropped her off at Mary's house for a sleepover. The bosomy blonde with blue eyes said she called all the relatives and the minister, Cindy's favorite teachers and her last principal. Then she called Mary, Cindy's best friend, who said Cindy was going to Scott Ream's birthday party.

Don thought the name Ream sounded familiar, but he knew numerous people in this line of work. He did not want to alarm the family, but the Reams were known as riff-raff.

Ed denied Scott was Cindy's boyfriend, saying Cindy knew the rule about boys. "She was too young for anything besides a casual friendship," he said. However, he admitted he knew Cindy was interested in this particular boy. He explained to the officers how he and Linda encouraged their children to be open and honest with them.

When Don asked the family to describe Scott, sixteen-year-old Liza who, like Cindy, was the spitting image of Linda, spoke up saying, "He's different." Although he played drums and sported a green Mohawk, he seemed nice.

Linda claimed when she called the Ream household, the father rudely answered saying his son was not home, then hung up on her. When she called back immediately, telling Mr. Ream Cindy was missing, he claimed Cindy was never at his home and he had never met her.

Don then suggested that perhaps Cindy had friends unknown to her family since, in his experience, it was common for adolescents to keep secrets from their loved one. Liza adamantly denied that accusation, saying, "Detectives, Cindy and I are very close." She described her relationship with her baby sister as "very close" saying, "We trusted and confided in each other. If there was someone special in her life, she would tell me."

Linda admitted that the last time she was with Cindy, the girl was angry and moody. She believed Cindy was holding something back.

Don knew that meant Cindy did keep secrets and felt she could not converse with her parents about anything. Ed admitted Cindy was upset with him and Linda for forbidding her to see Scott. The parents denied Cindy ever ran away from home when she became upset, but they did admit she sometimes stayed away from home for hours when she did not get her way, and her favorite hideout was in the woods behind the high school. They were unsure if she was alone during those times.

When detectives stood and prepared to leave, Ed was surprised at their non-alarmed attitudes for a young missing girl. Don assured the family that police were searching for their missing daughter, but admitted that now it seemed like an ordinary runaway.

Ed stood and became angry, recalled Derek. The detective thought that shortly the situation would become physical. Ed insisted the authorities take the situation seriously. Don assured him that his office took every situation seriously. The parents insisted Cindy was not the type to run away from home; something drastic had happened to her.

Don explained that since no foul play was detected, and many girls Cindy's age do tend to stay away from home if they are angry with a family member, right now, she was considered a runaway.

The officers left the home. Once outside, they saw the youngest Zarzycka child, eleven-year-old Dennis, in the yard. Derek claimed he told the child he and the police department would do everything they could to bring Cindy home.

The skinny, smaller version of Ed, told the officers he

tried following his older sister that morning, but she told him to "beat it." He admitted he spied on Cindy upon his mother's and father's request because they were aware of her interest in Scott Ream. When she left the house, he said, she carried a gift. When she would not allow him to go with her, he hit her with a pebble, saying, "I'm real sorry now. Do you think she knows I didn't mean it?"

Derek reassured the boy his sister had forgiven him. The detective then handed the lad his business card and asked him to call if he remembered anything else.

What Don knew of the Reams was all bad. The authorities suspected the father of committing neighborhood burglaries but had no evidence strong enough to take to court. The man, from all accounts, lived a respectable lifestyle. He held down a job and kept his bills paid up. Since the Zarzycka family had combed the neighborhood, the detectives saw no reason to canvass the area. Derek recalled how he was the rookie and knew Don, being the veteran, knew the ropes.

Don surmised that since Ed Zarzycka had done a majority of the legwork, his next step would be to let other officers know to keep on the lookout for the girl. He also knew to patrol the Reams' trailer. Let the slob know the cops suspect him of something. Don knew if Cindy Zarzycka were hiding out there, they would find her. Don recalled how the case upset his partner. What he did not want to see was Derek becoming obsessed with the missing girl.

Over the next few days, the detectives interviewed students at Cindy's Junior High School. None of the teenagers said anything of importance. According to Mary Dooley, she was sleepy when she and Cindy last talked. She had already talked with Linda and had nothing new to tell the officers.

Twelve-year-old classmate Shirley Knox remembered

talking with Cindy the Saturday night before she went missing. What she remembered was that Cindy was upset with her parents about an older boy whose name she could not remember. However, she did not believe Cindy would run away from home over the incident. She claimed Cindy spoke lovingly of her family, but she believed something evil had happened to her friend. Little did she know then that her last words with Cindy would haunt her for the rest of her life.

Derek then talked of safety precautions, telling her danger was everywhere, and she should always travel in pairs, never alone.

Nothing became of the interviews with Cindy's classmates. Derek wrote his daily report meticulously. He took his job seriously and hoped for Cindy's safe return.

The detectives' next stop was the trailer of Art and Scott Ream. The man of the house allowed the officers entrance. They sat at the kitchen table. The detectives immediately noticed how nervous their host seemed. Don recalled how he joked with the man by saying, "Are ya gettin' married, Art? You're shakin' like a leaf."

The forty-something twice-divorced potbellied slob attributed his nervousness to having a pregnant girlfriend, saying, "Like I need another kid." He nervously laughed, said the detectives.

Don got down to business by grilling Art about his conversation with Linda Zarzycka. Art admitted the mother seemed worried that her daughter was missing and perceived the girl to be a runaway. He then said he hoped the girl was found, but the detectives disbelieved him.

When Don asked to speak with sixteen-year-old Scott, Art said his son was at a friend's home practicing for an upcoming gig. When asked where he was on Sunday morning, the eighth of August, Art claimed to be doing paperwork at his employer's with his lady boss in attendance. However, he said the woman was angry with him for owing her money, and he did not believe she would vouch for him. The detectives found his entire alibi, chain-smoking and jumping bean act questionable.

Art allowed the officers a look around his home and claimed to be watching his P's and Q's, saying he learned his lesson and had nothing to hide. After a thorough search, the officers left disappointed. There was nothing significant to take to a judge, no weapon or body, and just having a hunch would not get the detectives anything.

Derek recalled how creepy Art's eyes were. He felt himself getting personal, the first no-no for an officer. Along with no sign of Cindy noticed by the surveillance officers, Derek had a sick feeling in his stomach.

The media also heard about the missing youth. Her parents insisted she did not leave home but met with foul play, saying, "All her belongings are still in her room."

Her money and clothes were left where she last put them, it was discovered. Ed and Linda insisted those facts were not the act of an angry girl, but of one who's been abducted.

The search for Cindy was extensive. Her family posted flyers throughout the neighborhood, and Ed routinely patrolled the neighborhood searching for her. Each time they spotted a friend of Cindy's, they stopped and asked the person if they heard from her. The story was always the same: No!

Liza tried talking to Scott, but he was evasive. One day after a track meet, she approached him. His father had forbidden him to speak with police or any of Cindy's relatives. According to Scott, his father told him police were trying to frame him for the girl's disappearance. He was angry, Liza recalled, asking her, "Why would you think me and Dad harmed her? I was her friend."

Liza claimed she reassured the frightened youth that all they wanted was Cindy's safe return and was not framing anyone. They simply needed to know the truth about that warm Sunday morning.

Scott insisted he was not at home that entire weekend and knew nothing. He grew defensive when Liza insinuated that perhaps Art was lying to him. He told Liza that he knew others looked down on him and his father since they lived in an old trailer and he plays drums and dresses oddly. He again told Liza his father is innocent of any wrongdoing and asked that they be left alone.

The days turned into weeks. Summer came and went, but no Cindy. Ed Zarzycka always set a dinner plate for his beloved daughter each night. During family cookouts, an extra hamburger and hot dog were grilled just in case Cindy came home.

School started up, but not for Cindy, whose fourteenth birthday had just passed. One day as he left a fast food restaurant, Derek recalled noticing Dennis Zarzycka walking home with a friend.

To Derek's surprise, the boy remembered him. After small talk, Dennis told the officer they were all sad that Cindy missed her birthday. He said the family bought her many gifts and Linda baked her favorite cake, German chocolate with coconut and walnut frosting. Dennis believed his sister to be dead. Derek recalled how that statement broke his heart. He vowed to not stop looking for her.

Derek said Dennis mimicked his promise before rejoining his friends. Weeks turned into months, and Cindy's photo was added to the long list of missing children and persons on the back of cereal boxes and milk cartons.

When after the one-year anniversary of Cindy's disappearance, Don received a surprise telephone call from

California. He and Derek flew there immediately. Don recalled being skeptical of the caller's sincerity, since all the other dozens of leads led nowhere. Her now faded photograph hung on Derek's chalkboard.

Now that Derek was the proud father of a daughter, he knew how Ed and Linda felt when Cindy disappeared, saying, "I curse the person who killed her." He had now come to the realization that she was probably six feet under. The missing persons case was now a homicide.

He did not believe that a person could just disappear into thin air with no one knowing what happened. He believed the man who grabbed Cindy was still out there killing, saying, "He's either in prison, or moved away, but he's still killing."

Don kept his head about things. He knew without a witness who can connect Cindy to a suspect, or some kind of solid evidence, police had nothing. However, he did believe that, with the grace of God, if the case was solved, it was going to be him or his rogue partner.

As the years drifted by, more dead-end leads came through the police department -- leads of Cindy spotted in Florida, or sitting in a diner in Pittsburgh, or pumping gasoline at a filling station just across town. Some of the callers were genuinely concerned and helpful citizens; others were heartless bastards looking for a thrill. Derek recalled cursing out more than one joker over his office phone concerning pranksters.

Each tip was taken seriously, but nothing came of any of them. Derek became obsessed with solving the case. With his love for his family and his church, he kept grounded and kept his sanity. He also expanded his family with two sons. He earned a Master's degree in Criminal Science through night school, and he and his wife were content with their quiet, peaceful lives.

The school years came and went. Liza graduated and went on to college, then marriage. Soon she had a daughter she named Cindy. She and her family kept Cindy's memory alive by keeping Cindy's bedroom the same. They bought Cindy Christmas gifts that were never opened but simply packed away.

Three separate times since his daughter went missing, uniformed officers escorted Ed Zarzycka to the city morgue to identify deceased bodies of young girls. Each time, they were not Cindy.

Ed told reporters he did not know if he should be happy that the dead girl was not his daughter or not. He described his feelings during those times as sad that some parent somewhere lost a beautiful child and happy that the girl on the slab was not his Cindy, saying, "I just want her to come home so we can hug her to pieces."

Six years after Cindy's disappearance, Don's beloved wife died, and he devoted his spare time to five-card stud and volunteering for the local little league. He transferred out of missing persons and into a comfortable desk job. Although he and Derek parted ways as crime stoppers, they stayed in touch over the years and remained good friends.

With no evidence and no viable suspect, the case stayed cold and was pushed into storage. The detectives assigned to the Zarzycka case became involved with different cases, but one detective never forgot about the blonde-haired girl who loved to dance and sing.

By the time the use of DNA was established, Don had retired and Derek had moved on to the newly organized cold case youth squad Detroit, Michigan, had started. It was now 1995, and Cindy Zarzycka had been missing for nearly nine years.

The first officer to greet Derek on his first day in the cold case unit was the pretty 24-year-old peeking into the office of the now 36-year-old Detective McLaughlin.

The now father of four recalled smiling at the young woman whose ambition reminded him of himself when he first joined the force. Tameeka was not only the number one weather reporter for the town but also the boss's daughter and a tall leggy Mulatto.

She recalled entering Derek's semi-furnished office while he removed personal items from an old cardboard box and placed them strategically around the room.

As the two new friends made chit chat, Derek placed the group photo of his wife and children on his desk. Next to those pictures, he placed the photo of Cindy Zarzycka.

Tameeka recalled telling Derek of her secret plan of joining the police academy, but she still needed to break the news to her father who was against her becoming a police officer. While she and Derek discussed her plans, her father entered the office carrying an even larger box than the one Derek was rummaging through.

The boss immediately boasted of Tameeka's enrollment in law school without realizing she had not actually enrolled, but instead used the money he gave her for the police academy and for her new Z-28.

Derek recalled how the fifty-year-old Captain Nathan Rollins threw the box atop the already cluttered desk and joyfully announced, "Welcome to the cold case squad. Here's your first headache." He said he wanted the case solved, and photo age enhancement could do just that. He then handed Derek a new photograph of Cindy Zarzycka.

Derek admitted he had heard of this new technology to find missing children but never had the opportunity to use it. He said he felt honored to get the chance to solve the case that ate at him for years.

The boss explained how officers had circulated the new photographs of Cindy throughout the United States. He admitted he also doubted Cindy was alive after all this time, but he said he would take any help he could get. He also had for Derek a statement analysis, how a person answered the questions would allow interrogation experts to detect any lies or deceptions. It not only dismisses suspects but also can detect suspects.

Lying on top was a large overstuffed manila folder with August 8, 1986, written in black letters. "Could it be?" he whispered. He carefully removed the faded and tattered binder that held all the information the original investigators knew of the disappearance of 13-year-old Cindy Zarzycka.

It took four hours to re-read and re-examine the entire box of evidence. When Derek was finished, he was exhausted, hungry, and felt he needed to start at the beginning to have any chance of solving this tragic and heartbreaking case, the strange, twisted case that haunted him.

After the second mug of coffee, the officers relaxed in a corner booth for shop talk, their feline entertainment long gone. They planned to re-interview Cindy's friends from 1986. They knew that might be difficult since some might have moved away and changed their names or even died, but that was the best plan they had.

Derek relaxed that evening with his heart on his sleeve, telling Mack he never got over Cindy's disappearance, mainly because she was a minor and how her disappearance devastated her family. He still called them from time to time. Cindy would be twenty-one next month if she were alive, married and with children perhaps. With advanced forensics and new eyes, authorities had a shot at solving the case.

They decided to use the Internet and other social networking devices. They knew Cindy's girlfriends from that summer might be married and using their surnames. They hoped their interviewing persons would refresh someone's memory of that Sunday when she disappeared, something that they forgot back them.

Both admitted they were lousy at computers and decided to bring Tameeka into the plot -- without telling her father. They knew she had no police training, but she knew karate, owned a .45 and was a computer geek -- just what detectives needed to help solve this nearly decade-old case.

Mack, who was smitten with the tanned and green-eyed woman, had reservations about bringing her into a potentially dangerous situation, but Derek knew she could handle herself in a tight situation, and using her help he felt was no different than using an informant except Tameeka was not a criminal, as most stool pigeons were.

Involving a civilian bothered Derek. He talked it over with his wife who convinced him that any work Tameeka did now would help her in the future if she did get into the police academy or law school.

Derek knew investigations were dangerous and was concerned with Tameeka's safety. Police were searching for a killer, not a traffic ticket dodger. Reluctantly, he agreed to allow Tameka her place in the spotlight.

While on his way to work the next morning, he recalled having his speech prepared. Little did he know he would not need it. As soon as he walked into his office, he spotted his favorite morning brew atop his desk. He placed his briefcase on the floor against the coat rack, then removed his coat and hung it up.

When Mack showed up, the three ironed out the rough spots in their plan. Derek knew they needed a new set of eyes to find witnesses that he and other original detectives might have overlooked or omitted back in 1986. Derek now believed the kidnapper might be a female working with one or two men.

"Mack was an aspiring boxer before a dislocated shoulder wrecked his career," explained the captain. "Every so often, he runs into someone he arrested when he was a recruit, and the guy tries him."

Rereading the case file, the detectives discovered that Mr. and Mrs. Dooley were never interviewed in 1986. There were a large number of officers assigned to the case in the initial investigation -- too many for all of the officers to compare notes at the time. He believed that if he were allowed to stay on the case, he would have solved it. He hoped not to let the Zarzycka family down again.

Once they reached the Dooley residence, a one-story home surrounded by a white picket fence, Derek removed an old photograph from his breast pocket. The home had never changed. No remodeling or improvements of any kind were visible.

The wooden porch swing and rose bushes next to the front steps made it seem as if the homeowners were locked in time.

Mack knocked on the door. A small woman with hints of gray in her dark hair and wearing glasses answered. After they flashed their gold, she allowed them entrance. They followed the small woman into the living room where they shook hands with Stanley Dooley.

After Derek explained to the homeowner that he and Mack were re-opening the Cindy Zarzycka case, Mrs. Dooley said she hoped the case could be put to rest since it had been way too long to not know what happened to her friend.

Derek removed the statement analysis, clicked on the tape recorder, then explained that sometimes persons forget facts concerning crimes, but as time goes by, they come to remember something they might have forgotten years earlier.

According to Mrs. Dooley, Cindy was very polite and she loved her homemade apple pie, saying, "She always had a second helping."

They then talked about the Saturday night that Cindy spent with Mary. The couple recalled Cindy showed up happy and left happy, although they recalled Cindy stayed in their daughter's room most of the time. They admitted only five persons were inside the home the evening Cindy slept over: them, Mary, Cindy and their sixteen-year-old son Richie.

Immediately, Mr. Dooley became defensive, believing the detectives were accusing Richie of being a kidnapper. Mrs. Dooley brought to the detectives' attention that her son sang in the church choir.

Derek tried calming the parents but explained that any boy Richie's age would be interested in a pretty girl like Cindy. The detectives needed to clarify his whereabouts for that evening, since officers never took their statements in 1986. That was not correct protocol, said Derek, and he did not want to repeat history.

The couple insisted their son was out of town on a Boy Scout trip and ended the meeting without filling out the forms. The detectives did not like being asked to leave, but with an alibi for Richie, they had some new leads.

After a background check on the Dooley boy, and verifying his alibi for that fateful Sunday in 1986, the now grown man was cleared for Cindy's abduction. The detectives were back to square one and had no viable suspects.

Tameeka, on the other hand, had better luck. Both Mary Dooley and Shirley Flowers were still single and living in the area. Mary accepted the statement analysis and agreed to fill it out and return it to the police station.

Then, in detail, she relived the last time she saw her

best friend Cindy. She explained that Cindy spent the night even though she was not allowed to because she was grounded for something. She recalled how excited Cindy was about a birthday party she was invited to that was also a secret from her parents. A party that involved Scott Ream.

She described her and Cindy back then as "just two silly, sometimes boy-crazy girls." She recalled Scott as being tall and a bad musician. She said she was not friends with Scott, and he and Cindy had only recently met. She remembered how Cindy and Scott snuck around to see one another. Sometimes they met at the local library or at the pool or in her backyard to sit and converse about music or school, saying, "He is always a gentleman. I remember that"

She recalled Shirley Flowers was invited because the girl admitted to Mary that she had a gift for Scott. She said Cindy made two phone calls that evening -- one to Shirley and one to Scott, but he was not home.

Tameeka recalled that during the interview, Mary became solemn. She then recalled something she had forgotten for all those years. She remembered that when Cindy called Scott, his father answered the phone, so Cindy talked to him. She told Scott's father she needed a ride to the party, because his trailer was too far away to walk. Cindy agreed to meet him at the Dairy Queen in the morning and ride with him to the party.

She remembered driving to church the next morning, being Sunday, and they passed the Dairy Queen. She looked for Cindy but did not see her, but she noticed a white van parked in front of the store. She was very upset that she had not remembered those major detail years ago.

Tameeka reassured her that it might not have saved Cindy anyway.

Mary explained how she tried talking with Scott about Cindy's disappearance, but it always seemed to upset him. After high school, she heard he turned to alcohol, then drugs. He said he was a bad boy, and she always liked nice guys.

Tameeka immediately telephoned Derek with the newest evidence. The detective knew that information was enough to pay Art Ream another visit.

Shirley Flowers also agreed to co-operate. The factory worker described Cindy as nice and smart. She never believed Cindy to be a runaway. She said Cindy loved her parents, and her disappearance made no sense to any of her friends.

She said she, Cindy, and Mary Dooley were very close. She showed the reporter turned cold case investigator pictures of her, Cindy, and Mary Dooley riding their bikes or at the park playing baseball. She claimed she and Mary really missed the skinny girl with the white sunglasses and matching go-go boots, another secret from her parents.

Shirley recalled Cindy buying the boots and sunglasses at a yard sale, and hiding them in the Zarzycka family garage, saying Ed seldom used the garage. She said Cindy loved those boots because she thought they made her look older, but she and Mary never thought so. She said she and Mary went along with Cindy and humored her "because that's what friends do."

She said Cindy's disappearance had a profound effect on her, making her respect others more and not to take life or love for granted. She recalled going to the party and knocking on the door and no one answering, so she left.
She recalled how the trailer looked dark inside as if no one was home. She looked through a window but saw no party decorations. She told her mother, who waited in the car, and they left. She also recalled deep buried memories too frightening to remember until then.

Shortly after Cindy went missing, she ran into Scott

at the candy store and asked him what happened with his birthday party. She said he gave her the oddest look, telling her his birthday was nine months away. Then he said something that terrified her so much, she never talked to him again.

She claimed Scott told her to stay away from his trailer because his father abused girls. She said she ran off as fast as she could. She remembered seeing Scott get into a white van with an older man. At the time, she thought it might be his father. With this new statement, Tameeka said authorities now might have two persons who could help put a killer behind bars.

Tameeka recalled telephoning Derek about the white van and the phony birthday party. The detectives now believed Art Ream set Cindy up for a kidnapping. Now they had to prove it.

On the eve of what would have been Cindy Zarzycka's twenty-first birthday, her family held a candlelight vigil in her memory. The media televised the event. Holding tight to his daughter and new wife, Ed spoke of the hardship of losing his youngest daughter. "I still miss my little girl greatly," he said, choking back tears. "Each day without her is like a knife to the heart."

"Cindy, if you're out there, please come home, if you can," said Linda. "We love and miss you terribly. We will never forget you and the joy you brought to our lives."

Liza Zarzycka stood beside her husband and child as she spoke to the cameras. "Cindy and I were the best of friends. I miss our talks and doing each other's hair and nails. I know someone out there knows what happened to her. Please come forward and help us find Cindy and help bring her kidnapper to justice."

The youngest member of the family and only son, Dennis, became a Marine. He took liberty to be with his family on this memorable night. "I never got to say goodbye to my big sister," he said. "The pain of not growing up with her is unbearable. We will never stop hoping she is alive or looking for her."

Derek and his team were also there. "We're getting closer to solving this case," he told the reporter. "It's just a matter of time before we execute a warrant. With the technology within the forensic field now, the person responsible cannot hide much longer."

Unfortunately, the detectives were unable to locate Art Ream or his son for interviews. They also had no hits off either one's Social Security numbers. Derek knew that if either was working off the books, they were not going to find them soon. Their only shot said Derek, was to notify other officers the pair were wanted for questioning. Derek said he hoped that one or the other would mess up and get arrested.

However, that took time. Months went by without any new information on the case or the whereabouts of Art and Scott Ream. Then one wintry day, a call came in from Kansas. A young woman caller claimed she had information about the Cindy Zarzycka case.

She claimed her friend Justine sings in this band, and she told her when she lived in Michigan in '86, she helped a man bury a body. That statement caused Derek to perk his attention. He immediately went to see the caller. After clearing the flight with headquarters, Derek and Mack were on the first plane to Kansas City.

Once the detectives arrived, they waited until evening for the band to perform in a local bar. They entered the premises of Harley riders, drug dealers and prostitutes to question the woman they hoped would close this cold case forever. They soon spotted the tall, skinny, bleach blonde with the rose and skull tattoo on her artificially tanned forearm, with a cigarette hanging from her dark painted and pouted lips.

They asked the woman, who was obviously under the influence of something, to speak with them in private and she agreed. The detectives recalled the look of fear smeared across her small angel-like face when they flashed their armor. She escorted the detectives to a semi-dark corner in the far side of the room.

After the detectives explained to Justine that Kristy called their office accusing her of helping a man bury someone in Michigan in 1986.

Justine shook her head in disbelief and then became angry. She then told the detectives that she watched a movie where a girl got herself mixed up with a serial killer who made her help bury his victims, saying, "I never told Kristy I helped buried someone."

The detectives then left for the airport, disappointed once more. Another misinformed tip.

Each person Derek and Mack re-interviewed agreed to fill out and return the questionnaire. Waiting for the returns, and then for the experts to read the documents and decipher them for any discrepancies between their first interviews with police in 1986 and now, took several weeks. During that time, Mack and Tameeka grew on each other in the nicest way.

Concerning the questionnaire, the one person the newly hired interrogation experts became leery of was Ed Zarzycka. Derek went to Ed's job site and requested he come into the station for a polygraph concerning the statement analysis.

Ed insisted he only told the truth.

The polygraph worked in the father's favor. Ed passed and was eliminated finally from being a suspect. The detectives' best suspect remained Art Ream, who the detectives discovered was doing time in a Michigan Prison for rape.

According to Scott's relatives, after his father's arrest, Scott drifted around doing odd jobs. Trying to locate him hampered the investigation. Scott was never interviewed in 1986. More inept police follow-up work, according to Derek.

The entire police department knew that if Scott was located, he was to fill out the questionnaire and take a polygraph. If he refused, he was hiding something.

When the team's computer genius, Tameeka, was not searching the Internet for Scott Ream, the man who they believed knew more about Cindy's disappearance than earlier thought, she was preparing her wedding. Derek, of course, was best man.

After a two-week honeymoon in Hawaii, it was back to work as usual for the three musketeers. Tameka soon joined the police academy. Her dreams were coming true, but not so for Derek, who struggled with the knowledge that he may never solve the case that touched so many lives all these years.

As winter changed to spring, then to hot sticky summer, good news came in the form of a traffic ticket. The payroll department discovered a paid ticket from a Scott Ream living in Michigan.

According to Tameeka, she had earlier located Scott who arranged with her for an interview at 3 o'clock. Not wanting to scare him off by seeing uniforms at his apartment, Mack canceled the pick-up just as the sounds of the EMS and fire truck whizzed by the station. That sound, all three remembered. Mack believed it to be early trouble with 4th of July, which was the following day. A second fire truck soon followed. Derek recalled his desk phone ringing. It was a call that once again turned the Cindy Zarzycka case and beer and allowed them to watch porno movies. She said Art had always preferred thirteen- and fourteen-year-old girls, right up until he went to prison this last time.

After Wilma left, the detectives discussed her accusations against the man she now loathed. Mack believed her to be an angry ex-wife. They made arrangements to interview Art in prison. They would let the man know what others said of him -- see if he got antsy.

The captain said he would allow it as long as the interrogation experts went along. If Art Ream lied, they would know it.

Arranging the meeting took three weeks. In the meantime, Derek and his team worked on locating possible burial sites for Cindy's remains. They had Tameeka get blueprints of all properties belonging to Art and his relatives. Since the man had been able to conceal his crimes for a long time, the officers knew not to underestimate him. Everyone, including Art Ream, knew he had everything to lose if he went down for murder one.

Tameeka and Mack shook their heads in union. Then the big day arrived -- the interview with Art Ream. Derek rode with Mack and Tameeka. The professional interrogators took their company van, loaded down with the needed equipment, to the correctional institute that housed Art Ream and Michigan's most vicious prisoners.

During the hour-long ride to the prison, the lead interrogator discussed their suspect. According to the prison warden, Art Ream was a model prisoner. He worked in the kitchen and helped illiterate prisoners learn to read and write.

Once the team was inside the prison, they installed hidden camera and audio equipment inside the room the prisoner would be questioned in. The interrogators and Tameka watched and listened on close circuit television from on its ear.

He explained to Mack and Tameeka that the call was from their captain. Scott Ream just died in an automobile wreck just one block away. All that hoop-la down the street was for him. They were all stunned, said Tameeka. It was back to the drawing board.

Days passed, and the team continued building a case against Art Ream. Then, there was another lucky break. Wilma Ream walked into the police station wanting to talk about her ex-husband, Art Ream.

She had information on Art, she said. "Right before that girl went missing, Art sent Scott out of town on some kind of trip. After the girl disappeared, Art was acting very funny. He junked his van he used for work, and he refused to allow Scott to mention the girl's name. You need to look at him closer."

She told the detectives she had no knowledge of what Art did before they married, claiming he was incarcerated in an Illinois prison in the late 1970s for raping a young girl. She claimed Art's sister confessed that information to her the same day she gave birth to Scott. She said the whole family was "sick."

When asked about Scott's birthday party on Sunday, August 8, Wilma said Scott's birthday was in May and he was gone the weekend of August 8.

Derek contemplated Wilma's statement, realizing Art was setting up the murder. Telling Cindy to keep the party a secret. Getting Scott out of town. Discarding the van.
Wilma's statement and the statements of Shirley and Mary were still not enough for an indictment. They needed a confession or a body.

Wilma claimed that after she and Art were divorced, and every other weekend when Scott was with her, Art held parties at his trailer for teenagers. He gave them cigarettes the adjoining room. Armed guards then retrieved the heavily shackled Art Ream from his cell. Armed guards waited outside. He sat at the elongated wooden table, the only piece of furniture the small unfriendly room held beside its four chairs.

The prisoner's excessive confinement pleased Mack who jokingly told the now obese gray-haired man that the state of Michigan was serious about not allowing him to escape.

Art in turn told the smirking detective that prison was not great, but guaranteed for three hots and a cot.

According to Derek, he locked eyes with the man who denied knowing why they wished to speak with him, even though Art agreed to the meeting weeks earlier. The detectives knew the man was toying with them still.

When told they were here because of Cindy Zarzycka, Art again denied knowing or ever meeting the girl. The detectives then dropped a bombshell, telling the prisoner they now had a witness who could verify he and Cindy were acquainted.

"Baloney!" he said angrily. "Who's this witness?"

Derek claimed he calmly informed Art they could not reveal their sources, but he also enjoyed the man's visible discomfort. He sweated profusely. His thin hair was now wet and matted to his head. Derek asked for his whereabouts for Sunday morning, August 8.

Reportedly, Art scratched his large nose with his equally large hand and said. "I stand on my original statement."

According to Mack, he asked Art what his original statement was, hoping he forgot the lies he told police years ago.

After releasing a deep sigh, Art retold his story of the detectives visiting his trailer asking questions about the missing girl. He again denied ever meeting Cindy Zarzycka.

Tameeka recalled watching Art Ream twitch as if he had ants in his pants. She knew he lied through his rotten teeth. She and the interrogators noticed how Art could not bring himself to mention Cindy by name, saying, "He calls her the girl."

Mack then brought up Scott's funeral, which infuriated Art who said, "That bastard warden don't care about prisoners' heartache."

Mack then lit up, offering Art a smoke also. "Sure!" he said, grabbing the item with shaky hands. "This stuff is gold in here."

The detectives allowed Art a deep inhale, then a slow exhale. It was obvious; the man missed his freedom, his vices, and his only child.

Then Derek told Art he should own up to kidnapping Cindy, saying her family needed closure, to bring her home for a proper Christian burial. He again denied knowing "that girl," saying, "I'm not the guy you're looking for."

Derek again told the prisoner they had enough evidence to take the case to court. He hoped that would scare Art into a confession, but it had the opposite effect.

Art dared the detectives to charge him with murder. However, Derek and Mack knew it was too soon for an arrest. The officers then played on the man's sympathy for his own deceased child, saying, "Be a man for your son's memory. Confess your sins."

Again, Art denied being involved in any way with Cindy's disappearance and presumed death, saying, "I'm just biding my time 'til I'm up for parole."

To the interrogators in the next room, Art Ream's denials spoke volumes. "He knows he's guilty, so he dances around the questions."

When Tameeka asked if Art could be forced, since he

was a prisoner, to take truth serum, the interrogator explained that there was a large amount of red tape involved with that type of procedure, the prisoner's civil rights for one thing. He said it was highly unlikely any judge would sign such an order.

Tameeka admitted she knew the case was wearing Derek down. He was now sleeping in his office most nights, which she believed meant problems at home.

The detectives then informed Art they knew he and his relatives owned a large acreage. The prisoner remained poker faced, saying, "I'm minding my P's and Q's in here. I'm doin' my time." Then he noticed the statement analysis. Once he learned the form was a tool used by professional interrogators to detect deception, he was comprehensive about agreeing. When he discovered others complied without having a problem with it, he agreed and accepted the form and a stamped envelope.

When asked where he was on Sunday, August 8, he claimed he was at his employer's warehouse filling out paperwork. He denied knowing anything about a birthday party for his son, accusing the officer of trying to frame him for murdering "that girl." Art's continued disrespect for Cindy Zarzycka boiled Mack's blood, forcing him to lash out. He accused Art of being Cindy's killer before Derek calmed him down and he left the room. Art accused Mack of being high-strung before wiping his brow of sweat.

When Derek asked Art why their witness, a person who has never met him, would lie, he said Art shrugged his broad shoulders and said, "Heck if I know. Some people just like to make up stories, I guess. Do ya think I can get a soda?"

Derek claimed he stomped out his smoke and said, "Go to hell!" He too left the room. The interrogation ended. Art was re-shackled and returned to his cell. The team disassembled their gear and left for home.

1997

By now the warehouse Art Ream had his carpet business in came under scrutiny.

Derek issued a search warrant for the monstrosity. The only business in the place now was a butcher shop. It had never been checked out.

Ten minutes later, the detectives were in front of the now abandoned carpet shop that, back in 1986, was Art's bread and butter. They entered the dilapidated building and greeted by the woman who owned and operated the butcher shop downstairs.

Derek explained to the sixty-five-year-old owner that he was working on an old case and hoped to look through the old carpet business that was in the back of the building. She immediately knew the detective was referring to Art Ream's business.

She voluntarily told the officer she closed the business down when Art went to court one day and never returned. She discovered through the local news that he was in prison for sexual assault on a teenager. He got her drunk and attacked her. The woman claimed that if she had known he was a pervert, she would never have rented the place to him. All his belongings were still in the attic because she did not know what to do with the items considering he was locked up.

She gave the detectives permission to take what they wanted. The detectives knew this information might possibly yield new clues to the disappearance of Cindy Zarzycka. Derek now believed Art killed Cindy inside the warehouse.

The officers promptly dove into the age-old abandoned property. After an hour of searching box after box, Mack found a photograph of his victim. They knew murderers kept souvenirs of their victims. Derek believed they were closer to proving Art Ream was the killer. Everything from the attic was carried downstairs and placed inside their vehicle.

Once the detectives were back at the station, the captain had more negative news about the Zarzycka case. The Chief informed them the Prosecutor refused to issue a warrant for Art Ream's arrest on the basis of statements from Mary Dooley and Shirley Flowers which were insufficient to prove their case.

The Chief said they needed hard evidence to take to the Prosecutor, not just faded memories from the victim's thirteen-year-old friends who never saw Cindy and Art Ream together. It had to be a confession from Art Ream, or blood, or a weapon.

The captain suggested turning up the heat. He instructed the detectives to let the bastard know that we know he killed Cindy and he will pay. "Put some scare into the creep," said the captain.

Once again, arrangements for an in-house interrogation with the prime suspect were arranged, but Art refused. Another disappointment.

According to the captain, the department could do nothing if the prisoner refused to cooperate. It all had to do with the man's civil rights.

Derek admitted their captain was right, and their hands were tied for the time being. Still more leads came through the station, but nothing ever panned out until one snowy day when a local psychic called in concerning her visions of Cindy Zarzycka.

Mack was hysterical with laughter at hearing that, saying, "Are you serious? We're not that desperate for clues. are we?"

Derek, on the other hand, said he would try anything at this point in time. The partners hit the pavement. Within minutes, the men arrived at the shop of the fortuneteller. Before entering, they removed their badges and placed them inside their pockets.

Derek admitted he pictured a young beautiful woman sitting at a table overlooking a crystal ball, but he was so wrong. The psychic was a tall, lanky elderly man wearing jeans and a ball cap.

The man sat at a small round table where Derek joined him, while Mack stood nearby. After Derek informed their host that they heard through the grapevine of his visions about his missing teenager, he admitted the rumors of his powers were true.

"Let's see what the spirits can tell us," said the psychic. The detectives watched as he fanned a deck of tarot cards upon the table. He turned over the first card, revealing The Death card.

Derek acknowledged that the one they sought was presumed dead. The second card revealed The Peacemaker, with the spiritualist realizing his guests were police officers. The detectives nodded their heads in agreement. The psychic then instructed Derek to turn over the third and last card.

Hesitant as to what the old bearded man with the long robe was up to, Derek claimed he gazed at his partner, who was primed for action, then cautiously turned over the card, which was The Meeting. The psychic predicted within two weeks the officers would visit a man.

The psychic pushed the cards to one side and gazed into his crystal ball positioned in the middle of the table. Then he explained that their victim was near water with a steel bridge above the water and purple flowers nearby. He then rubbed his eyes as if to clear his mind, saying, "That is all I see."

Once outside, Derek said he got the heeby-jeebies and shivered like a frightened rabbit. Mack was shocked by his partner's sudden worried appearance.

Derek then explained his sudden uneasiness. He had received a telephone call from Art Ream that very morning wanting to speak.

Upon hearing about the second interview, Tameeka wanted in. Derek initially said no, feeling it was too dangerous with Art's known deadly attraction to the fairer sex. Tameeka insisted she could safeguard herself since she was trained in martial arts, saying, "I beat Mack in wrestling all the time."

Tameeka admitted she had longed for the chance to face off with Art Ream who they referred to as "the human animal." To drill into the sick mind of the creep she had spent many years investigating would be a pleasure. She said her time on the case had been both painstaking and rewarding. She had met and married Mack. She knew children were just around the corner. She was accepted into the police academy. Her plans for a happy and fulfilling life had come true. Now, she had to get Art Ream to confess to killing Cindy Zarzycka, or find out where Cindy's remains were buried.

Just hours before they were to leave for the prison, the lead interrogator entered Derek's office with alarming news that the handwriting of the signature and the answers did not match. It was obvious to the interrogator, Art Ream did not fill the questionnaire out but had another prisoner do it for him.

He explained that he became suspicious, so he drove to the prison and examined known handwriting samples of Art Ream the prison had on file. They also did not match the handwriting on the form. Both knew that meant Art Ream was hiding something. Mack was ecstatic, saying, "The fox is in the henhouse." The team high-fived each other.

The next time the detectives met up with Art Ream, the detectives held nothing back. They entered the second interrogation in an accusatory frame of mind. "Stop lying, Art," said Derek in the man's face. The detective let the prisoner know they knew he kidnapped and killed Cindy Zarzycka in his white van in 1986. He denied the accusation, but the officers were relentless. They knew Art disposed of the van immediately after Cindy's disappearance to hide evidence of her murder. Art insisted the engine blew in the vehicle, but again the officers accused him of lying. Derek and Mack tag-teamed the man.

Mack told Art to be a man and to save himself from the hot seat. Tell them where the body was. He continued denying any involvement. Art asked for a cigarette, but he was refused. The detectives wanted the truth and were not leaving without it.

They asked their suspect if Cindy screamed and begged for her life, or did he shove a sock in her mouth to drown out her cries for help. They mentioned finding Cindy's photograph in his possessions at the warehouse, insinuating that was evidence that he was involved. Art called the officers "crazy." He sweated like a dog in heat but would not break.

When asked who filled out the questionnaire for him, Art claimed he did, but the detectives disbelieved him, claiming his constant lies proved he was the killer. He then asked for a glass of water, and that was denied.

The detectives said they ignored his pleas and took a break. They immediately went into the adjoining room and watched their suspect on video.

Tameeka recalled handing them each a bottle of cold water. The interrogator claimed Art was scared, which proved his guilt. Derek suggested they give the man a few minutes to compose himself before hitting him harder. They all knew if Art Ream did not break, they would all go home empty handed ... again.

The detectives gulped their beverage. Derek grabbed the property maps they brought with them and left for the adjoining room for another round of twenty questions. Tameeka grabbed a can of soda from their cooler and followed. Once in the hallway, she recalled asking if she could have a chance at the prisoner.

She said since they were unable to budge him, perhaps her wiles would. She knew she was over the age limit for Art's pleasure, but she was still the youngest woman Art had had contact with since his incarceration. She thought he might give something up for her he would not for a man.

Derek and Mack both recalled how she then twirled her long dark hair around her slim finger and smiled innocently. They said, "Why not?" She unbuttoned two extra buttons on her silk blouse before grabbing a soda and entering the room. The detectives and investigators listened from the next room.

She offered Art the drink and he accepted. She handed him the soda and laid the maps in the middle of the table. She could tell he was interested. She then introduced herself and allowed him to call her Tameeka. She described his voice as low and sinister sounding.

She became serious and sat on the edge of the table close to Art, crossing her long, slender legs as her skirt climbed her thighs. She said Art did not miss a thing. She asked him to stop his charade and tell them where he buried Cindy.

The men in the adjoining room knew Tameeka was driving Art Ream crazy, while they watched everything from closed circuit TV.

Tameeka claimed Art told her he could not tell her anything, for it would open Pandora's Box, getting others into trouble.

Then she laid her cards on the table, letting Art know what she had on him. She spread the maps onto the table they sat at. She told him that authorities knew Cindy Zarzycka was buried somewhere with a ten-mile area, saying, "As you can see, we know she's buried somewhere inside this area."   Using her long index finger complete with long polished nail, she twirled it in a slow seductive circular motion atop the map. She said Art followed her hand intently, before leaning in and whispering, "You're getting closer ... but still no cigar." He then retained his upright position.

The detectives noticed. Even the interrogator did not catch Art's last words. He turned up the volume on the audio equipment. She again asked if Cindy was buried in the campsite area he and his son visited. She leaned inward toward Art while twirling her finger over different areas of the map, including a good spot for fishing. Her silk blouse was slightly opened, she said, which allowed Art to strain his neck for one small peek at her bosom before pulling back.

Again, he refused to answer, saying, "That'll open Pandora's box."

After six hours of interrogation, Art gave up nothing of value. The interrogators knew he was lying, but still that was not enough to take to the Prosecutor. Art returned to his cell for the night.

Tameeka recalled that interview as "creepy." She surmised all the "Pandoras" was just more bullshit on Art Ream's part to keep authorities guessing.

The next morning, with lots of black coffee, Derek held a meeting between him, Mack, Tameka and the captain, in his office. He asked for and was then granted permission to use a certain informant inside of Art Ream's cell. He described this plant as a "real pro" at getting others to trust and confide in him. Derek knew Art was a killer, but he was no fool. He knew if Art even smells a trap, they might never get him for Cindy's murder or get another interview with him. They all knew the informant could be the team's last shot with Art Ream, and his parole was scheduled for the end of that year. They knew it was crucial to find a way to keep in him locked up.

    The prison stoolie was everything Derek said he was, and then some. When he first entered the prison, he made sure he ran into Art, accidentally on purpose. He recalled asking Art directions for the prison infirmary. Once Art answered, the stoolie told him he was a "cool guy." Art was impressed as if he had never been called "cool" before.

    Introductions were then made with the informant calling himself Randy. The friendship cemented. Within three weeks, the "plant" won Art's confidence. Derek soon received the good news.

    The detectives drove to the prison. The long-haired and tattooed career criminal waited inside a holding cell in chains. He immediately claimed Art confessed to killing Cindy Zarzycka inside his van and then burned her body before he buried it. He said the grave was by a bridge and a river. Derek was furious that Art was bragging about murdering a thirteen-year-old girl. They now had the evidence to take to a grand jury hearing.

    After working on the Cindy Zarzycka case for eleven years, the persistent detective convinced the State Prosecutor to issue warrants for first- and second-degree murder.

January 2008

A smiling Derek entered Art Ream's cell as he placed the man he always believed killed an innocent girl under arrest, saying, "Read him his rights." According to officers, Art Ream showed no emotion as if he knew the arrest was forthcoming.

Mack noted that as the prisoner walked from his cell down the hall toward the front door, fellow prisoners jeered and threatened his life. Once outside, Art entered the cruiser for the ride to the courthouse for arraignment.

As they rode along, Derek tried again to get Cindy's burial location from Art, the only person who knew her whereabouts. Derek ordered Mack to pull over. Derek exited the vehicle and walked into a nearby florist shop. Minutes later, he emerged with a bouquet of mixed flowers. When Mack asked his partner who the flowers were for, he was told, "It's a surprise." Derek then instructed Mack to drive to the Hindenborough Cemetery.

Minutes later, the men exited the vehicle and Derek handed Art the flowers, saying, "Put these on Scott's grave. Let him know you still think about him."

According to the detectives, without uttering a sound, the prisoner accepted the flowers and proceeded to his son's resting spot. Art admitted he had never visited Scott's grave since he was incarcerated. He then thanked Derek for his kindness.

That was the moment Derek said he had waited for. He then told Art to be a man and not an animal and to reveal Cindy's grave, saying, "Your child got a decent burial; now let the Zarzyckas bury theirs. Do the right thing."

According to the detectives, Art stood from his son's grave, looked Derek straight in the eye and, with the same deep sinister voice he used with Tameeka, said, "That's a low blow. Get me out of here."

The detective's ploy was unsuccessful again. He knew he may never get Art to reveal the body's location. The Zarzycka family may never have the opportunity of giving their daughter a decent Christian funeral.

Later that night inside the county jail, the detectives, along with Tameka, continued to question Art for the whereabouts of his thirteen-year-old victim. Again, the property maps were displayed for Art, but he kept mum of Cindy's resting place. All he would say was "Can't let Pandora out of the box," then released a sick laugh.

The detectives and Tameeka used every tactic they knew. The good cop, bad cop routine; threats; shame; clearing his conscience; meeting his maker. Nothing worked on the cold-hearted man. He was as hard as stone and twice as thick-skinned. It looked like Art Ream would take his secret to the grave.

According to the interrogators, the things Art did not say spoke volumes. He could not say her name, which might hint at remorse, but not enough remorse to tell the truth. Now he knew he was looking to at least life in prison. That certainly would not make him reveal the grave site. There was a good chance he might never break his silence.

The detectives were not giving up on locating Cindy's remains. Because of Art's history of sexual assaults against minors, the state decided to seek the death penalty.

The detectives tried keeping the re-opening of the case a secret from reporters, but soon after the arrest, the case became front-page news. When the media discovered a twenty-year-old cold case was reopened with a suspect in custody, they had a heyday. Local reporters camped outside the courthouse for the grand jury hearing. The estimated time for the case to reach a jury was two years.

The Zarzycka family was ecstatic that police arrested someone. Ed Zarzycka announced to reporters that he and his family had waited a long time for justice for their little girl.

A local woman and ex-neighbor of Art Ream's told reporters that after Art and Wilma were divorced, countless parties with teenagers running in and out of the trailer occurred. Beer cans were everywhere, she said, adding, "He was always a strange guy."

An old classmate of Scott Ream's told reporters that she believed Scott knew his father killed Cindy Zarzycka but was afraid to tell. Authorities knew that kind of knowledge was hell to conceal. She believed Scott's suspicions of his father caused him to deliberately crash his truck into that telephone pole that afternoon.

The detectives kept a close watch on the news for the next two years. They meticulously went over their evidence. They made sure they knew how to describe to the jury the details of that sinful day of August 8, 1986.

June 14th came soon enough. The accused baby killer Arthur Ream stood trial. Every member of Cindy's family attended the trial each day, but no one from Art's family was present. The defense counsel insisted the case was purely circumstantial and the missing girl was merely a runaway. Although reports of her existence had been reported throughout most of those twenty-two years, no evidence ever emerged to prove she was alive.

After four weeks of testimony, Art Ream was found guilty of first-degree murder on August 7, 2008 -- almost to the day of Cindy Zarzycka's disappearance. His sentencing hearing was one month later. At that time, he would know his fate: life without parole or death by Old Sparky.

The press waited outside the courthouse for anyone who wanted to talk. Photographers, victim advocates and thrill seekers stood by to see the convicted rapist and murderer taken away in chains for the last time of his miserable life.

According to Linda, the conviction that day was not the answer the family wanted. They wanted her body, she said, but at least now, they know what happened to Cindy.

Ed told waiting reporters that when Art Ream killed his daughter, he took not only her life, but also her dreams and his dreams for her, saying, "He took a lot that Sunday morning."

Derek explained to reporters that when he heard his station was developing a cold case squad, he jumped at the chance to be a part of it. He said he had become fascinated with this case over the years as a police officer. Cindy's parents were devastated by her disappearance, and he had promised them he would bring her home. He admitted it took longer than he had hoped, but in some ways, he kept his promise. The little girl who never really lived. Who never married or experienced the love of a man or knew the joy of raising a child. A girl who touched so many lives, even after her untimely death.

The detectives and the family attended the sentencing hearing. Art Ream received life without parole. Derek, desperate to find Cindy's remains, made one last visit with Art. He went alone for he knew it would be short and to the point.

According to Derek, he told Art that they both knew no one gave a shit about him. Telling him he was completely alone now, and if he and Scott were close when Scott was alive, he was his only friend. Derek then threw down a piece of paper and pen in front of Art and asked that he draw a map outlining where he buried Cindy, saying, "There's nothing more you can do to the Zarzycka family. Just tell us where she's at."

The prisoner refused, pushing the items away. Derek claimed he made it clear that he was not here to play games with him. He told Art that Cindy's family had accepted her fate. They buried their sorrow with Cindy the day he was found guilty of her murder. There was nothing more he could do to the Zarzycka family to hurt them.

According to Derek, Art became angry, realizing the Zarzycka family found closure, saying, "What parent would accept their kid been missin' all these years?"

Derek explained that the Zarzycka family were no longer grieving and were happy because they know the truth about what happened to their daughter. They can sleep peacefully now. He could no longer hurt them. Their suffering was over. They can now sleep easy at night.

According to Derek, Art's anger grew into rage at the realization that his victim's family found peace, and he was miserable. He insisted he could not sleep and had not slept well for twenty-two years.

Derek's anger showed also. He insisted Art confess to where Cindy was buried, saying, "Clear your conscience now or I'm leaving." According to Derek, Art released a deep sigh. He just sat there fuming but never revealed his pent-up secret. Derek told him to go to hell, grabbed the pen and paper and began to leave, telling Art no one needed him anymore.

Derek returned to his wife and family with the satisfaction of closing one of Michigan's coldest cases. When he thought he would never recovery Cindy's remains, he accepted that fact and concentrated on other cases. However, two days after his last conversation with Art Ream, the man telephoned Derek and agreed to show the detective where he buried Cindy's body.

Derek said he did not know what made the man change his mind and, frankly, he did not care. He was just glad for the Zarzycka family that they had their daughter back home.

Art Ream was again transported from the prison. He, along with Derek and Mack, uniformed officers, Tameeka and a news crew, directed the group to a secluded spot near a bridge and river.

Art looked around, moving from one area to another. He commented that it had been a long time since he was last here. He claimed not recalling some of the trees.

However, Derek did feel the location was familiar. Eerily familiar. He told the group that it resembled the location the psychic had foretold. Art moved about and soon located what he was searching for. He pointed to a small hill only yards from the bridge where the purple flowers predicted by the psychic grew.

Art located several spots he thought the body was in, but each time that an officer dug, only an empty hole was found. It began to get dark, and an officer suggested they stop for the day and start early the next morning.

Derek refused to stop the search by retrieving the shovel from his subordinate. He then walked several feet away poking the ground with the tool until he felt something peculiar, something he could not explain to the group. Within the first scoopful of dirt, Derek found what he had been searching more than two decades for, saying, "Now we really can tell the Zarzyckas we found their daughter."

Inside the grave were the charred and broken bones of Cindy Zarzycka. Her white go-go boots and sunglasses she loved so much lay beneath her. It was a heart-wrenching moment for the team.

Tameeka recalled how joyful Art Ream was that day, saying, "He had the attention he so craved." Derek and Mack were present. The news media was there. He was once again in the spotlight, the centerpiece of this giant puzzle he had created. He walked around pointing to spots he might have buried her with that sick, twisted smile for young girls on his face. "It was pure evil," she said.

Immediately upon finding the remains, Derek telephoned the family. According to Liza, they were ecstatic. She said now they can put Cindy where they wanted her, not where some animal in the night hid her. The Zarzycka family now had a place to go and speak with the girl not forgotten if they choose.

According to Linda, bringing Cindy home would not stop the pain that her being gone all these years caused. It just meant the family would not wonder where she was anymore. They knew where she was. She was across the street in the cemetery.

The Spell Casters Murders

It would have been a nice day in California except for two things: the vicious and bizarre murders of two Asian women and the whereabouts of their killer.

When Detective Marcus Brown and partner Jonas Nutter entered the mansion-like home, they discovered what looked to be a robbery gone wrong. Detective Nutter described each room inside the home as ransacked as if the killer or killers had been searching for something. However, nothing at the time seemed to be missing.

The home was supplied with expensive furnishings and electronics, with money and jewelry lying out in the open. The detectives believed that if a robbery had occurred, the missing merchandise had much more value than material objects.

Detective Nutter explained that in one rear bedroom, officers discovered several cages with snakes of different species and sizes. One family having a large number of reptiles was baffling to officers, but in police business, no two cases are alike.

The entire neighborhood became suspects and were horrified when learned that two of their most respected citizens, 42-year-old Ha "Jade" Smith, and her 21-year-old daughter Anita Vo, lay dead for nine days before relatives found the discolored and bloated bodies of the once vibrant and voluptuous women and called police.

Jade's older sister, May Ling, told police that when Jade was absent from bridge, she knew something was very wrong, saying, "She never miss a game."

Immediately the detectives alerted animal control to

remove the reptiles and allow officers to inspect the home for evidence. On a shelf in the snake room were dozens of glass jars with various fluids inside them. Some of the liquid resembled blood, but until the lab checked it out, the liquid could be Kool-Aid.

Once the forensic team arrived, the property was taped off. The officers knew that the more time that elapsed, the harder it was to solve such a crime. They also knew they were on a time restriction since the victims had been dead for an extensive amount to time.

The victims' hands were bagged as evidence since they defended themselves. The evidence lay in their broken artificial nails and strands of their long black hair found in different parts of the living room and kitchen. Splattered blood stained the carpet in various places proving the victims tried fleeing from their attacker or attackers, explained Nutter.

Found on the bodies was what appeared to be dark semi-short coarse hair that Detective Brown said reminded him of a pony he had as a child. Since finding the snakes, he claimed not to be surprised by anything found in the home.

While Brown and Nutter inspected the inside of the home, they had the uniforms canvass the area and look for witnesses who either saw or heard something. They soon found an elderly couple who believed they heard arguing coming from the home, but they ignored it. They said they kept their noses to themselves.

The upper-class neighborhood was occupied with mostly retirees. Residents in that area were mostly working class and were gone most of the day with employment, errands or socializing.

Detective Nutter described the neighborhood as very tight-knit. Each person the uniforms talked to wanted the person or persons responsible caught. The authorities knew they had a large amount of support behind them from the public, and that always helps everyone concerned.

What they found to be peculiar about the condition of the bodies was that the women were doused with white paint. Their faces, arms and legs were covered. Detectives had neither seen nor heard anything of that caliber. They did not know what kind of lunatic they sought, but they wanted the responsible party caught for the sake of preventing further victims.

Detective Nutter said he took it upon himself to make sure the police photographer had a sufficient supply of photographs of the victims and each room of the home. Once the interior was examined, the detectives discovered many freakish items. "We didn't know if we were looking for a witch, a sexual pervert, or a devil worshipper," he said.

With no knowledge of the peculiar lifestyles of the victims, the detectives thought it best to bring in a police expert on witchcraft and Demonology. They knew they were in over their heads with this strange case.

When Detective Derrick Waltz from the special crimes unit saw the bodies, he knew the white paint meant someone believed these women were deceitful in some way. Further findings made it clear: one or both of the victims dabbled in fortune telling. Officers found candles of various colors as well as incense and oils used for various spells. A deck of tarot cards lay scattered around the victims. "Something twisted took place inside that home," he said.

During the initial questioning of the neighbors, none mentioned the victims being involved with mystic arts. Once detectives knew more about the victims, they were sure the neighbors were skittish to talk about the hocus pocus that went on inside the home. Many of the neighbors were known businesspersons, and persons of that nature usually do not become involved with any mention of black magic.

Their first clue pertained to a young neighbor who remembered seeing a middle-aged woman loitering around the victims' home two days before the victims were presumed to have died. The neighbor was immediately brought in for questioning; with a police sketch artist, she gave a description of the woman.

So far, the woman in the sketch was the only suspect. She was Asian with long bushy black hair and a stocky build. Unfortunately, that fit quite a lot of Asian women in the town. The victims lived in an Asian neighborhood.

Nine days after the bodies were discovered, police received an anonymous telephone call, providing their first good lead. The detectives learned that Jade was not only a fortuneteller, but also a spell caster.

According to Waltz, most do not believe in voodoo, but within the Asian culture, it thrives, both religiously and financially.

After discovering the victims were charging people for casting spells, Detective Brown claimed he knew this case was going to be the oddest case of his career. That explained the charms, potions, and books found inside the residence.

Waltz explained that the use of, or having the gift, as many persons believe it to be, of telling the future, whether that be with cards, a crystal ball or tea leaves, goes back thousands of years and is found in every culture known to mankind. Literally millions of people believe in some sort of predicting the future or of being able to change one's life through magic, he said.

According to Detective Nutter, once the community learned of the double slaying, the phone rang off the hook at the police station. He said many were convinced the murderer was a serial killer or involved with occult activity.

One such lead led the detectives to the home of a twenty-six year-old Asian woman named Kim. They brought her in for questioning. Detective Nutter described the woman as "frightened", but she obeyed. The detective sat across from her and lit a cigarette. He then offered her one, but she declined. After a long exhale, the officer got down to business, asking her to explain her relationship with Jade and Anita Vo.

She explained that she had paid Jade $13,000 for a love spell; however, the spell failed to work. She said her husband left anyway. "I very angry, but I no killer," she said. She then claimed to be out of the state during the time of the murders. She said her passport would prove her story. The detectives took her written statement, fingerprinted her, then released her.

According to Detective Brown, Kim was their best lead, but it went nowhere. She had nothing to do with the murders.

That was the only lead for six months. The detectives feared the case would go cold -- until they discovered someone had used the victims' credit cards. The charges were coming in from the Los Angeles, California, area. The detectives boarded the first plane to Encino.

Within minutes of landing, the detectives were at the first store at which the cards were used. When they viewed the store video, they could not believe how familiar the woman on the screen looked to their composite sketch.

After getting a printout of all the victims' credit card activity since the murders, the detectives discovered $75,000 worth of merchandise had been charged. The new suspect was blatantly spending Ha "Jade" Smith's money. "She looked as cool as ice on the video," said Detective Nutter. The detectives watched in awe as their suspect just walked through the store picking out items to purchase as if she had no cares in the world.

According to Waltz, the woman was bitten by one of the world's deadliest sins: good old-fashioned greed. It was her downfall but the officers' good fortune. In addition, the detectives knew this mystery woman would soon find her world of diamonds and furs crumbling down on top of her fast and hard. They kept track of the credit card activity and discovered this woman bought two airline tickets to North Carolina under the name of Ha "Jade" Smith.

Detective Nutter felt the woman had no shame for what she was using the credit cards for. It was as if she thought she was entitled to them, he said.

The detectives immediately flew into North Carolina and waited for the plane to land. They had already notified North Carolina police of their intentions of arresting the woman. The local police department sent two uniformed officers to assist with the apprehension.

The detectives had photocopies of the woman in the video and gave one to each of the local officers so they would know whom to look for. Then once at the airport, as each person exited the plane, they stood at a distance and watched the passengers unload so as not to be spotted by the target. They did not want her to flee. They had waited this long to catch their killer and did not want to lose her in a sea of people.

Detective Brown recalled that within thirty minutes, they spotted their woman, and she had a friend with her. They were then surrounded and read their rights before being handcuffed and taken to the North Carolina headquarters for questioning.

Detective Nutter described that feeling as "one of the best days of my career." He claimed that having a double homicide murderer off the streets was worth all the footwork and hard work the officers put into the case.

Once inside the interrogation room, the woman clammed up. She was described as calm and collected just like on the video. "Her silence spoke volumes," said Waltz. She apparently knew the jig was up and she was going down for the murders.

While inspecting the woman's purse, the man's wallet and both their luggage, officers hit the jackpot. They discovered her real name was Tanya Jaime Nelson, a forty-year-old Vietnamese, and her accomplice was a forty-six-year-old Puerto Rican named Phillipe Zamora.

The detectives not only found their killers' identities, but also inside their belongings were found the driver's licenses, Social Security cards and passports belonging to Jade and Anita Vo.

According to Waltz, there was no reason to keep those items unless they were mementos from the crime. Like many murderers, he said, they tend to keep something personal from their victims to remind them of the crime, and that they were in control of their victims.

After finding the I.D. of the victims, the detectives got a search warrant for the house of Tanya Nelson in North Carolina, as listed on her driver's license. Inside that home was found the missing three hundred thousand dollars.

Detective Nutter said, once approached about what detectives found inside the home, Silas sang like a canary. He claimed he killed one and Trudy killed the other, and it was all her idea.

Like most partners in crime, said Waltz, once caught, the killers started pointing fingers at one another and looking for the best deal even if that means putting your partner in the hot seat. Even though Silas and Trudy were lovers and childhood chums, he was out to save his own hide that day.

When asked why he and Trudy tore the Vu's home

apart, Silas said they were looking for the $5,000 Trudy paid Jade, but finding the $300,000 was even better. Trudy thought she deserved it because Jade did not do her job of making the spell work.

When asked why the women were killed, Detective Nutter stated that Silas gave the most twisted and unbelievable reasons for murder the detectives had ever heard. Silas said Trudy found Jade's business over the Internet and paid her $5,000 for a love spell to get an ex-lover to return to her. Silas said the spell did not work, and Trudy asked for the money back, but Jade said she did not give refunds.

Silas said his reason for going along with the killings was because Trudy promised to pay for male prostitutes for him. By Silas's account, he had always been curious about men, and he finally had gathered the nerve to try it, but he did not know how to go about getting these men. He said Trudy offered to hire professional high-class male prostitutes for him if he helped her. "So he did. Crazy!" said Nutter.

According to Waltz, when you have two dysfunctional people on a rage-fueled rampage, do not expect things to make sense because they will not.

When Detective Brown asked Silas if money was the reason for the murder, he said that was only part of it. Silas claimed that, in Trudy's mind, she felt justified in killing Jade when the spell did not work. Not only was Trudy out $5,000, but she was also without her ex-boyfriend. Silas said that made Trudy extremely angry, and that was when she wanted Jade dead.

When it comes to sex and money, you can be sure some kind of perverse and twisted love was involved, explained Waltz. He described Silas as clearly not the sharpest pencil in the box which was probably why Trudy chose him as her strong arm.

He explained that Silas could have saved his friend and taken all the blame for the crimes, but he did not do that. Instead, he chose to push most of the blame onto Trudy. A person does that for two reasons, to make himself less culpable of the crime and to appear less of a monster then he was, or to get a lesser sentence at hearing.

When asked why they killed Veronica, Silas said she was just like her mother, a "phony snake," and deserved to die also.

Phillipe Zamora took the plea deal and received life without parole. Tanya Nelson took her chance at court and was found guilty of first-degree murder; she became the second woman in Orange County, California, to be on death row.

Her twisted love for revenge against Jade overpowered her rationality, destroying her and everyone around her.

All for The Family

If nineteen-year-old Molly had listened to her mother, perhaps the slender, freckled-faced felon and her now-divorced felon husband Clayton would not be sitting in a Texas prison. The way the auburn-haired Molly chose to make a new life for her and Clayton shocked the town and became forever known for being the cruelest and dumbest action one could do when one wants to do "all for the family."

Candy will say she tried talking her daughter out of marrying the lazy, drinking, sandy-haired, blue-eyed Clayton, but Molly was "starry-eyed head over heels in love," so she thought.

Molly insisted she knew the seldom-employed Clayton well enough to be his wife and allow him to be the only father her four-year-old son Matthew knew. Even though Matthew was conceived from an earlier relationship, Molly insisted the uncouth and chain-smoking Clayton treated him respectfully. "He loves me and Matthew," Molly would say.

After a two-month courtship, Molly married twenty-two-year-old Clayton Wayne Daniels. Candy hated Clayton and wanted everyone, including Molly, to know it. She told Molly she was making a drastic mistake by marrying Clayton, but she said her eldest daughter insisted the two were soul mates. "He's the one," Molly said.

In a simple backyard ceremony with the theme of Harley Davidson motorcycles, the pair exchanged wedding vows. As if something straight from the pages of *American Rider*, the bride wore jeans and a sleeveless Harley shirt. The groom donned black leather chaps and a vest embossed with the famous cycle logo.

Their friends and relatives, who happily toasted them with keg beer, surrounded the glowing couple. The reception followed with grilled hot dogs and burgers as the main course. They received numerous wedding gifts and money to help them on their way to a long and happy life together...or so the giddy couple thought.

It was not just Candy who disapproved of the courtship. Baby sister Janie was as different from Molly as igloos are from tropical huts. Janie was known as the "pretty" sister and Molly the "plain Jane." Janie thought Clayton was a loser, as most of Molly's family did. She believed her big sister thought she was in love because, according to Janie, Clayton was the first man to pay attention to Molly in a long time.

Molly called Janie jealous. Afterward, she thought it best to let Molly find out for herself what a "bad apple" Clayton was. She gave the marriage two years, saying, "Good things come to those who wait."

The next move for the newlyweds was buying that dream home Molly so wanted. According to Molly, when she saw the two-story ranch style house in a quiet, family-oriented neighborhood with an adjoining playground and dog park, she knew, "This is the one for us."

She said Clayton picked her up and swung her around, telling her the house would be theirs. They called the realtor and, three weeks later, moved in -- but as renters, not owners. Both had inadequate credit. The loan officer informed the couple that with neither earning more than minimum wage, and Clayton's upcoming legal matters, he did not see a home in their near future.

Molly was devastated, recalled Candy. Besides being a mother, Molly wanted so much to be a homeowner.

Another who had doubts about the couple getting the home was Rita, Clayton's mother. Tall and skinny with waist-length red hair, Rita dressed and partied like a teenager. When she learned of her son attempting to purchase a home, she told relatives, "With Clayton's credit and legal matters, he couldn't get a loan for a candy bar."

However, the couple stayed happy and made the best of their financial problems. According to Clayton, it was his idea to meet the neighbors. "Let's go for a walk," he told Molly one day.

The neighbors agreed the newlyweds and Matthew made a seemingly happy family. However, Molly's relatives were stumped as to what the college graduate saw in the pudgy man with the rough exterior. Molly thought her Prince Charming walked on water and regularly defended her family's attacks against the love of her life.

Molly's co-worker was twenty-two-year-old Melinda, a brunette with a big smile and a big heart. She recalled meeting Clayton, describing him as a "dumb hillbilly." She claimed he was chewing tobacco and wearing a hat with fishing hooks in it when they were introduced. She also believed her friend could do better.

Molly and Melinda worked together at an area insurance company, Molly as the receptionist and Melinda as an agent. Although the women disagreed greatly about their taste in men, they were good friends. Even when they were not at work, they talked on their cell phones, saying, "If she didn't call me, I called her."

Within their first year of marriage, Molly gave birth to the couple's first child, Harley, named after none other than Clayton's favorite motorcycle. According to relatives, Clayton was ecstatic about his daughter's birth. "She looks just like me, doesn't she?" he beamed while holding his daughter in the hospital shortly after her birth.

Candy was present for the birth, and she informed Clayton it was too premature to know which parent the child would resemble, saying, "All babies are red and wrinkled at first." She then kissed Molly goodbye and left on the ruse of preparing dinner for her husband.

She recalled Molly telling her to have Janie stop by before she left the hospital, saying she did not care if Janie's boss wanted her to work late. "Family comes first," Candy remembered her eldest saying. She nodded her head and exited. Once in the hall, Candy said she met up with her youngest.

Janie overheard Clayton bragging that the baby resembled him. She hoped that was untrue, claiming naming a child after a vehicle was bad enough.

Candy reassured Janie that Harley looked nothing like Clayton. The two laughed their way to the outside.

Although his wife's relatives did not care for him, Clayton was there to help them whenever possible. Candy admitted Clayton mowed her grass during the time her husband had back trouble, calling Clayton "a handy backyard mechanic" who often never charged for his labor. "He was a good ol' boy in a lot of ways," many said, but he could be as mean as a rattler on a dime, said others.

Melinda recalled that three weeks after Harley was born, she offered to watch Harley and Matthew while Molly and Clayton had a date night. When they arrived at her home with the kids, Clayton thought her upstairs neighbors were overly noisy, so he took it upon himself to go upstairs and tell them to " shut the hell up."

According to Melinda, the neighbors called police. Clayton and Molly were gone by the time the officers arrived. "Clayton is a real Jekyll and Hyde," she said, recalling that it was after midnight when Clayton and Molly retrieved their children. It was obvious Clayton was inebriated, she said; he burped and slurred his words.

Melinda offered to drive them all home, but Clayton insisted he was okay to drive since their home was only five minutes away. She remembered seeing him stumbling out the door with Molly and the kids in tow.

Melinda recalled never seeing Molly so inebriated. She claimed Molly seldom drank before Clayton entered the picture, but from then on, Molly showing up at work hungover; it happened frequently. Melinda said she tried talking to Molly about her excessive drinking, but Molly insisted, "It isn't a problem."

Clayton seemingly left a bad taste in everyone's mouth. Molly's relatives claimed that Clayton's laziness and alcohol abuse led to them visiting the couple less and less.

When Janie learned Clayton had quit his job, she called her sister Janie. Molly and Clayton felt it would be better for Clayton to become a stay-at-home dad. Molly's excuse was since she and Clayton had two children, it was not feasible to pay a babysitter when he could "'watch the kids for free.'"

Janie claimed that when she explained to Molly that her job did not sustain the family's financial needs and they needed two incomes, Molly said she and Clayton had a solution to their financial problems. Janie said she immediately thought the couple were dealing drugs or running a chop shop, but Molly assured her they were not. Molly became defensive, saying she and Clayton were not criminals, and then abruptly ended the conversation by hanging up.

Molly and Clayton soon handled their money and other problems in a way that rocked the small town to its core. However, that was not the couple's only major problem. Only weeks after Clayton quit his job, Molly got a heated telephone call from Candy concerning Clayton's arrest for raping his minor cousin.

Candy recalled that Molly defended Clayton and adamantly denied his involvement, calling the alleged victim a liar. '"Clayton would never hurt a child. He loves kids,'" replied Molly.

Candy claimed she called her daughter a "love-struck fool," advising her to file for divorce. Molly insisted Clayton was innocent until proven guilty. However, Candy felt Clayton, like most sexual predators, was a master manipulator, and Molly was putting her children in danger. She then threatened to report the situation to the children's services, which most likely would result in the removal of the children.

Molly begged her mother to not call CPS, telling her she would never forgive her. She then hung up sobbing straight to Clayton about the conversation.

She found him drinking beer and smoking dope in their garage while giving their car a tune-up. When Clayton heard about the threat, Molly said, he remained quiet for several minutes. Then in a soft, calm voice, he said. "Well, I got a friend that gets things done for good. I can call him if you want."

Molly said she slapped him hard across his face, making it clear she was no killer. She ended the conversation by telling Clayton she would handle the problem.

When the stout, dark-haired Sgt. William Mays brought Clayton in to discuss the aggravated rape charge brought against him, he denied it entirely. Clayton said he would never do something that horrible to another person. The sergeant did not believe him at all, saying, "He wouldn't look me in the eye and was very nervous."

He said Clayton then asked what made the rape charge aggravated. Mays said it was aggravated because of his physical assault against the girl. Clayton looked at him and said, "'I didn't beat her before I raped her.'" Mays said as soon as Clayton said those words, he knew he had signed his death warrant. "I immediately placed him under arrest and took him to county lock-up," said Mays, describing the moment as a "good feeling."

After Clayton's arrest, Rita and Molly begged for money from everyone they knew to bail Clayton out of jail. After his release on his own recognizance, Clayton kept a low profile. His arrest was reported in the area newspaper along with his photograph. "Everyone knew who Clayton was then," said Molly.

Molly's relatives claimed they again tried to convince Molly to leave Clayton, but she insisted he would be proven innocent at trial. "She was determined to stand by her man, worthless that he was," said Candy.

Molly tried making the best of Clayton's upcoming trial. He was looking at twenty years in prison if convicted. That was twenty years too long for Molly.

Melinda recalled how upset and haggard-looking Molly appeared during the time of Clayton's legal problems. She remembered that sometimes while at work, she found Molly in the break room crying. Other times she heard Molly crying over the cell phone to Clayton, asking, "Why? why?"

Melinda believed that as time went by and the trial was nearing, Clayton admitted to Molly that he did rape his then seven-year-old cousin years earlier. She said Molly forgave Clayton, but she was no longer the same happy, perky Molly anymore, saying her story book marriage was gone.

Molly continued showing up each day to work as normal. Although Clayton made bail, she said he had no intentions on showing up for his trial date. No one knocked on their front door wanting to remove the children from their care, and there were no more frantic phone calls from relatives. Each time she checked in with Clayton, Molly said, he and the kids were okay. Neighbors recalled seeing Clayton taking the kids for walks in the nearby park, out for ice cream, or playing hide-n-seek in the backyard. "To the outside world, we were a content family, so it seemed," she said.

Janie agreed with that statement. She admitted Clayton appeared to be a good father saying, "Sometimes I think he liked being a dad more than being married." However, she admitted she never told her sister that, describing Molly as the jealous sibling. Janie recalled that while she and Molly were children, if one parent paid excessive attention to her, something of hers "came up missin' or got mysteriously tore up. That was Molly," she said.

Candy claimed she and her husband never played favoritism, but she believed some people required more attention than others. She referred to that symptom as an inferiority complex. She defended Molly by claiming every family had one, and Molly was theirs, saying, "Sometimes that girl was real hard ta love."

On June 18, while preparing for bed, Molly recalled two local police officers paying her a visit. She said she greeted them in her doorway, at which time they asked to come in. Once inside, Molly said they followed her into the living room where she offered them a seat. She said they declined, and then said she should sit.

According to the officers, their statement puzzled Molly, but she sat anyway. They then told her Clayton was found dead earlier that night. They described Molly as being surprised and she asked for details.

The officers told her the police station received a telephone call from a motorist, stating a car had run off the road and plunged down an embankment, catching fire. They said Molly then covered her face with her hands and sobbed, asking, "'Are you sure it's Clayton? He left to go to his mother's house. It can't be him.'"

The officers reassured Molly it was Clayton inside the vehicle, telling her they checked the registration of the vehicle. When they asked Molly if Clayton drove a green Chevrolet, she answered "'yes.'"

Molly explained she and Clayton had been married for less than two years, and she seemed genuinely upset, saying she did not know how to tell her children their father was dead. She then asked to be alone, and the officers offered their condolences and left.

The fatal accident made front-page news. The outpouring of sympathy for the young widow and now single mother was overwhelming. Melinda said she could not imagine what Molly was going through when she heard Clayton was dead. "She worshipped that man," she said, recalling how their boss allowed Molly two weeks off to get her nerves together. "We all felt so sorry for her," said Melinda.

Candy recalled being in shock when Molly called and told her of Clayton's death. She recalled going to Molly's home immediately to comfort her, saying, "She was a bag of nerves." Candy said she took the kids for a week to allow Molly to gather her thoughts. She felt remorse for disrespecting him earlier.

According to fifty-seven-year-old Fire Marshal Sterling Tupper, the fire consumed the car to the point of Clayton's remains turning to twelve pounds of ash. That was the worst traffic accident in the history of the town, said the silver-haired grandfather of four, who stood of average height and weight and sported glasses.

First on the site was Trooper William Mays, a thirty-year-old with a black flat top and dark eyes. He said he was amazed at the intensity of the flames. He hoped the victim died before the fire started, saying, "That's one bad way to die."

If Clayton's life was filled with petty crimes and poverty, and his death grisly and sudden, he was spoken well of and mourned at his funeral. A die-hard rocker, Clayton's friends said they knew he would have no such music as gospel hymns at his wake. As the song Free Bird spilled from the speakers and mourners shared a bottle of Jack Daniel's, there was a flood of attendance, with some complete strangers. Many appeared only for the sake of the now grieving widow and fatherless children.

One was Melinda. She told the crowd that although she did not know Clayton exceptionally well, she knew he loved his family, saying, "Molly and those kids was everything to that man."

Molly's side of the family reported that showing up late, tipsy, and dressed like a teenager on prom night was Rita. After staggering to the podium, she told the mourners she knew her son had problems, but she also knew, as God was her witness, her boy was committed to three things. "Fishing, motorcycles, and his family," she said.

"Hear! Hear!" reportedly shouted the crowd, as one by one, the attendees said their farewells to the young, wild and rambunctious, sometimes foolish man that warm June evening of 2005.

Molly might have been a wreck at Clayton's funeral, but according to Melinda, the young mother of two did not like wearing mourning black. Four days after the funeral, Melinda recalled Molly calling her and asking her to accompany her to a new bar that just opened up. Melinda said she was shocked but shrugged off Molly's odd behavior as her being confused with Clayton's death and her having financial problems including defaulting on bills. Melinda said she agreed to go.

Melinda was not the only person shocked at Molly's sudden burst of cheerfulness so soon after her husband's ghoulish death. Rita noticed Molly and Melinda at the bar and recalled Molly sporting a new hairstyle and manicure and "was all smiles." Molly was dancing with any man who asked her and receiving free drinks. "She was definitely not the grieving widow that evening," said Rita.

Neighbor and professional babysitter, Chloe Lins, remembers that just weeks after Clayton's death, Molly began searching for a babysitter. She recalled that while walking her young son around the block, she noticed a help wanted ad nailed to a telephone police. The ad stated an area mother with two small children was looking for a sitter.

Chloe claimed not knowing Molly or her relatives or of hearing about Clayton's death. She approached Molly and offered to watch her children for thirty dollars a week, saying, "That was dirt cheap anywhere."

Molly wanting to go back to work was confusing for her mother. Candy offered to help her daughter financially if that should be the reason for her sudden interest in returning to work.

To Candy's surprise, Molly said she did not need outside financial help because her friend Jake was helping her. Candy said she assumed "Jake" was a co-worker concerned about Molly and the children. The reason Candy gave for not questioning her daughter about Jake was because she knew heartache and stress often "makes a person act strange."

As it turned out, Molly was giving some people one answer for returning to work and others a very different answer. Many thought it strange for Molly to return to work so soon after her husband's death, including Melinda.

According to Melinda, the answer she received from

Molly was that work took her mind off things, and she needed the money. Apparently, Molly had not collected Clayton's $115,000 life insurance policy. The wreck was still under investigation by the Fire Marshal, and the post-mortem report was incomplete. Melinda claimed when she informed her and Molly's boss of Molly's financial situation, office employees donated money to help with bills and groceries.

Relatives also helped in various ways. Janie and her mother took turns watching Molly's children to allow Molly time to herself. They ran errands for Molly and helped with house and yard work.

Clayton's family, on the other hand, was as worthless as Clayton had been. Molly never heard from any of Clayton's relatives after the funeral, although Janie knew some of Clayton's relatives had asked about Clayton's life insurance money.

Molly informed Candy that with the help she received from friends and family, she and her children would do fine until Clayton's life insurance came through. Candy claimed Molly seemed worried that the insurance company holding the policy was taking so long in closing the case and mailing the check. Molly shrugged off the delay as the insurance company being overworked, saying, "'Insurance companies investigate hundreds of car wrecks every year.'"

Yes, the insurance company investigated dozens of such horrible accidents, but Clayton's death started looking more suspicious with each passing week.

According to Sgt. Mays, his first thought when viewing the wreck was how could one car burn so badly, just by driving off the road and crashing? Was there foul play, he wondered, for insurance money? On the other hand, did someone want the husband out of the way, like a jealous lover? "Stranger things have happened," he said. However, he was not the only expert baffled by the facts of the wreck. The local Fire Marshal, after reviewing the photographs of the wreck, found several oddities.

Arriving minutes after Sgt. Mays, the Fire Marshal claimed his first concern was for the victim inside the incinerated car. From the outside of the vehicle, he and Sgt. Mays saw the victim in the driver's seat, but the head was missing. He thought that might have occurred due to the extreme heat, but once the fire was extinguished, the men discovered the legs were also missing. After a search of the vehicle, they discovered the missing body parts on the floorboard of the passenger side of the vehicle. When paramedics tried removing the victim from the car, the remaining flesh nearly crumpled under the touch. "I've never seen anything so bad," the Fire Marshal said. Immediately everything was sent to the county medical examiner.

With the fire now ruled suspicious, the insurance company refused to release the money until authorities solved the case. According to Melinda, the insurance company she and Molly worked for held the policy on Clayton's car. When the report came in, she kept it confidential so as not to alarm Molly to the details of Clayton's death.

Melinda claimed not wanting Molly upset any more than she was. When Melinda read the fire report, she said she was amazed as to how badly Clayton was burned. She found it upsetting to read.

The report revealed that what was found were only scraps of clothing; the victim was wearing what seemed to be blue jeans and a baseball cap with one fishhook attached. "It sure sounded like Clayton Daniels," she said. The report described the body as charred beyond recognition. Melinda knew that meant dental records were needed to identify the body, causing a delay in releasing the insurance check.

The total details concerning the crash were never released, not even to Molly, claimed Janie. She said that with the age of Clayton's car, she found it odd that it traveled at such a high rate of speed that investigators claimed it was traveling for Clayton to lose control and crash and burn. Janie said she and her family suggested to investigators that perhaps Clayton fell asleep at the wheel, or was intoxicated, which was one of his favorite pastimes. "They say one shouldn't mix drugs and alcohol, but Clayton never was one to follow rules," she said.

Like Molly, Candy said she also assumed the insurance company would pay the policy soon after burial. According to her, the medical examiner ruled the death as accidental, claiming few remains was recoverable for burial. The examiner reported an autopsy unnecessary. "It should have been an open and shut case," she said.

The Fire Marshal wrote in his report that at the crash scene, he saw no visible signs of skid marks. He had the impression the driver never attempted to stop. He concluded that the driver was either unconscious inside the car, or he committed suicide, in which case the insurance policy was void.

Once the Fire Marshal contacted the office of Sgt. Mays concerning a possible insurance fraud, the officer immediately ran a background check on Clayton Daniels. What he found revealed that Clayton was no stranger to law enforcement.

He said what jumped out at him were not the petty robberies or cultivating marijuana Clayton had on his record. It was not drunk-and-disorderly charges and bar fights; it was a sexual assault charge pending against him. "Now that's big news in a small town," he said.

The pending rape charge against Clayton shocked and worried many, according to Melinda. She recalled how calm Molly took the news about her husband. She claimed she talked with Molly about the repercussions of Clayton being a registered sexual offender and how such a charge such as that would hamper their lives. She claimed Molly said she "had everything worked out."

As many thought, Clayton pled guilty to rape, making a trial unnecessary. When Candy heard the news, she said she worried constantly about her grandchildren. Then days before Clayton's sentencing hearing, he dies in a fiery crash. "Strange how things worked out," she said.

Many thought Molly's behavior soon after the wreck was odd. Three weeks after Clayton's death, Melinda recalled the two lunched together. Molly asked right out of the blue when would be the proper time to begin dating again. Melinda said she was shocked. First, Molly had vowed her undying love and devotion to Clayton, and now faster than sunburn in July, she was ready to go man hunting again. "It was weird," said Melinda.

The cracks in Molly's still unknown scheme were starting to show. Chloe had only been Matthew's and Harley's babysitter for one month when Matthew started acting out. Right after the child's fifth birthday, he began instigating fights with her four-year-old. She recalled not being overly alarmed with Matthew's behavior since he was a boy, and boys were naturally rowdy. However, she brought it to Molly's attention.

It was not only Chloe who noticed a big and strange change coming over Molly after the funeral.

A few weeks after the funeral, Candy visited Molly and the children one Sunday afternoon. She said she got the shock of her life when Molly answered the door in a short sexy nightgown and tousled hair.

Candy recalled Molly said the children were at the babysitter's who lived only a few houses away. Candy thought the whole incident strange but did not pursue it and simply left. Later, when she discussed the matter with Janie, Candy said Janie theorized Molly was entertaining a man, the reason she would not allow her mother entrance into the home. Janie recalled a bizarre conversation she had with Molly while at Clayton's funeral. According to Janie, Molly told her and their mother to call before dropping by. Jane and Molly found that strange, since neither ever had to call ahead. When Janie questioned Molly's reasons, she said Molly got angry with her and snapped, "'Just call first.'"

Many thought Matthews misbehavior was due to Clayton's sudden death since Clayton was the only father figure the boy had. Chloe noticed Matthew's behavior worsening and shrugged it off as being with a new sitter. She recalled theorizing about the child's anger problems, which included his spitting and urinating on her bathroom walls. When she warned Matthew to stop or she would tell his mother, she said he begged her not to tell on him, saying, "Please don't, because Jake will get mad."

This mysterious man named "Jake" would not be a mystery for much longer. When Matthew mentioned Jake, Candy immediately called Molly and wanted to know who this man was that was living with her young grandchildren.

Candy remembered how irate Molly became during that phone call, telling her she was on her way to retrieve Matthew who was visiting Candy. When Molly arrived at Candy's home, she was very angry with Matthew for mentioning Jake, which apparently was supposed to remain a secret. Candy said Molly left immediately with her son and refused to answer any questions.

Melinda also found Molly's behavior odd. She recalled that while at work shortly before Clayton died,

Molly often researched various sites on her office computer. Whenever Melinda approached, she said Molly minimized the screen as if to keep secret what she was viewing. At the time, Melinda thought Molly was surfing dating networks looking for a boyfriend.

While others saw Mollys's out-of-character behavior confusing, Rita called her daughter-in-law's behavior downright shocking. According to Rita, two weeks after the funeral, she noticed Molly at the area shopping center purchasing a complete new wardrobe, clothes no decent widow with small children should wear. When Rita approached, she said Molly claimed she was Christmas shopping for her sister, Janie, even though Christmas was six months away. "She didn't fool me none. Those sleazy clothes were for her," said Rita.

Matthew's behavior never subsided either. Chloe recalled that a few days after the urination incident, she questioned Molly about Jake, saying, at that point, everything was about Jake, Jake this and Jake that. Molly said he was a family friend. Chloe said, at the time, she believed and understood that, since she had platonic male friends. That all changed, Chloe said, the day her car stalled. As she fidgeted with her vehicle, Chloe said Jake came out of Molly's house wearing only his boxer shorts and a T-shirt to help her. She said that was when she said, "Whoa, this guy was more than just a friend." Matthew's behavior never got any better, she said.

It was not only Molly's home where strange happenings occurred. Things for the county and medical examiner became twisted when a cemetery groundskeeper came upon a sickening site.

Sgt. Mays said when he discovered a grave had been uncovered and the corpse removed, he did not know what to think. He knew the county had never experienced problems with body snatchers before. After checking with the groundskeeper, he discovered the corpse was an eighty-six-year-old mentally handicapped woman from an area nursing home. According to court records, the woman was indigent with nothing of value buried with her.

The woman might have been alone in the world with no visitors during her entire stay at the nursing home, but nursing assistant Helen said Charlotte was loved. Helen recalled receiving the disturbing news, saying, "My heart just broke." According to nursing home staff, they adored Charlotte, calling her a joy to care for. Helen knew Charlotte had no family, so she and the other employees took Charlotte under their wing and became the woman's family.

Charlotte's desecrated body was reported in every local paper. When Candy read about the missing corpse, she recalled being disgusted, saying, "Now there's one sick person out there."

According to the Fire Marshal, he continued discovering bizarre circumstances with the investigation. He said when tire treads on the crash site pavement were absent, he suspected the driver was either unconscious or already dead when the car went into the ravine.

As part of his investigation, he went to the junk yard where the Chevrolet was towed, taking several samples from the inside of the vehicle. He noticed the driver's side of the vehicle sustained the worst damage. He knew then that it would be several weeks before the results came back, so he took it upon himself to notify the insurance company, telling them not to release the insurance check.

That decision by Marshall Tupper did not sit well with Molly. Melinda said when Molly learned there was a hold on the insurance claim, she threw a fit. Melinda claimed Molly stormed into their boss's office the morning after she was notified by the insurance company of the stall and read the man the riot act.

Melinda said the entire department heard Molly yelling and cursing. However, Melinda knew releasing the insurance check was not up to the boss, it was the coroner's decision. There had to be a death certificate for Clayton Daniels. "I've never seen her that mad," said Melinda.

Janie saw that not receiving the insurance money added financial problems for Molly and her children. The bills soon piled up, and the collection plate was empty. Even worse, townsfolk heard rumors of Molly being investigated and people were whispering about her. She was getting irritable more easily with people. It was obvious to many that something far more serious than financial woes bothered the young widow.

With a career of twenty-one-years under his belt and investigating more road wrecks then one could throw a stick at, Marshal Tupper said he could not shake the haunting feeling that many details of the accident did not add up.

He contemplated that perhaps someone pushed Clayton off the road in a fit of road rage, or maybe someone retaliated against him for the rape of the young relative. However, when he learned Molly Abbott took out a life insurance policy on her new husband, Clayton Daniels, immediately after were married, it "smelled like homicide," he said.

One person who sided with the Fire Marshal was Rita. When Sgt. Mays came to her house and inquired as to whether or not she believed Molly Abbott could murder her husband, Rita said she answered with a resounding "yes," saying, "I wouldn't put anything past her."

Rita then informed Trooper Mays of Molly's strange behavior soon after the funeral, behavior completely bizarre for a grieving widow. Rita claimed that while at Clayton's funeral, Molly talked non-stop on her cell phone. She repeatedly snuck away from the mourners to an adjoining room to talk. Then the new wardrobe, the dating, Matthew's sudden hostile behavior. "There was definitely something going on with her," said Rita.

Within a matter of a few weeks, the Fire Marshal was convinced there was foul play concerning the suspicious death of Clayton Daniels. The autopsy revealed an absence of soot in the lungs of the burned driver.

According to Trooper Mays, he then reviewed the autopsy report on his own. The problem with that was the original medical examiner was now retired, and a new ME had taken office. When Trooper Mays read that the report mentioned no male genitals found on the burn victim and no soot in the lungs, those two facts should have raised red flags, but, unfortunately, no one communicated with each other through the proper channels. "The county messed up, big time," he said.

Once Chloe realized Jake was the new man in Molly's life, she began quizzing Matthew with questions about the man. Matthew told Chloe that Jake stayed inside the house all the time, playing videos and wrestling with him. That right there was strange, she thought. Who stays in the house in the summer time on a beautiful day? She said she answered herself, "Someone running from the law, that's who."

Once Trooper Mays and the Fire Marshal connected with one another, they discussed the various theories of the cause of the wreck. According to Marshal Tupper, they decided that perhaps the new boyfriend they recently learned of had bumped off his competition...and maybe Molly was or was not involved.

The Marshal then requested the body of Clayton Daniels exhumed, which was a delicate situation. "No judge likes signing this type of order, and it was seldom done," he said.

When Molly found out authorities wanted to exhume Clayton's body, she went ballistic. Molly used Candy's telephone to call the Fire Marshal, venting her anger, calling him everything but a white man. "I thought she had finally flipped," said Candy.

To their surprise, or maybe not, when Molly refused to give her consent for the exhumation, Janie suspected her big sister was involved with Clayton's death. Janie claimed that if her husband had died the way Clayton died, she would want to know if it was homicide, unless she was the one who killed him.

Melinda reported that during the time of the exhumation, Molly continued working. However, she began taking lunches outside the office on a daily basis, which in itself caused eyebrows to rise. The employees knew of Molly's financial problems, for now Molly's life was an open book. When she received a shut-off notice for the electric bill, Melinda said she assumed Molly's new friend was helping.

It took an entire week for the judge to agree to exhume the body presumed to be Clayton Daniels. According to Trooper Mays, bone marrow from the left hip was tested. Rita was asked for and then gave a DNA sample to match to the body. At this point, Trooper Mays said he did not know what to believe. "Molly's strange behavior so soon after her husband's death seemed fishy," he recalled.

Rita claimed she agreed to the DNA test because she needed to know who was in that grave and whom she mourned over at the funeral. According to Rita, Molly was giving her the runaround when she was not dodging her phone calls. Molly said one thing, and the authorities said another. She said all she wanted was the truth about what happened to her son.

By this time, Chloe realized Matthew was completely out of control, with Molly still in denial of his constant tantrums. She claimed she informed Molly that Matthew's behavior was abnormal for a small child to be so malicious. Chloe said she suggested Matthew see a counselor but claimed Molly denied ever seeing the child acting out, saying, "'He's not rowdy at home.'" Molly then accused Chloe of inciting Matthew's behavior, which threw Chloe for a loop. She was shocked to hear Molly blaming her for the boy's misbehaving, saying, "I tried to help Matthew."

During the next few months, Molly continued being secretive, taking her lunches out, mum about the mystery man hidden inside her home, and still angry about the insurance claim not paying up. One afternoon after work, Melinda spotted Molly retrieving boxes from the dumpster behind the insurance building.

According to Melinda, when she asked Molly why she needed the boxes, Molly informed her she might be moving out of town. When Melinda suggested that might not be wise, since she was under investigation, Melinda said Molly became irate, telling her if she were truly a friend, she would not doubt her innocence, and if she was not a friend, to "mind my own business."

The investigation had its toll on everyone involved, it seemed. Candy saw less and less of Molly and the kids. Candy claimed that when she asked Molly where she was keeping herself, the girl said she and Jake went out of town for entertainment. Candy said she did not push the subject but prayed Molly was not involved with criminal activity, saying, "The last thing I wanted was a jailbird in the family."

When Janie heard Molly went out of town for entertainment, she believed Molly was dating someone of Clayton's caliber. Janie said Molly saw through a man's rough exterior and looked for the good, finding love through rose-colored glasses. She believed that was the reason Molly made the choices she made.

After five weeks, authorities received the DNA results from the lab. According to Trooper Mays, many believe it only takes a short time for the results, but in reality, it was nothing like on television, saying, "'Nothing about lab work was fast.'"

When Rita received the news that the burned body from the wreck was not her son, she said she could have killed Molly and her new "friend" with her bare hands. She accused Molly of causing nothing but drama and pain for her family. She said she and her relatives all wondered, "If we didn't bury Clayton that day, who was buried, and where's Clayton?"

When the ghoulish news reached Candy and her family, she said they were all scared for Molly. They were all equally confused. Candy knew Molly was crazy in love with Clayton. They theorized that one of Clayton's shady friends done him in. Candy prayed her daughter was not involved, saying, "I sure didn't want my baby girl mixed up in murder."

The burn victim's identity was not the only confusing detail in the insurance policy case, it seemed. Janie said each time she saw Matthew, all he talked about was Jake. She said getting information out of Molly concerning her ghost boyfriend was like pulling teeth.

Janie claimed she and Candy received different answers from Molly concerning Jake's identity. First Molly said Jake was a neighbor. Then Molly said he was a friend of Clayton's. Then Molly told her family Jake was a truck driver, which made no sense to the relatives, since Matthew said Jake was at home all the time and did not own a vehicle.

Melinda recalled that one day while at work, Molly left her cell phone on her desk while she went to the bathroom. While Molly was gone from the room, Melinda confessed to checking the stored messages, finding Molly had texted a man named Jake, saying she loved him. Melinda said she felt it was too soon after losing a husband to be making such personal statements to another man, but she stayed quiet.

Chloe knew it was Molly's business only as to what she did with her life and the choices she made; however, with Matthew's behavior and Molly lying to her about Jake being just a friend, she wanted the truth, and she believed only Molly had it.

That was when she made the decision to confront Molly concerning her relationship with Jake. Chloe claimed when she asked Molly where she met Jake, Molly said in a bar. When she prodded for more information, Chloe said Molly clammed up.

What Chloe did not want was for Molly to become suspicious of her, the reason she did not press the subject. However, Jake came about, so soon after Clayton's death, made little sense to her. She believed Jake was upsetting Matthew.

After discovering the burned body was not Clayton Daniels's, Fire Marshal Tupper said he knew he had some kind of insurance fraud case in front of him, but exactly what kind was baffling. He immediately notified Trooper Mays.

According to Trooper Mays, the case now pointed to fraud -- and possibly murder, since no one knew where Clayton Daniels was, or who the burned corpse was. Realizing he was in over his head and needed outside help, he contacted the Texas Rangers.

When Ranger Jared McCoy initially met Molly Abbott at her home, he said she invited him in, but just inside the door. He recalled Molly appearing nervous with his presence, but overly calm to the fact the burned body in the Chevrolet was not her husband. According to Ranger

McCoy, Molly insisted if Clayton was alive, she did not know where he was, and she did not appear to be anxious to find him.

When Rita learned the body was not that of Clayton, she told Molly she had a lot of explaining to do. If Molly and Jake killed Clayton, Rita was going make them pay, she said.

According to Candy, Rita's threats to find the truth came true. Candy claimed she and her family received constant harassment and threats from the Abbott family after the corpse was identified as Charlotte Davies. Rita and her clan followed Candy and her family everywhere, accusing them of "being in cahoots with Molly to get the insurance money," she said.

Ranger McCoy knew Clayton Daniels had a checkered past from talking with local police, but where was he now? Was he dead perhaps and authorities had a second dubious case on their hands?

First, he said, he wanted to find out about Jake. From the persons he interviewed, no one from Molly's family or Clayton's family saw or talked with Jake. In addition, he did not want Molly to discover he was searching for Jake. He said with all the odd incidents involved in the case, he did not want anyone else to go missing.

Immediately the Texas Rangers posted a surveillance team outside of Molly's work place and at her home twenty-four seven. Authorities believed Molly was the key to solving everything. From what Chloe Lins told Trooper McCoy, "this Jake fella did not scream family man."

When the Texas Rangers asked Melinda to monitor Molly at the office, she said she did not want to become involved. However, with Molly's odd behavior and her anxiety, Melinda said she felt her once best friend was up to something, and she was afraid of her.

Melinda had never known anyone who was a murder

suspect; she found it very frightening. She agreed to help the authorities. When Molly told Melinda she was meeting Jake for lunch, Melinda called the Rangers and informed them to be on the lookout for Molly.

After Melinda's phone call, Trooper McCoy said he felt they were wrapping up the case. He recalled his men tailing Molly for over a month with no boyfriend sighting. They also had no probable cause for a search warrant for her home, he said. The only option was to wait for Molly to slip up, and she did.

The investigation continued for months after the identity of the burned victim was known. When Trooper Mays received the okay to close in on Molly and her friend, he was elated, saying, "This who-dun-it had gone on for nearly five months."

Molly was not the only one taken by surprise that day. According to Candy, she was getting a perm at the area beauty shop when she saw police cruisers surround the Taco Bell restaurant. "I thought it was a robbery in progress. Boy, was I wrong," she said.

Rita was equally shocked, she said. She, like many others, were in the dark about Clayton's arrest until it was reported in the local papers. "I couldn't believe my eyes," she said. "I didn't know whether to faint or jump for joy."

According to Trooper Mays, when he and fellow officers entered the restaurant through the front doors, he immediately recognized Jake as being Clayton Daniels with dyed black hair and sporting a mustache and glasses.

Ranger McCoy remembered how peaceful and nonchalant Clayton looked while eating his burrito as if he had no cares at all. "That just shows how callous the man really was," he said.

Apparently, when Clayton saw the officers, he only said two words, "Oh shit!" Trooper Mays said, "Welcome back, Clayton Daniels, you're under arrest." He just hung his head.

Clayton Daniels may have handled the arrest like a man, but that was not the case with Molly Abbott. According to Ranger McCoy, she immediately jumped to her feet, screamed and cursed at the officers, so officers arrested her also.

Janie recalled seeing the arrest on the local news stations. Clayton at least knew the jig was up, but not her big sister. Molly showered the officers with vulgarities, exited the restaurant kicking and screaming, to a chaotic scene of news cameras, and shocked on-lookers. Janie said at that moment she knew why Matthew's once gentle disposition had turned hostile the past few months. "His daddy wasn't dead, he just disguising himself as his mommy's new boyfriend. Sick!" she said.

When Candy realized Clayton was alive, she said she was somewhat thankful. She knew then that Molly was no killer. She thought everything would be settled and be fine and dandy, but "again I was wrong," she said.

Once officers restrained Clayton with handcuffs, they searched him, discovering a driver's license with his new identity on it. Trooper Mays noted the new identification contained not only the name of Jake Ashboard but also a new Social Security number. The husband and wife crooks were booked into county lock-up.

Initially police charged Clayton with failure to appear and arson and Molly with insurance fraud. That was the extent of the couple's criminal activity known to authorities, but the story did not stop there.

While Clayton was in custody, Trooper Mays contacted the man's probation officer for a positive ID on him. After one look, the probation officer positively identified Jake Ashboard and Clayton Daniels as being one and the same. A quick fingerprinting again identified Jake Ashboard as being Clayton Daniels.

After the arrest, pieces of the puzzle fell into place: the burned corpse minus male genitalia, the missing cemetery body of Charlotte Davis, the large insurance policy, the faked death, the mysterious new lover, and Matthew's sudden misbehaving.

It quickly became obvious to authorities that Molly and Clayton Daniels faked Clayton's death for the insurance money, to begin a new life together somewhere else. Now all authorities needed was to put the few remaining missing pieces together and close one of the strangest cases in Texas history.

Once Clayton and Molly were booked, they clammed up and asked for attorneys. Rita said she knew Clayton was in for a hard ride with the rape conviction hovering over him. Even though he was alive, she knew she would not see him for a very long time, saying, "It felt like he died all over again."

When Melinda discovered to what lengths Molly and Clayton went to for new identities, she said she was in disbelief as to why and how Molly's life had regressed, saying, "She could have been so much more than a felon and the wife of a rapist."

Even though both refused to talk with law enforcement, Trooper Mays said he knew neither could stay quiet for long, not with the type of charges against them. He suggested Clayton be celled with an informant with a wire in case he sang, and it worked.

According to the informant, within three weeks of his incarceration, Clayton admitted he was going to prison for rape then registered as a sexual offender for the rest of his life. His wife said that would hamper their lives forever. Clayton said it was Molly's idea to fake his death and use the insurance money to start a new life. Clayton said Molly found everything she needed for their plan over the Internet.

Once authorities heard that bit of news, they immediately confiscated Molly's work computer which was sent to the crime lab. Within days, they discovered every website Molly Abbott had surfed.

Melinda and co-workers were shocked when police officers executed a search warrant at her insurance agency. She recalled being in awe of the entire scene, saying it reminded her of the movies; cops everywhere, searching Molly's desk while wearing white gloves, labeling what they confiscated before sealing the items in evidence bags. "It was so surreal," she said.

After Chloe learned of Molly's and Clayton's arrest and the charges against them, she immediately thought them trailer trash. She thought what Molly put Matthew through was unforgivable, saying, "They completely messed with his head."

According to Trooper Mays, only when Molly heard Clayton's confession to his cellmate did she agree to an interview. He said once she revealed the entire story, it was a story he had never heard and hoped to never hear again.

According to a reporter, Molly celebrated her twenty-first birthday while incarcerated and awaiting trial. She entered the room in a white jail jumpsuit and wore makeup. Her long brown hair pushed behind her back. She was calm and polite throughout the interview.

When asked why she and Clayton put their families through such a horrendous ordeal, she calmly said three words. "For the family. I did it all for the family."

When asked about being a body snatcher, she said she knew there would be consequences for their actions, but rationalized her actions by saying, "To start a new life you have to take chances."

She said Clayton being a registered sex offender would dictate their entire lives. Where they could live. What jobs Clayton could get. How people viewed them. She then described Clayton as a "bad boy" and "a pain in the butt," but said she fell for him anyway.

She said she liked to fix things, and she believed she could fix Clayton. She believed she could make his past mistakes better with her outlandish plan. She believed her scheme would wash their mistakes from their lives, leaving behind a fresh beginning. At the time, she felt faking Clayton's death was the only solution. She admitted Clayton set the car ablaze with gasoline after driving it into a ravine.

Clayton had admitted earlier to authorities that within thirty seconds, the vehicle became a fireball. He said he stood back and watched the vehicle burn, saying, "I heard the tires pop." He admitted to having stashed a motorcycle in nearby bushes the previous day.

Molly told the reporter that the burning of the car was no clean getaway. Moments after Clayton sped off, a driver on the same road, noticed the wreck. He tried using his cell phone, only to discover there was no reception on that part of the road, so he drove off looking for help.

Clayton then immediately drove to Abilene, Texas. a two-hundred-mile journey. As soon as he arrived in Abilene, Molly said he called her from a pay phone, saying only two words, "It's done." In Abilene, Clayton met an elderly farmer named Mr. Ross and became his hired hand, Molly said.

When asked why she and Clayton did not leave the area after the funeral, she said she actually believed the insurance company would pay up, but Trooper Mays became suspicious. That, said Molly, was when her plan began to unravel.

Things in Abilene were going fine for Clayton, she

said, until Mr. Ross caught Clayton and her in his barn with their pants down, literally. She recalled Mr. Ross came looking for Clayton one morning, and when he opened the barn door, he caught them both butt naked. He told them they had ten minutes to get out or he was calling the police.

She claimed the homeowner had no weapon, but just his threatening to call authorities was enough to scare then into leaving. That was the day plan two, Clayton being Jake, came into play. With Clayton fired, no money, no place to live or hide, and their not having the finances to rent him an apartment in Abilene, he had to return and hide at her place under a new identity.

She said she honestly thought Matthew would not recognize Jake as being Clayton, since Clayton changed his hair color and wore glasses, but the child did. She admitted Matthew was very confused and had a hard time dealing with the identity scam. With Matthew being only four, she believed she could convince him into believing Jake was Jake, not Clayton, but that did not work out according to plans.

That confusion for the boy was the beginning of his behavior problems. However, she rationalized his behavior change as being typical for a child of that age.

When confronted by the reporter concerning Matthews spitting on the babysitter's furniture, picking fights with other children and urinating on walls, Molly said she talked to him about his unacceptable behavior but claimed he was calm in her home with Jake.

She claimed she underestimated her son's emotional well-being when it came to calling Clayton Jake. She realizes now how big a mistake it was but says she cannot go back and erase her mistakes.

The reporter then told her she seemed to be taking her charade with a grain of salt and had shown no remorse for anything she and Clayton did. She claimed, since her incarceration, she came to realize her and Clayton's actions were wrong for many reasons, but again insisted she saw no other way around Clayton's past.

She claimed her plan would have worked if it were not for authorities asking questions. She explained how she surfed the Internet concerning how one would change their identity, how to fake one's own death, how to get new Social Security numbers, new birth certificates. She said she searched crematory websites to determine what temperature fire had to be in order to burn a body beyond recognition.

She admitted to planning the insurance and identity frauds after Clayton's rape conviction, knowing their lives would never be normal again. She had researched websites for weeks before the crash, with Melinda suspicious of her behavior.

She knew her bizarre plan would not be easy to pull off, considering the amount of thought and research involved. However, she now knew using her work computer was foolish.

When asked how she found a body, she said she searched for two days. Her initial plan was to get an unclaimed cadaver at the local mortuary but decided getting one from a cemetery would be more confidential and cheaper.

She claimed Clayton dug up the corpse while she stayed home and played homemaker. That way, in case someone came over, they would at least see her at the house.

Clayton told authorities that digging up the corpse was the grossest thing he had done. "It was covered with maggots," he said. The smell was stomach turning, and he tried not looking at her by concentrating on his new future with Molly.

Molly said Clayton also applied his clothing to the corpse before putting it into the driver's seat. Molly said Clayton told her he then sat on the legs "like when you're a kid," and drove the car to the fire spot. He told her it was "disgusting and more," but he looked beyond that.

She claimed from the research she did, if the body burned beyond recognition, no autopsy was required. The police would check the car's registration to identify the owner. That, she said, was the reason Clayton dressed the body in his clothing. "By all accounts, the plan should have worked," she said.

When asked how she came upon the body of eighty-six-year-old Charlotte Davis, she said the websites explained the body used should have no known family, such as a drifter. That way, no one would inquire about the deceased or visit the grave. That was the reason she thought a male corpse was unnecessary. If the body burned beyond recognition, the genitals would burn away.

As for the age of the body used, Molly explained that according to the websites searched, the body can't be buried for a long period or it would burn too quickly due to the lack of flesh. However, the corpse cannot be freshly buried or it would burn too quickly because of embalming fluids.

She claimed she discovered the old abandoned cemetery by searching for cemeteries where the homeless and indigent were buried, a Potter's Field, where she discovered Charlotte Davis, buried just six months earlier, "just the right amount of time," she said.

She said she had no qualms about desecrating a bod since the woman was deceased, saying, "it's not like we killed someone." She does realize that her actions were ghoulish, but said Charlotte was in heaven and "it's just a body."

The reporter called her callous. She again justified her actions by saying, "I did it all for the family."

She talked about her and Clayton spending time in restaurants. She said she often went to see Clayton while he worked for Mr. Ross. She explained how she drove to Abilene, arriving at dark. She then parked her car away from the farm and out of sight before walking to the farmhouse, saying, "The road was empty late at night."

She and Clayton would often stay inside the barn drinking and dancing by candlelight with a battery-operated radio. Other times, they would go into the town of Abilene to drink or see a movie. She recalled how free and safe they felt while in Abilene where no one knew them. They did not need to hide or wear disguises and could be their selves and enjoy their time together. She said she and Clayton were happy in Abilene. She described their time in Abilene as a peaceful, secure time in their lives, away from the law, the fire investigation, and Clayton's legal problems. "It was a nice time," she said. However, Mr. Ross found out and everything changed; Clayton became Jake.

She explained how Clayton being Jake caused various problems within their family. Clayton had to stay in the house the entire day, emerging only at night. The babysitter was irate with her concerning Matthew's behavior, and the coroner would not sign the death certificate. She said without the insurance money, and the judge wanting a DNA test done on the remains, "The jig was up."

Once they discovered there would be no insurance money, Molly said she and Clayton decided to just move to Florida and begin a new life there. That was when they let their guards down. They ventured outside the home more often, believing Clayton's disguises would hide his identity. They were no longer concerned being caught, she said, since they were leaving for Florida within a few days, but then they were arrested.

She said everything came crashing down on her and Clayton. All her hard work creating the plans went right out the window. She received twenty years to life, with her children raised by relatives. It seemed like a lifetime, she said.

She described her incarceration as "being really hard behind these cold, uncaring walls." She said her only salvation was the visits by her children and mother, and knowing that when she and Clayton are released, they can be together. She claimed to love Clayton and called him her "soul mate" and the father of her children, saying they deserve to be together as a family.

After his interview with Molly, Trooper Mays claimed she never shed one tear during the discussion. He said some of the officers who watched the interview through the two-way glass were amazed to discover she was the mastermind behind such a fantastic and unbelievable plan.

However, Trooper Mays knew Molly Abbott was a twisted and cold-hearted woman who would do anything to get what she wanted. He believed prison was exactly where she belonged.

The case destroyed many lives and left everyone asking, why? Janie said she was not ready to forgive her big sister. She claimed the impact of Molly's selfish choices was devastating on Matthew. He suffered the most, she said, and will need counseling for years to help him deal with the lies Molly and Clayton fed him all those months.

Melinda said she also felt completely betrayed by Molly's actions, saying, "Molly so messed up her life, and for what? A loser! Money!" Melinda believed everyone who loved Molly and Clayton lost something due to their misguided choices, and it will be a long time before Melinda can consider Molly a friend again.

Matthew hates changes. Janie explained how she colored her hair a different color one month, and he had a fit. She said she had to return to the beauty shop and re-dye it the color she usually wore to calm him down.

Clayton Daniels's trial was first. In the January 2006 trial, Helen, Nurse's Aide and friend to Charlotte Davis, gave a witness statement. "I want the court to know what a caring and loving person Charlotte was. When we buried her in January of 2005, she should have been able to rest in peace in that back part of the cemetery she loved so much. Not cremated in a car fire. She wanted to be buried under the big shady oak, so the hot sun wouldn't be in her eyes."

Clayton and Molly and the twisted and monstrous deeds they did for love became their downfall. The jury deliberated for less than two hours. Clayton received twenty years for the rape conviction and ten years for arson and the desecration of a corpse.

Molly got fifteen years for arson and ten years for the desecration of a corpse. She justified her actions until 2006, when she divorced Clayton .

Thicker than Water?

According to fifty-eight-year-old Fire Chief Reginald Whitehall, a phone call came into the station around 9 p.m. on June 18, sending the short, plump salt-and-pepper-haired man and other personnel rushing to the scene. When they arrived, it appeared a Molotov cocktail was tossed through the living room window. A Molotov cocktail is homemade device considered a simple and cheap form of arson. Minutes later, area police arrived.

The caller identified herself as being fifty-two-year-old Jenny Michaels, owner of the bombed house. The tall, round woman with grey hair and brown eyes made it safely outside and waited on the sidewalk, being comforted by fellow neighbor, thirty-six-year-old Bonny-Jean, a petite red-head with blue eyes, when fire trucks arrived.

The first thing veteran detective forty-four-year-old Erick Bowers said he noticed was the glass from the alcohol bottle was mostly on the outside of the window, lying on the ground. That alone screamed inexperienced arsonist, such as a young person, the sandy-haired and green-eyed bachelor said. That area was known as a drug-infested, high-crime neighborhood.

According to the Fire Chief, the home was insured. There was minimal damage to the burned area. He knew of Jenny's neighborhood watch, and within that area, she was known for being a hero. He said it took guts to stand up to drug dealers and gang members, but she did it.

Jenny kept tabs with the officers assigned to her home arson case, recalled older sister Rachel. Jenny informed her she wanted the crime solved. She wanted the bastard responsible for setting her beloved home on fire to pay. She was a determined woman, and she was not letting up.

Detective Bowers had his officers out in full force. Officers canvassed the entire area for five city blocks looking for witnesses who might have seen or heard something peculiar around the time of the bombing. Reportedly, nothing useful was learned to explain the bombing, or who the bomber might be.

Unfortunately, before the minor damage was repaired, the home was bombed again. This time, two bombs came into the master bedroom of the home, Jenny's bedroom.

The Fire Chief was not the only one involved with the initial investigation that thought it was strange for the same house to be bombed twice within two weeks. He said he wondered if maybe the Good Samaritan videotaped the wrong crime, and her good luck ran out.

Talking with Rachel, police discovered Jenny was a very caring daughter to their ailing parents. The father built the couple's house in 1940, when he and his wife first married. Jenny grew up in that house and kept it immaculate. She never married nor had children. She worked hard throughout her life and saved her money.

With the fires so close to one another at the time of their happenings, the Fire Chief theorized they might be retaliation bombings toward Jenny Michaels. She was known for videotaping the streets outside her house for drug activity. She then turned the tapes over to police, which had resulted in the arrests of several drug dealers.

Also on the case was Detective Willard Stallman, a thirty-nine-year-old brown-haired man with hazel eyes and twin boys. He knew Jenny's neighborhood to be relatively respectable, but over the decades, it had become seedy.

Most people stayed inside their homes after dark. The night brought all the undesirables out. The prostitutes, drug activities, and various other crimes blanketed that side of town.

Rachel claimed she was not surprised when Jenny's home was bombed the first time. She knew of Jenny's neighborhood watch activities. She had been doing it for years, and the criminals in that area knew about the cameras.

Rachel said she warned her little sister about the negative effects of videotaping criminal behavior, but she said Jenny was determined to make her neighborhood safer in one way or another.

With Detective Bowers having two decades of police experience under his belt, he was the best man for the case that was nothing like it seemed.

He said the second fire, which occurred on July 1, was an almost total destruction of property. This time, the assailant got it right if their aim was to destroy Jenny's home or possibly to kill her.

He said he knew he was looking at no ordinary fire, but an attempted murder and felony arson. He sent the broken bottles to the same crime lab where the first bottle was examined for comparison.

With Rachel living in another state, she claimed she did not hear about the second fire right away. She later heard from news media that Jenny was badly injured with third degree burns. By the time she learned Jenny was hospitalized for her injuries, she had been in the hospital for three weeks already.

With eleven children in the family, and many living out of state, Rachel said it took some time to notify them all about the first fire. However, when she heard of no alarming news from Jenny, she assumed everything was okay.

The story of Jenny's plight and of being a crusader against crime was broadcast nationally. Detective Stallman said he was amazed by the media frenzy surrounding Jenny's case. The governor of California then offered a fifty-thousand-dollar reward for the name or names of the responsible party. He said he was sure someone would come forward with information for the reward money alone. "All the decent people wanted the case solved," he said.

When Detective Bowers learned of the large reward, he also believed persons would crawl out of the woodwork. With a reward that large, people, and especially drug addicts, turn in their own mothers, but they got no hits, he said.

He claimed no one called in about the bombing asking for the reward. The streets were quiet, he said. It was baffling. He wondered what authorities were dealing with. With two bombings on the same house within a two-week period, some officers involved wondered if the victim was involved with the crime herself. The police wondered if perhaps Jenny was targeted for more than being a bother to the area drug dealers. Was there more to this seemingly nice, friendly, middle-aged woman than met the eye?

Detective Bowers received Rachel's name and telephone number from one of Jenny's neighbors following the second fire. Bowers indicated Rachel was shocked to learn the police suspected Jenny of setting fire to her home.

When the detective asked Rachel if she thought Jenny was involved with illegal activity, she became extremely angry. She made it clear that Jenny was the most hard-working and honest person she knew, and she put the detective straight about her baby sister.

Detective Stallman admitted he hoped to gather more information about Jenny from her sister Rachel, but what he received was "a good old-fashioned chewing out."

He said the next time he or his partner spoke to Rachel, they chose their words carefully.

What physical evidence the forensic team gathered from the first fire was both confusing and contradictory. The results from the first fire were not even in when the second fire occurred.

When the Fire Chief returned to the house in search of evidence of arson, he found everything saturated from fire hoses. Even though he felt there was nothing of usefulness to gather, he and his men searched through the debris for any signs of arson. With the fire being a felony, he wanted the responsible party to pay for the financial loss, but also for the physical injuries Jenny suffered.

While searching the debris, one officer discovered in the kitchen area a chest freezer that had partially survived the blaze. It was apparent the freezer was no longer working or salvageable, but then the men noticed the lid heavily taped shut. That raised some eyebrows, Bowers said.

Detective Stallman recalled that before officers opened the freezer, they got a whiff of rotting meat. He said he first thought the frozen meat inside had thawed, then rotted, because the electrical wires were fried by the fire.

When Rachel received the news that the officers found a human body inside Jenny's freezer, she said she almost fainted. All kinds of confusion and gruesome ideas run through her mind with nothing making sense, she said.

When Coroner David Rasp, a sixty-seven-year-old with a receding hairline, received the call about a body in a freezer, he said he knew police were looking for a monster. "Only a psychopath cuts up a body and saves it."

The first thing Detective Bowers wanted to know when learned of the body, he said, was the victim's identity. Then he thought, maybe the sweet and always smiling homeowner had a terrible tale of her own?

Once the coroner removed the body parts, packed inside heavy-duty black trash bags, out of the freezer, he opened the bags and discovered the body severed into several small pieces. He said he had seen murders such as this before in his thirty years of being the county medical examiner, but you never get used to such brutality against another human being.

Once the bag that held the victim's head was located, officers immediately realized the cause of death was blunt force trauma to the back of the skull. Detective Bowers saw that the entire back of the skull was crushed. No one could survive that type of attack.

The coroner advised the time of death was difficult to pinpoint. The freezer had preserved the flesh. He claimed the victim might have been dead for weeks, months or even years. The freezer was turned full blast to ensure no decomposition. "Whoever killed this woman wanted her to remain a secret," he said.

Immediately police had a ton of questions for Jenny. Investigators wondered if she was the killer. If she did not kill the victim and place the corpse inside the freezer, Detective Stallman and Bowers believed she at least knew who did, and they wanted that person's name.

When Rachel learned about the body inside the freezer, she said she immediately thought that perhaps it was her mother. The woman had recently died, only weeks before the first fire. Although Rachel said she attended the funeral, it was a closed casket. If it was not her mother inside the freezer, then who was it?

When Rachel informed Detective Stallman of her mother's recent demise, he grew suspicious that perhaps the body in the freezer was that of the late Mrs. Michaels.

Mrs. Michaels was presumably buried after her funeral -- a funeral consisting of over fifty mourners. The last thing the detective wanted to do, he said, was exhume the mother's body and look inside her casket. He believed this case was morbid enough without digging up the dead.

When Rachel discovered Jenny was at the hospital, she said she called but was told Jenny signed herself out. There was a forwarding address, but Rachel claimed being unable to locate the telephone number for the hotel listed. She did not want to write Jenny because the home was being demolished. Rachel said she had to wait for Jenny to contact her.

When Detective Bowers checked with the hospital, he, too, was informed Jenny was no longer there. Jenny, however, left the front desk her hotel address in case there were any more monetary donations for her.

Once the body was found, the process of searching for blood evidence inside the burned house commenced. The dark residue around the freezer was reportedly too disintegrated from the fire to yield any usable DNA. Afterward, they located the bathtub in the back of the home.

It was apparent to the officers that the bathtub had what appeared to be saw marks on the inside of it. The police photographer was called in.

Believing the body was dismembered inside the bathtub and with the possibility of locating blood residue under the floorboards, officers removed the bathtub and held it for evidence. Afterward, using the station's saw, large parts of the burned bathroom floor were sprayed with luminol.

Unfortunately, no evidence of blood was found. To Detective Bowers, that sent investigative clues right out the window, for he was sure the victim died in the bathroom.

The fire chief explained that the finding of no blood in the bathroom might have been caused by the severity of the burned floorboards. A hot enough blaze can destroy anything, even blood trace, he said.

Officers then searched through the rubble to find the master bedroom. After searching, an officer discovered four lines of what appeared to be blood running down the wall next to the window that the second bomb came through.

According to Rachel, her father died six years before her mother died. With Jenny being the only child who stayed single, it was feasible she would care for the parents and in return, she would get the home after mom's death.

Rachel claimed she had no problem with Jenny getting everything, but she knew other siblings resented that. No matter how much siblings love one another, when there's money involved, there was trouble, she said.

It took several days for the coroner to determine who the victim was. The woman had no arrest record, making it difficult to learn her identity. He was very shocked to discover who she was. He also took notes of all the identifiable marks on the body, such as a surgical appendectomy scar and a large mole on the lower back; in addition, the victim wore dentures. He believed that if this case went to court, the information would be crucial.

When the fingerprints on the body came back as belonging to Jenny Michaels, Detective Stallman said he knew detectives would add identity fraud to the list of crimes concerning this case.

Once Detective Bowers received the coroner's phone call about the fingerprints, he and Detective Stallman located Jenny, or the woman who claimed to be Jenny, at the hotel. She agreed to go to the station. On the drive there, officers said she was pleasant, cooperative, and seemed to want to help with the investigation.

Once the detectives were inside the interrogation room, Detective Stallman relieved the suspect of her purse and searched it while Detective Bowers interviewed her. Detective Bowers said he noticed the woman's burn injuries all seemed to be on the front side of her body. With the type of fire, that Jenny was involved with, he determined the injuries should have been more on the backside of her hands and arms. Her injuries were more like a splash pattern. He said his gut told him he was looking at a murderer.

Inside the purse, Detective Stallman reportedly found two driver's licenses. One was for Jenny Michaels and the other was for a Sarah Mitchell. The women could pass for twins, the resemblance was so close, said Detective Stallman.

The detectives said the woman insisted she was Jenny Michaels and agreed to be fingerprinted. Within minutes, the prints came back as Sarah Mitchell. The detectives also discovered an arrest record for Sarah Mitchell which included theft and prostitution. The detectives now believed her arrest record would include cold-blooded murder. Detective Bowers said he immediately asked for a search warrant for the hotel room.

The woman denied being Sarah Mitchell, even after confronted with her fingerprints and arrest record. She also claimed to know nothing about the body in the freezer, said Detective Stallman.

She claimed she took several trips out of town to visit friends, and perhaps the body was placed inside the freezer at that time. That made no sense to the detectives and they told her so. She then said she occasionally allowed friends to stay with her at the house, and perhaps one of them committed the murder.

With Sarah denying she was Sarah Mitchell and having two driver's licenses, she was booked for identity fraud. Detective Bowers said he did not want to release her for fear she would disappear. He also knew police could not charge her with murder without hard evidence. "We needed to find that evidence before this mystery woman lawyered up," he said.

Three weeks after the second fire, Rachel received a telephone call from her brother, Clint, who lived in a nursing home in the next town. He said while watching the second fire on the news, he noticed the woman taken by paramedics to the hospital was not Jenny, but younger sister Sara.

Rachel said she was unsure as to whether or not to believe Clint because he suffered from Alzheimer's. She told him she would relay the news to the detectives assigned to the case. "His phone call only perplexed and saddened me more," she said.

According to Detective Bowers, after receiving Rachel's telephone call, he realized Sarah Mitchell was a sister to Jenny and Rachel. He said he immediately went to county lock-up and re-interviewed Sara, confronting her with the newest evidence.

Only after detectives informed Sarah that her brother saw her on the news did she admit she was Sarah Mitchell. However, she denied any involvement with Jenny's murder.

According to Rachel, her parents and Jenny supported Sarah most of her life. Sarah had two failed marriages, and although Sarah's children were adults, they, according to Rachel, were just as impoverished and emotionally unstable as Sarah was and incapable of helping her financially.

When authorities informed Rachel of Jenny's death, and believed Sarah responsible, Rachel was devastated. Rachel told the detectives that Sarah was the youngest of the family, and her actions would have overwhelmed their parents, saying, "I'm glad our parents weren't alive to see all this. What Sarah did would have crushed them."

Rachel admitted she knew Sarah resented Jenny's successful life but claimed she never realized Sara's jealousy and hatred toward Jenny had progressed to murder.

Detectives now believed the second arson was a cover-up for the murder of Jenny Michaels. With forensic evidence found in the master bedroom next to the window, authorities believed that room was where the murder took place.

When questioned, Sarah denied knowing how Jenny's body came to be in the freezer even though she often lived with Jenny. Detective Stallmans stated that Sarah admitted to identity fraud but continuously denied murdering her sister. She then clammed up.

Once officers were granted a search warrant, they discovered inside Sarah's hotel room check books and blank checks belonging to Jenny Michaels. Further checking revealed Jenny's checking and savings accounts were drained of nearly all the funds. Sarah Mitchell stole thousands of dollars that Jenny Michaels worked for, authorities believed.

Officers located writing tablets which appeared to be practice pads for Sarah practicing her sister's signature to be able to write checks and cash them. By all accounts, Sarah had completely taken over Jenny Michaels's life as if she wanted to be Jenny Michaels.

To prove murder, the detectives knew they needed clear signs of foul play. Once they discovered the house was a homicide scene, they cancelled the demolition.

According to the coroner, the saw marks found in the bathtub and on the victim's bones were smooth and consistent with marks made by a circular power saw. A handsaw, he said, would leave coarse marks from moving back and forth over the bone.

Authorities then re-interviewed neighbors. What Bonny-Jean revealed blew the case against Sarah wide open. The authorities were convinced the killer used the bathtub in the crime, but where was the blood?

Detective Bowers claimed he began with Bonny-Jean who confronted Jenny after the first arson attempt. What she said blew the case against Sarah out of the water.

Further damaging accusations against Sarah came from Rachel. She claimed Sarah routinely accused their parents of caring for Jenny more than her. While at their mother's funeral, said Rachel, Sarah became irate upon discovering Jenny inherited the parents' entire property. "It almost came to blows, but I never dreamed Sarah had it in her to kill," said Rachel.

Bonny-Jean claimed that when Jenny's mother was alive, Sarah was a frequent boarder. She was aware of Sara's alcohol and gambling habits, often overhearing Sarah and Jenny arguing about Sara's behavior.

Jenny told Bonny-Jean that Sarah had stolen money from her purse several times. Sarah refused to work and collected welfare checks or made money from illegal behavior. "Sarah always had a different man dropping her off at the house," said Bonny-Jean.

Rachel recalled while at their mother's funeral, Jenny confided in her that she could not tolerate Sarah anymore and she was going to insist she leave. Sarah was a pathological liar, according to Rachel and her siblings, which caused further conflict within the household.

While her mother was still living, Rachel said, Jenny's and their mother's jewelry went missing. Jenny believed siblings should respect one another, but with Sara, she said blood was not thicker than water.

Reportedly, Jenny asked Rachel to take Sarah in, but

with Sarah being an undesirable, Rachel refused. After the murder, Rachel regretted not distancing Sarah and Jenny, saying, "Maybe Jenny would be alive. She really was a sweet person."

Talking to Bonny-Jean, detectives discovered the bathroom inside Jenny's house was renovated. They believed that was the reason no DNA belonging to Jenny was found.

Once again, the forensic team turned to luminol with the hope of finding evidence needed to charge Sarah Mitchell with her sister's murder. Between the water hoses and the bathroom being burned the worst, the possibility of not locating evidence for a murder charge was high.

Once the blood from the bedroom walls was diagnosed as being human, officers used a saw to dismantle the floorboards. Underneath they hit pay dirt. The blood was still moist, not dried or damaged by the fire or water. Authorities believed Sarah killed Jenny, then started the fire in that area.

Afterward, officers sprayed luminol over that entire area. Within seconds, an outline of the bed appeared, a large square outline in blue. The officers were ecstatic, they reported. They had discovered the murder scene; Jenny was killed in bed while she slept.

The coroner agreed the number of blows on the victim's skull proved Jenny was asleep when attacked. In his professional opinion, there was no way a person could be awake and sustain that many hits to the head. There were no defensive wounds on the victim's arms or hands to indicate she fought back. She was completely off guard while asleep. The forensic evidence told the story of the last hours of Jenny Michaels's life.

The detectives believed that when Jenny told Sarah at the funeral that she would have to move from the house right away, Sarah formulated her plan to kill Jenny and assume her identity since the two could pass as twins.

Sarah never admitted her guilt, but from the forensic evidence, the victim's wounds, and from talking with persons who knew both women, Detective Stallman believes they know what happened that night. They believe Jenny went to bed and, after falling asleep, Sarah snuck into her bedroom and bludgeoned her to death with what authorities believed was a tire iron. She then put Jenny into the bathtub and cut her up, leaving saw marks on the inside of the tub. Then Jenny was placed into trash bags and into the freezer.

Sarah then hired a remodeling crew who renovated the entire bathroom including new floorboards, leaving no trace of Jenny's DNA. Then Sarah used the first fire, started by the drug dealers Jenny videotaped, as a way to start; the second making police believe both arsons were drug related. Without forensic evidence and the determination of officers, Sarah Mitchell almost got away with murder.

Sara's twisted love for money and material possessions destroyed her entire family. In 2001, she was found guilty of forgery, arson, and first-degree murder. At her sentencing hearing, her sister Rachel spoke. "We have already lost one sister, we don't want to lose another." Sarah was spared the death penalty and was sentenced to life in prison without parole.

Mail Order Murder

Few women find themselves in such a bizarre relationship as did eighteen-year-old Anastasia Solovieva, a Kyrgyzstan native. Speaking minimal and badly broken English, the family had high hopes for their tall, voluptuous, raven-haired daughter. An only child to senior and ailing parents, Anastasia's mother said she and her husband only wanted the best for her.

In a country where the average yearly income was three hundred dollars per person, Anastasia's parents believed Anastasia's future happiness lay with the United States.

Anastasia's mother recalled how Anastasia did not want to leave. It was the parents' idea for her to be a mail order bride. According to her mother, Anastasia said, "'What if I don't find husband? What if you and Papa waste your money?'"

Anastasia's father recalled telling his tall, curvaceous daughter that she was never a waste of their money. She was everything to them, and they wanted her to have everything America offered.

Anastasia's parents then took Anastasia's photograph in the dress she made, not like the other women posing for the magazine, loose women half naked. "No good man want them," they said.

Anastasia was a lady, explained Anastasia's father. A good Christian girl. Hardworking and responsible. She was raised the right way, they said.

In the spring of 2016, Anastasia became number M245, in a Kyrgyzstan mail order catalog with a circulation of over twenty million viewers. The magazine burst with dozens of glossy full-color photographs of young hopeful women looking for husbands to rescue them from their poverty-stricken and unhappy lives.

It was not long before Anastasia had her first letter from a prospective admirer. She returned to her small four-room home from her part-time job at a nearby bakery when her glowing parents greeted her just inside the front door.

Anastasia's mother recalled how surprised Anastasia was when she saw her and her husband smiling. She then handed her daughter the pink envelope with trembling hands.

At first Anastasia was afraid to open the letter, said Anastasia's father, but he told her it was from an American man. He said he and his wife watched as Anastasia read each word silently, her large dark eyes wide with anticipation. They said she was hesitant to respond to the sender, and maybe friendship will bloom. "If not, you brush up on language skills," said her mother.

That made Anastasia laugh, recalled her father. He still remembers her pretty laugh, saying, "as if a small child without cares."

The sender was a man by the name of Indle King. He claimed to be a successful executive in Seattle, Washington. When Anastasia asked "where Seattle," the family retrieved their family atlas from the windowsill near their kitchen table.

According to Anastasia's mother, when they discovered Seattle was near a large body of water, Anastasia was pleased. The family had, in the past, spent countless weekends at a nearby lake where Anastasia would swim and play with her cousins. There would be picnics and conversations between the adults. "It was a happy time," she said.

Anastasia did write to Indle King. She explained herself and her music teacher parents. She talked of being an accomplished pianist and winning minor contests in Kyrgyzstan. She wrote about how she was fluent in several languages, but her English was of poor quality. "She loves music, animals, and life," they said.

According to Indle King, he was shy and clumsy around women. He was overweight, bald and, for the most part, unattractive. He claimed not to drink, so the bar scene was not an option in finding a wife.

Then one day a co-worker suggested a mail-order bride, foreign magazines of gorgeous young women looking for friendship or marriage. He began searching and soon found Anastasia's photograph and profile. He said he was smitten and amazed that someone as pretty as Anastasia would respond to his letters.

When twenty-nine-year-old Detective Stella Blat, an attractive brunette with hazel eyes, became involved with the case, she described Indle as a blow-hard as were most men who turned to long-distance love affairs. He built himself up claiming to be an entrepreneur. In reality, she said, "he was a slob who couldn't hold down a job."

When Indle King offered to pay Anastasia to visit him in America, Anastasia's parents thought it a good idea. Her mother helped Anastasia to choose what clothing to take with her, including her best pair of shoes. Her parents recalled how happy Anastasia was that day.

Anastasia's first letter arrived in Kyrgyzstan one week later. Her biggest complaint, said her mother, was the physical size of Indle King. Anastasia called Indle loud and pushy, saying he wanted to hold her, even when she took her meals. When they went to clubs, Anastasia said Indle videoed her while she danced.

Anastasia wrote her parents weekly telling them she

slept on Indle's couch. She called him a gentleman, but she knew he wanted sexual favors. Her letters described how she told him no sex without marriage, and he left her alone.

Three weeks after arriving in America, Indle King proposed to Anastasia. She wrote her parents with the news and, according to them, they told her marry him for the green card, and perhaps she would learn to love him. Her mother said she blamed herself for what came later.

Anastasia's only Kyrgyzstan friend after arriving in America was the equally gorgeous and bosomy fellow Kyrgyzstan mail order bride, Vida. When first meeting Anastasia, she was very happy to be in America, but said all her husband Indle wanted was to keep her in bed.

Her parents echoed that sentiment and claimed Anastasia often wrote of Indle King's bedroom habits. Her mother claimed she told her sexually inexperienced daughter, "All husbands want that." She told Anastasia women should view sex as just another chore, saying, "Just do it and mark off list."

According to Indle, the first six months of marriage with Anastasia was the best time of his life. He described Anastasia as perfect. He said she cooked like Betty Crocker. kept the house so clean it could be in Better Homes and Gardens. and made love like there was no tomorrow. "There wasn't anything she wouldn't try," he said. "We were happy."

That, according to Detective Blat, was untrue. From her investigation of the couple, within a year of the marriage, cracks developed. Anastasia took a part-time job as a hostess for a local restaurant. That was where Anastasia met Vida and her group of Kyrgyzstan friends.

Indle King insisted he did not mind Anastasia working outside the home. He claimed he wanted his wife to enjoy her youth and experience some forms of freedom. He did, though, insist she stay faithful to him and keep her promise of having a child within the next year. Indle said Anastasia agreed to obey his wishes, saying, "I did trust her."

Vida disagreed with Indle's claim of trusting Anastasia. She claimed Anastasia called Indle possessive, even to the point of videotaping her in the shower and dressing. Vida also said Anastasia confided in her saying she did not want a baby right away, like Indle did. "She wanted to go to college and get education."

Anastasia's parents encouraged their daughter to further her education. Her mother said Anastasia was highly intelligent and could accomplish any goal she set, but Indle watched her like a hawk and did not trust her.

Indle King claimed he trusted Anastasia until she proved unfaithful. He claimed Anastasia went to Las Vegas with a Kyrgyzstan man she met through her Kyrgyzstan friends. He went to Las Vegas and brought Anastasia back, then made her quit her job at the restaurant. "It was destroying our marriage," he said.

Anastasia wrote her parents of Indle's increasing jealousy and domination over her and his resentment of her Kyrgyzstan friends. Her mother and her husband informed Anastasia she could return to their home, but Anastasia insisted on remaining in America where she was preparing for college.

After Anastasia's affair in Las Vegas, recalled Mr. King, she came up with an agreement that we would spend fifteen minutes a day with one another. During that time, we could do anything, talk or have sex. It was her idea, he said, because she did want the marriage to work, saying, "We were happy."

The idea of spending fifteen minutes a day with each other was not Anastasia's idea, said Vida. Anastasia said it was Indle's idea, with Vida telling Anastasia she was crazy to agree with such a ludicrous agreement, because all Indle wanted was sex. "He never wanted just conversation," said Vida. "Anastasia was his possession. His prize."

When detectives discovered dozens of videos at the King home, Detective Blat said they knew Indle King was a sex freak. It was not only the age difference that made the pair an odd couple. It was obvious to the detectives, Indle wanted a trophy wife. "Who videos their wife's private parts while she's dancing in night clubs?" Indle's obsession for everyone to see him with a young hot Kyrgyzstan woman was his drug, said Detective Blat. It became clear to many who knew Mr. and Mrs. King, Anastasia was Indle's slave.

Back in Kyrgyzstan, when Anastasia's parents discovered their son-in-law was all show and no blow, they were disappointed and angry with him. They both agreed that if they wanted their daughter to marry a pauper, she could have stayed in Kyrgyzstan.

Vida knew of the couple's financial problems first-hand. Anastasia and Indle received a shut-off notice for utilities, which only added to the couple's already rocky relationship. She claimed Anastasia and Indle began quarreling constantly, saying, "Anastasia see through lies." She claimed Anastasia said she did not love Indle and feared becoming homeless.

Anastasia's complaints to her parents continued. She wrote of relinquishing her job at Indle's insistence, a job her parents said she enjoyed, and it did help somewhat with bills. Anastasia saw her losing her job as another way for Indle to "keep her nailed to the house." Anastasia complained of numerous chores and of having no personal time. Anastasia told her mother Indle always found something around the house and yard for her to do, saying, "Anastasia say she feel like a servant."

Anastasia's father agreed that Indle's unfairness

toward Anastasia was abuse, saying, "Indle not love Anastasia. His love twisted." The couple fought non-stop, he claimed, and with Indle unable to keep steady employment, the household bills piled up.

Uncovered was that Indle had a string of menial employment. During Detective Blatt's investigation, and from interviews with Anastasia's friends, Indle was controlling, with Anastasia working herself ragged to please him. She kept the home immaculate and had dinner on the table when he came home from work -- "when he was employed."

As the marriage progressed, Indle's restrictions for Anastasia progressed also. Anastasia wrote to her mother of Indle's forbidding her to associate with Vida and other Kyrgyzstan friends and how he kept her at the marital home constantly, and how she was "very sad and lonely."

The situation for Anastasia became worse, when in December 2017, Indle took in boarders to supplement the household income. Most of the boarders were male drifters with criminal backgrounds who ogled over the beautiful Kyrgyzstan girl.

Vida knew of Anastasia's fear of these strangers in her home, saying, "Anastasia lock self in bedroom if husband not home."

When detectives learned one of the boarders was twenty-two-year-old Daniel Larson, they knew to keep an eye on him. According to Detective Blat, Daniel Larson had a past conviction for rape and was a known drug user.

Anastasia wrote her parents of Daniel also. Her mother recalled Anastasia wrote about fearing Daniel, who claimed being a prophet, saying, "I tell her, Daniel crazy like husband."

Reporter Rod Cooke also found Daniel to be one strange person. According to him, when he learned Daniel claimed to have been a child actor with a microchip implanted in him, "I about fell off my chair. Who says things like that?"

By this time, Anastasia's parents wanted their daughter out of the marriage and back on Kyrgyzstan soil. Anastasia asked Indle to allow her to visit her parents, telling him she was lonely for Kyrgyzstan and her parents. She no longer had American friends to converse with, and Indle had Daniel watching her when he was gone from the home.

The visit did not happen. Indle insisted there was no money for a visit. Anastasia wrote to her parents several times a week at this point. Her husband, as authorities would later discover, kept Anastasia's mail from her. The fighting between the couple escalated until one evening in April of 2018, when Anastasia called police and reported her husband physically assaulted her.

Indle King had another version of the incident. According to him, Anastasia assaulted him first, and he was only defending himself when he struck her. He claimed neither of them was arrested, but he did agree to stay at a hotel that evening and allow the tension between them to cool.

Vida remembered the night of the assault. She claimed to receive a telephone call from Anastasia asking her to pick her up at a neighbor's home. Anastasia refused to stay in her home with Daniel, saying Daniel talked to himself and kept odd hours. Vida said Anastasia told her Indle threatened to kill her if she left, saying, "I give her money for Kyrgyzstan."

Anastasia's parents were ecstatic to see their daughter. Her father recalled Anastasia being distraught and haggard-looking, saying, "She cry a lot when first arrive. She here two weeks when husband call."

Anastasia told Indle she was okay and would be

home soon. That happened sooner than any of them could imagine. The morning after Anastasia and Indle's telephone conversation, Indle showed up at the parents' front door, video camera in hand.

When Indle arrived, Anastasia's parents immediately saw an unhealthy change in their daughter. According to the parents, Anastasia became withdrawn and depressed around Indle. "She act happy when husband hold and kiss her, but I know she not love him," said her father.

When detectives discovered Indle King filed for divorce immediately after Anastasia left for Kyrgyzstan, Detective Blat said she "knew the fox was in the henhouse."

While in Kyrgyzstan, Anastasia and her mother paid friends a visit one day without telling Indle. When he realized Anastasia was gone, he emerged from the house wearing nothing but his underwear and T-shirt and berated Anastasia in front of their neighbors, shaking his finger at her, which embarrassed her terribly. They returned to America that day.

Her parents drove Anastasia and Indle to the Kyrgyzstan airport. Once there, they told her to call them as soon as she arrived in Seattle, saying, "She say she will call, but we not hear from her again."

When October 2 rolled around and still no word from Anastasia, her father telephoned Vida and asked her to make a missing person report on Anastasia. She agreed.

Vida said she immediately knew something drastic happened to her friend because Anastasia "very close to parents."

When the missing person report came across the desk of Detective Blat, she said she immediately recognized it as unusual. The report described Anastasia as a responsible person who would not wander off without telling those she loved. The detective also discovered

Anastasia prepaid for the first semester of college, including paying for her books. "It all smelled like foul play," she said.

When Reporter Rod Cooke heard a Kyrgyzstan mail order bride was missing, he became intrigued to learn the details. It became the most bizarre and sad story of his career.

When Detective Blat initially talked to Indle King about his missing wife, she claimed he said he returned to Seattle on September 22 without Anastasia. Indle said he and Anastasia argued at the Kyrgyzstan airport and she left. He then flew into Seattle alone. It did not take long for the detective to prove Indle a liar, saying, "The Seattle airport's video showed Indle and Anastasia returned together."

The next step for Detective Blat was to notify her parents. Her parents drove Anastasia and Indle to the Kyrgyzstan airport and watched them board the plane. Her father said he knew something horrible happened to Anastasia. Vida did not wait for the authorities to contact her. When she learned Anastasia was missing, she called Detective Blat, telling her what she knew about Indle and Daniel.

According to Detective Blat, when Indle King came into the station to discuss his missing wife, he was relaxed and seemingly unconcerned about Anastasia.

When the detective asked Indle King what his relationship with Daniel Larson was, she claimed he described it as a landlord-tenant relationship. When asked why he lied about returning to Seattle with Anastasia, Indle said it was to hide his marital problems and to save face, because he believed Anastasia ran off with another man.

Detective Blat stated, from the beginning, Indle King's story of his wife's whereabouts changed with each interview she had with him.

The police had no solid evidence to prove foul play in

Anastasia's disappearance. They continued to investigate and locate others who knew the couple and her possible whereabouts. It soon became a dead end.

Her parents kept in touch with the police. A few days after he returned to Seattle, Indle King called his in-laws and told them he and Anastasia had parted ways and he had no idea where she was. By November, Anastasia had been missing for two months. There were no new leads until late December.

Daniel Larson, after a financial dispute with Indle King, called Detective Blat asking to talk. He was not hard for the detective to find. He was incarcerated for one month in the town's local jail on an attempted rape charge.

When Larson called her from jail, Detective Blat checked with the jail attendant and discovered Daniel Larson's only other visitor was Indle King. That certainly raised eyebrows, since King denied any friendship between him and Daniel.

Daniel Larson was a small but very strong man, according to Rod Cooke. When the reporter initially talked with him, he described Daniel as "feminine acting and soft spoken." Daniel claimed he met the Kings when he called about the room for rent.

After Daniel Larson moved in with Anastasia and Indle, Vida claimed she saw him around town or in the Kings' yard.

Vida claimed she never saw Daniel help with yard work. She claimed it was Anastasia she saw mowing the grass and pulling weeds when she drove by the home. She claimed Indle stayed in the yard while Anastasia worked, directing her along, and he and Daniel smoked cigarettes and drank beer the entire time.

Anastasia described Daniel as a second husband to her parents. If Indle did not watch her, Daniel did. Anastasia told her parents she had no peace, and one of the men watched her constantly.

Anastasia complained to her parents of never being comfortable in her home once Daniel moved in. She always had to be fully dressed. She could not relax in her nightgowns and watch television.

Detective Blat said Daniel Larson was homeless when he moved in with the Kings. When asked to describe the marriage of Indle and Anastasia, Daniel said, "They had a normal marriage," although they did argue and Indle King controlled the home and handled the money. He also claimed Indle King murdered Anastasia the evening they returned from Kyrgyzstan.

After months of wondering where Anastasia King was, the truth became clear. Rod Cooke called it "a sad moment for all of us." He said he had hoped she had left her husband and was in hiding. He said he felt remorse for Anastasia's parents, saying, "Anastasia was their whole life."

For five hours, Daniel explained to investigators in detail what Indle King told him about the murder. Daniel claimed he was gone from the home during the time Indle King said he strangled Anastasia in the couple's garage. He said Mr. King cut Anastasia's hair off to alter her looks, then buried her naked in case her clothing held Mr. King's DNA.

Daniel Larson took investigators to the burial site. Handcuffed and surrounded by armed officers and a camera crew, Daniel directed the officers to a remote area thirty-five miles north of Seattle. It appeared to be a place for camping. Deer were seen roaming free and no homes were in the immediate area. One hundred yards off the road into the woods, they easily found the shallow grave. One hand partially protruded from the ground.

When her parents learned Anastasia's last minutes on earth consisted of pain and terror, they were devastated.

She was buried face down with her hands tied behind her back.

Her mother described Anastasia as a strong-willed girl, saying, "I know she fight back." They said Anastasia planned to divorce Indle and return to Kyrgyzstan. Immediately upon removing the remains from the grave, Indle King was arrested and charged with the first-degree murder of Anastasia King.

His first words to investigators during his booking were "Daniel Larson set me up. The man was crazy, a freak," said Detective Blat. He insisted Daniel was attracted to his wife, that he liked violence -- and had ten assaults on his arrest record. Indle insisted he was innocent.

When other area newspapers learned of the murder, reporters descended upon the city jail. The only information released by investigators was that the investigators sought witnesses and evidence.

Back in Kyrgyzstan, all hope was gone for Anastasia's parents. They explained how difficult it was to perceive. "To think the one thing we cherished the most, we will never see again," they said. For them to imagine how her short life had come down to being murdered was heartbreaking and unbelievable, said her father.

Investigators knew going into trial that Daniel Larson had a long history of mental problems. They also knew Indle King, like most killers, thought he was smarter than the police, but in reality he gave investigators the majority of the evidence needed to prosecute him.

In early January 2001, Anastasia's parents traveled to Seattle to attend their daughter's funeral and help with the investigation.

At that time, the couple had only the American legal system to put their daughter's murderer behind bars. All they knew about Daniel Larson was from Anastasia's letters and from what they read in the newspapers. They spoke very little English, so the police department hired an interpreter for them.

Five days after Indle King was officially charged with Anastasia's murder, Daniel Larson was interviewed a second time and threw the case for a loop. Detective Blat said Daniel was kept incarcerated due to the attempted rape charge against him. During his second interrogation, he gave detectives a different story of how Anastasia died. He now claimed he killed Anastasia on Mr. King's orders.

Anastasia's parents knew Indle King was involved somehow with Anastasia's death. "She was leaving him for college and a better life, and he would not have that," said her father.

After the arrest of Indle King, every newspaper followed the story. Rod Cooke described the case with all the earmarks of a Hollywood script: a beautiful and young mail order bride; an older jealous husband; a mental patient accomplice. Everyone was watching to see what happened next, he said.

In his second interview, Detective Blat said Daniel Larson claimed he received a telephone call from Indle King at the Seattle airport right after Mr. King landed. Daniel said Mr. King instructed him to kill Anastasia as soon as the couple arrived home that evening. The murder took place inside the couple's garage.

Hearing how both men ganged up on her friend sickened Vida, she said. "Anastasia so fragile and soft. Mr. King so big. She not stand chance."

When Rod Cooke interviewed Daniel Larson while he waited for trial, Daniel claimed he hid inside the garage in the dark. He told police he did not remember how long he was there, but he needed to go to the bathroom, so he urinated in a corner. He then said he noticed the headlights of Mr. King's car enter the driveway and then the electronic garage door opened. Mr. King entered the dark garage and turned off the headlights and then the car.

Daniel said he heard the couple arguing from inside the vehicle, but he could not make out what they were saying. He then watched from his hiding place as the couple exited the vehicle. Then when Indle King was beside Anastasia, he asked her for a kiss.

Anastasia's parents, like the investigators and Prosecutor, believed the kiss was a ruse, a trick, to throw Anastasia off guard. Her whole marriage to Indle King was a lie," said her father.

Daniel Larson said that before Anastasia reluctantly kissed her husband, she said she smelled urine. At that moment, Indle King embraced Anastasia and Daniel Larson sprung the attack into action.

Rod Cooke claimed Daniel Larson told police he initially had a large socket wrench he was going to use on Anastasia, but during the three of them struggling, he dropped it.

Daniel described Anastasia screaming and struggling to free herself from the men. That was when Indle King panicked and punched her in the jaw, knocking her to the concrete floor to keep her quiet.

Her parents said they can't erase the image of Anastasia fighting for her life on that dirty cold floor from their minds. They said an obese man such as Indle King straddling Anastasia while she begged him not to kill her, and while Daniel strangled her with his necktie, was pure evil.

The one defense Daniel Larson repeated during interviews, according to Detective Blat, was that Indle King threatened to shoot him if he did not kill Anastasia. He claimed he feared for his life.

Daniel Larson said he closed his eyes and did not look at what he was doing to Anastasia King. He then helped roll Anastasia into a dog blanket from the trunk of Mr. King's car, before helping to dig the shallow grave.

After the detectives received statements from Daniel Larson, his defense attorney struck a deal with the state. If he agreed to testify against Indle King, his first-degree murder charge would be reduced to second-degree murder, sparing him from execution.

Once Daniel Larson and Indle King were incarcerated, Daniel Larson claimed Mr. King wrote him bizarre letters, asking him to recant his testimony against him. Unbeknownst to Indle King, the correctional institution that housed him read each letter before mailing it.

Some things Indle King wanted Daniel Larson to admit to in the letters were that Mr. King did not know anything about the murder; that Mr. King was not present when Anastasia was killed; and that Daniel Larson did not receive any orders from Mr. King about killing Anastasia.

According to Rod Cooke, each letter Mr. King wrote to Daniel Larson became more and more strange and lengthy -- eight and nine pages long. Daniel received three and four letters a week, with Mr. King begging him to recant his testimony against him. "It was totally hilarious," he said. His said his Editor printed several of the letters, causing company sales to skyrocket.

The Prosecutor allowed the letters from Indle King to reach Daniel Larson, with the hope Indle King would hang himself. The ploy worked, and the man eventually dug his own grave. During his incarceration, Indle King often granted interviews with reporters. These interviews aided the prosecution into gathering evidence against him for trial.

Indle King asserted he loved his mail order bride until the day she died. He claimed from his cell that he still loved her. He insisted they were a happy couple. He admitted they had problems, saying every couple does.

He claimed he went to Kyrgyzstan because he loved Anastasia and wanted the marriage to work. He talked of the footage he shot of him and Anastasia dancing and laughing at her parents' home as evidence of his love for her and insisted that their marriage was solid.

He denied he controlled Anastasia or forbade her to leave the home, calling those rumors lies. He talked of his allowing her to work outside the home. He took her dancing. She enrolled in college. "Those are not the acts of a domineering and selfish husband," he said.

When Vida watched Indle King's interviews from his cell, she claimed he only took Anastasia out so he could show her off because she was beautiful and had a nice figure, saying, "She trophy wife. Not real wife to love and respect like Anastasia need."

On January 14, 2002, Indle King went to trial on first-degree murder charges. A packed courtroom spilled into the halls. Anastasia's parents were front and center the entire time. The presiding Judge allowed news media inside the courtroom. Local and foreign reporters and news crews hovered outside the courthouse waiting for the verdict.

The prosecution claimed the motive for the vicious killing was bitterness. Indle King paraded Anastasia King around town like "arm candy" wanting a domestic and sexual slave.

Also uncovered was the fact that Indle King was married once before to a Kyrgyzstan woman but denied that on his marriage application with Anastasia.

Once bitten, twice shy, was what destroyed the marriage and sparked a well-planned murder, according to Detective Blat. She told the jury Indle King felt used by Anastasia King wanting out of the marriage, and in his warped manipulative mind, he was not going to be used again by "someone who wanted a green card."

The Prosecutor surmised that the home video taken by Indle King in Kyrgyzstan was part of his plan to conceal his crumbling marriage with Anastasia.

Anastasia's happiness on those videos is clearly staged for her parent's reassurance, he told the jury. Anastasia was a very unhappy wife who wanted out of a bad situation, "but not if Indle King had it his way," he said.

The videos never fooled her parents, they said. Through their interpreter, both told the jury the videos "were phony." They knew their daughter was unhappy and did not love her husband. Indle King's words say one thing, "but his actions say different," they said.

When Anastasia's father took the stand, he informed the court that the entire time Anastasia and Indle King were in Kyrgyzstan, the couple never shared a bed. He explained that Anastasia pulled away from Indle each time he tried to kiss her. He told the court that Indle followed Anastasia around with the video camera the entire time, even when she went to the bathroom, saying, "Very sick videos. Who does that? He was sick."

Four weeks into the trial, Indle King, against his attorney's advice, testified on his own behalf.

He said that by February of last year, Anastasia stayed out late and at times never came home. Her excuse would be that she was too intoxicated to drive home, so she stayed with a friend.

Indle told the court he did not believe his wife's excuses, but they did not argue about it. He said he encouraged Anastasia to have friends and enjoy herself. He said it was Anastasia's idea to have a child by the end of the year. He insisted he trusted his wife, the reason he stayed with her and tried to make the marriage work.

The Prosecutor recalled staying quiet while Indle King hanged himself on the witness stand. He said he knew the more Indle talked, the more lies he told. Lies, according to the Prosecutor, he used against him in cross examination.

Indle insisted it was Anastasia's rule for the fifteen minutes a day. During those fifteen minutes, he said they took turns at what we wanted during that time. "Anastasia wanted to talk," he said. "I, of course, wanted sex."

The Prosecutor pounded into the jurors' minds the fact Indle King knew Anastasia did not want him sexually and was through with him. She wanted no part of him, and that was another motive for murder.

Indle insisted Anastasia lied to him repeatedly. He said she used ruses such as going shopping, but then disappeared for two and three days at a time. He insisted Anastasia was alive when they returned to their home from Kyrgyzstan. He said that after their ten-hour plane trip from Kyrgyzstan to the U.S., he needed to use the restroom. When he returned to the living room, he claimed Anastasia was gone from the home. He thought, "Well she's left me for real this time." He said he had no idea Daniel had killed her.

Under cross examination, Indle admitted he initially lied to investigators about him and Anastasia flying home together. He again said he lied to save face, saying, "I didn't want anyone knowing about my marriage problems. I was embarrassed."

He admitted he lied when he told investigators he filed for divorce when Anastasia left for Kyrgyzstan. He again claimed saving face.

Rod Cooke watched the trial from its entirety. To him, the testimony of Indle King was disturbing. He watched the jurors' faces twist with disgust as they listened to Indle, saying, "They knew he was telling one lie after another."

Detective Blat also watched from the gallery. She knew during her interviews with Indle King that his story of where Anastasia was and if they flew back to the States together or not changed on a weekly basis. "The more Indle King talked during his testimony, the more he contradicted himself," she said.

By February 21, the jury deliberated. It only took the nine men and three women six hours to find Indle King guilty of first-degree murder. Anastasia's parents were overcome with emotion.

Vida watched Indle King during the reading of the verdict. She recalled Indle King showing no emotion. "Cold like stone," she said.

When Anastasia's parents stopped crying, they and the Prosecutor hugged. It was a very moving time, the Prosecutor recalled. He said it was not a happy occasion, "but very satisfying to know Indle King will never harm another woman again."

Afterward, Anastasia's mother talked with reporters outside the courthouse. They said they entrusted Indle King with their most prized possession, and it got her killed.

Anastasia's mother said she hoped Indle King had nightmares every night, saying, "I hope he sees Anastasia looking down at him, and he is terrified."

Indle King's twisted sense of love was ruled by his lust for sex and control. He received the maximum sentence for first-degree murder in Washington State, twenty-eight years. He still insists he is innocent.

In February 2007, Daniel Larson, in his plea deal, received twenty years.

3381 Market Street

With a population of 35,313 people, Lancaster, Ohio, bragged of being the birthplace of many notable actors, authors, sports stars, and cartoonists. Founded in 1800, the famous merchant, trailblazer, pioneer and soldier, Ebenezer Zane incorporated the town in 1831. Yet, now, like all cities, it was not above murder -- the worst murder of a child in the county's history.

Twenty-eight-year-old Christina Sims hesitated many times before turning in her older brother John Engle for the murder of his four-year-old son Christopher. Torn between her love for John and Christopher and doing what was right, the soft-spoken slender blonde with dark eyes said she looked to Christ for guidance. After speaking with her minister, she made the devastating choice of walking into the Fairfield County Sheriff's Department on August 9, 2014.

While trailing the short, young dispatcher down the dark, colorless hall, she recalled her first meeting with one-year-old Christopher. Unable to walk on his own, it did not take the stay-at-home mom long to realize why the love-starved toddler was behind in his learning.

She described Christopher as her favorite nephew, saying, "All Christopher wanted was to be held and loved." Christina explained that she occasionally visited her brother and sister-in-law and their growing brood. She described Christopher as "pitiful" and told how his siblings were mean to him and hit him regularly. "All he wanted was to be loved," she said. When she visited the family in the spring of 2014, she asked where Christopher was. Edna Mae told her he went to live with his grandmother in Columbus, but then she started to cry. She said he was in a better place.

Christina recalled how mean the other children were to the child. She explained that when the child tried pulling himself upright to walk, the other children would not allow him to stand. They jerked his arms and legs out from under him, making him fall. She said Edna Mae ignored her pleas for the fragile, light-haired child, and her heart went out to him. She told the sheriff she wanted to love and cuddle the little boy forever. She wished she could have taken Christopher from that filthy, crowded trailer and never looked back.

She described the portly sheriff sitting in his sweat-stained uniform talking on the telephone. His office was not much bigger than an average-sized home bathroom, she claimed. It contained a large wooden desk, two hard-back wooden chairs, one telephone, and an overhead ceiling light. The prison-like chamber had one small window, minus air. She watched the sheriff light a cigarette, and after wiping sweat from his double chin, he asked her to explain the circumstances.

Fearing her brother's reaction to her betrayal, Christina said she chose her words cautiously. She calmly told the lawman that her brother John Engle, who resided in Rushville, confessed to killing his son, Christopher -- and burning his remains in the back yard. She recalled how light she felt once she had her heinous secret released.

The sheriff then asked her when and where did the murder take place. She explained that the child was killed inside her brother's trailer in Rushville, nearly two years earlier. She recently learned of the crime from her now fourteen-year-old niece Rebecca, a tall redhead with green eyes and freckles.

She admitted she and her brother were not exceptionally close, due mostly from John moving his family often. She remembered the sheriff removing a tape recorder from his antique oak desk and clicking it on and how his large fingers left fingerprints on the dusty device. Once he recorded the time, date and location, and she recorded her name and address, she retold her entire story from the beginning.

She explained that her brother and his wife Edna Mae move often and do not have a telephone. Some two years ago, she moved to Lancaster from Columbus and went straight to John's trailer to see Christopher and his siblings. When she arrived, all the children were there but Christopher. When she asked about him, John claimed Christopher was living in Michigan with Edna Mae's sister. When she asked for the phone number and address, she said John grew angry and walked away.

She said John's explanation quenched her wondering for a while. However, each time she visited, he and Edna Mae refused to talk about Christopher. "None of the family mentioned his name," she said. When she suggested they visit Christopher, John refused, as if the child never existed. This made her suspicious, she said. However, she never believed Christopher was dead.

She told the sheriff that she believed families should be safe havens where parents lovingly raise their children to be productive members of society. But this was not true for her brother, John Engle, and his 44- year old wife, Edna Mae.

She explained John and Edna Mae's brief courtship and life; how John returned from Vietnam, eager to marry and start a family. What he saw in skinny, homely, twenty-three-year-old Edna Mae Wilcox, Christina said she never understood. Virtually illiterate, Edna Mae came from a household of twelve children. Perhaps that was the reason she wanted so many children herself. Every two years, Edna Mae popped out another child while showing no maternal instincts for those she already had. John, on the other hand, revealed an unusual possessiveness.

Christina claimed John forbid Edna Mae to wear makeup or drive a car, John frequently moved his family before returning to Ohio. In an attempt to terminate Edna Mae's contact with her family, John refused to install a telephone. By the time of Christopher's murder, Edna Mae had enjoyed no contact with her family for several years. During Christina's last visit, she was horrified to see the conditions the family lived in. The rented trailer on Market Street was dilapidated, unfit for habitation. It had no working sewer system. The toilet was broken. The floorboards were crumbling. Electric sockets had been pulled from the walls. The entire structure, infested with cockroaches, leaning to one side with broken windows, attested to John and Edna Mae's drunken brawls.

Christina and John's home life had been the total opposite. Raised by loving, religiously strict parents, she and her five siblings looked forward to graduating and becoming adults. She married and had one young daughter. John, her brother – the eldest child and only son – resented any authority. Yet Christina remembered John as humorous an idealistic, before Vietnam.

Enlisting at eighteen against his father's wishes, John yearned to experience battle and defend his country. "The battlefield was no place for decent folk. Get married and raise a family. That'll get the military off your back," Christina claimed their father said.

However, John ignored his father's recommendation, though he wept as his family hugged and kissed his smooth young cheek goodbye. His hair styled into a flat top for the military, John shook hands with the man who called him son and told John he loved him. That was the last time John saw his father. A few months later, at forty-two, their father died from pancreatic cancer.

Christina recalled notifying John of their father's demise and welcomed his homecoming, which came sooner than expected. Seven months after his father's death, the military discharged John due to "battle fatigue," saying he suffered irreversible psychological trauma. Christina said she worried over his medical evaluation, as did his military physician. The doctor notified the family by mail and requested John receive psychological counseling upon returning to the States. He made Edna Mae and his children the unfortunate recipients of his rage. The last statement she made before leaving, was "I can't help Christopher, but I can help the other children."

She recalled the sheriff assuring her he would check out her allegations and report to her. She knew to now distance herself from John, believing if he discovered she reported the murder, she might very well be the next one dead.

Four days after her initial statement with Sheriff Norris, Christina received word that John and Edna Mae were brought to the Fairfield County courthouse for questioning.

Delivered in separate cruisers, Edna Mae and their children were placed in separate waiting rooms. With police officers posted in the hall, social workers interviewed the children. The Prosecutor questioned John first. A sworn deposition was taken. The Prosecutor felt he could get a conviction in this case, for Edna Mae, who sat just down the hall in another room, had minutes earlier admitted John scalded Christopher to death. Reportedly, unshaven and dressed in a dingy white T-shirt, and torn jeans, John was the prime suspect. He was read his Miranda Rights and instructed to sit in the chair provided.

Prosecutor Langdon informed John Engle that it had come to his attention that certain facts did not add up concerning the family's Government Assistance they received throughout their marriage. Therefore, he and Edna Mae were brought in for questioning. The Prosecutor then reminded the scrawny, unshaven man he was under oath. John stated he had nothing to hide.

When asked how many children he and Edna Mae bore during their relationship, John admitted there had been ten children born during his and Edna Mae's twenty-year marriage. When asked to name his children, the uneducated man used all his fingers to recall his brood. When John spoke the name Robin, the Prosecutor stopped him and asked about her death at the age of three months.

John proceeded to insist that while the child slept, their oldest, John Junior, accidentally poured a jar of black pepper onto her face and she suffocated to death. According to Michigan court reports, that incident was written off as an unfortunate accidental death. Afterward, John moved the family to Kentucky.

While asked about his third child, Ronny, also born in Kentucky, John admitted Ronny was removed from the home due to neglect and abuse. Reportedly, a relative of Edna Mae's noticed the child was drastically underweight and had what appeared to be cigarette burns on his arms and legs. John received probation for the incident; however, Edna Mae was never charged. John insisted that although he was a strict disciplinarian, he did not abuse his children. Prosecutor Langdon thought otherwise.

John insisted he and Edna Mae raised their children as best they could, acknowledging that children fall down and develop bumps and bruises, saying, "All kids have it hard growin' up. Some just have it harder."

When asked if he knew the difference between discipline and abuse, John ignored the question. He claimed what happened with Robin and Ronny happened years ago and no longer matters.

When asked if he and Edna Mae collected government assistance for themselves and all eight of their children including Christopher, throughout their marriage, John admitted he had, saying, "I guess I never found a job I like."

When asked directly if Christopher was living with him and Edna Mae in their Rushville trailer, John claimed Christopher was living with Edna Mae's mother in Columbus, Ohio, and had been for eight months. John was then informed that the Prosecutor's office contacted Edna Mae's mother who informed Mr. Langdon writing that she had not seen or spoken to Edna Mae in six years and had never met Christopher.

When told by Langdon that his office received a report of Christopher being deceased, John asked for an attorney. He and Edna Mae were then placed under arrest and initially charged with welfare fraud.

Once handcuffed, John and Edna Mae were transported to the county jail. There they were assigned bail of one hundred thousand dollars each and charged with welfare fraud and perjury.

Based on Christina's allegations of Christopher's disappearance, the search for Christopher's remains in John's backyard began on August 23, 2014, as a welfare fraud inquiry. Soon thereafter, cadaver dogs were summoned to the scene to search the nearby woods.

Officers from the Sheriff's Department and students from Ohio State University's Anthropology Department helped in the search. The Anthropology Department informed them that bones vary in color from white, to dark brown, to black. Investigators discussed using DNA to determine if any found bones were Christopher's. DNA, controversial at the time of Christopher's disappearance, offered little chance of a positive identification at the time. Shortly after the digging began, Prosecutor Langdon requested a special fund to help pay for any expensive tests, private investigators, witnesses, and DNA testing.

Langdon advised when authorities recover remains, they need to establish whether the remains are the product of John and Edna Mae Engle. He explained that by matching the parents' blood samples with the DNA test results, investigators could establish the parentage of any remains found.

However, he explained the condition of the remains has some bearing on whether or not DNA testing can be used. He said with a child so young when he allegedly died, any bones found would be small and fragile.

In addition, in order to perform DNA testing, there must be a certain amount of bone marrow available within the bones. Since the remains were set afire, he said there was always the possibility of contamination and an insufficient amount for testing.

Issued later, a warrant to search a junked 1993 Oldsmobile once owned by John Engle in the hope of finding articles of clothing or sheets used to conceal the child's body. Unfortunately, the vehicle's search yielded little information.

As each day brought little comfort to Christina, she thought of the horrible, short-lived life Christopher endured. She said for as long as she could remember, none of Edna Mae's and John's children received birthday parties. Christmas toys came from county charity programs, as did the family's clothing and furnishings.

On September 6th, Prosecutor Langdon told reporters, "The abusive home life of the Engle family was 'the sickest case I ever heard of.'" Four days later, he sought involuntary manslaughter charges against John and Edna

Mae in Christopher's disappearance and suspected murder. Shortly thereafter, the news media descended on 3381 Market Street.

According to Prosecutor Langdon, since John and Edna Mae Engle were unable to produce Christopher, the State believes there was sufficient evidence to charge the couple with the child's death, saying, "I'm obligated by law to bring the accused to justice." With those words, the media had a heyday, and Christina's life was never the same.

When one reporter asked where the body was, Langdon explained that in the state of Ohio, a physical body was not necessary for a finding of guilt in a murder trial. He claimed authorities had definite evidence to prove Christopher Engle was murdered two years ago. "It was not all circumstantial," he said.

John's neighbors immediately flooded the telephone lines at the city paper. The tabloids published statements which made the neighbors wonder what kind of people lived next door all those years. Former neighbor, Lucinda Joy, had moved to Bremen to escape the Engle family.

According to the tall, plump grandmother of seven, she and neighbors heard John and Edna Mae yelling and cursing one another or their children on a regular basis. The Engles' arguments were at times so loud, she said she turned up the stereo to drown out the noise. The kids were certainly neglected, she claimed, since they routinely wore torn and soiled clothing.

Joy's son, Roger, claimed he moved after John and Edna Mae's arrest, saying, "John always had strange-lookin' people comin' and goin' day and night." He also claimed seeing signs of abuse and neglect on Edna Mae and the children.

The whole tragedy left landlord Eddie Newman wondering why he did not evict the Engles family sooner.

Many believed Newman was worried the housing association would hold him responsible for the trailer's unfit living conditions. Hoping to conceal his slumlord persona, Mr. Newman told one reporter that, in the beginning, John and Edna Mae were okay, but as time went on, things were not so rosy. They started drinking and fighting all the time, he said. The place was never clean. The grass was knee deep with broken windows and trash everywhere, claiming, "I told the cops years ago John Engle was a basket case.

Newman said he contacted the Sheriff's Department and County Children Services several times, but nothing was done. Newman never explained why he allowed his rental property on Market Street to deteriorate to the point it was condemned. Many believed he should have been fined by the city or state for even allowing the Engle family to live in a structure so unfit and dangerous. Many felt Mr. Newman knew for a long time the children and Edna Mae were being abused and tortured by John but ignored their plight, as did the entire legal system. He claimed Edna Mae and the children were terrified of John.

When Sheriff Norris learned of Newman's comments, he told reporters that being terrified was no excuse for allowing the four-year-old to die. He claimed through his investigation that the older kids and Edna Mae were allowed to leave the house, meaning "They could have informed the authorities."

Authorities believed John was a serial killer in the making. It was obvious to them; John had killed for years and concealed the crimes with lies and drifting.

Reported in the July 31 edition of the Lancaster *Eagle Gazette* was the fact that an old blanket, a plastic bag, and a neck bone belonging to a child under the age of seven were unearthed, caked with lime, a substance used to conceal the odor of decaying flesh.

The child's disappearance officially became a homicide investigation once human remains were found, said Prosecutor Langdon. There was no way John and Edna Mae could claim Christopher was alive and living elsewhere with relatives. When DNA results established the remains were Christopher's, investigators officially charged both parents with killing their son and 57 other counts between them.

Authorities then used a backhoe to locate more skeletal remains. A student who worked the Rushville site daily as part of her post-graduate work at OSU stated it was interesting work. She explained that workers dug four inches deep in half-meter squares, then everything at the site was taken for analysis. She claimed she and the others never left the site without a bag of something. She said they did the excavating by marking off an area, removed a thin layer of dirt with a trowel and a brush which was then sifted through a screen. With human bones differing from animal bones in shape and structure, it was easy to decipher the remains, she said. The condition of the bone depends on how much moisture it has been exposed to and on the pH level of the soil, among other things.

Sheriff Norris made it clear from the beginning that his men will dig until they have exhausted all their options and it was no longer feasible to go any deeper. He claimed he felt it was just a matter of time before authorities amass enough evidence to get a conviction.

When asked by a reporter about the living conditions inside the Engle trailer, the Sheriff replied that a search warrant was issued for the two-bedroom trailer where officers found a disaster area. He claimed it was rodent infested with the toilet built right into the floor. "The entire place held a rotten stench," he said. He claimed he gagged when first entering, calling the home the "worst livin' conditions I ever saw."

He explained that he increased security at the jail due to John and Edna Mae receiving death threats. He explained that homicide cases always put more of a burden on law enforcement, but he vowed justice would be done in this case. He said when he learned of a missing child, he exercised the proper steps, which meant determining if there was a Christopher Engle, saying, "You can't accuse someone of murder until you can prove there was a physical person."

He first contacted the County Vital Statistics Department and obtained the child's birth certificate before contacting Children's Services and the D.A.'s Office since a child was missing.

News reports alleged that soon after John's arrest, a cellmate, angry over Christopher's murder, attacked him with a sharpened spoon. Combat-trained, John kicked the weapon away and restrained his attacker until guards arrived. John then went into solitary confinement for his own safety. Edna Mae was not so fortunate. An emotional mess, she was an easy target for assaults by other female prisoners. After a severe beating by three women, she was placed in solitary confinement after being released from the local hospital.

Christina felt that with John and Edna Mae behind bars, their children were free from the hell they survived for years -- but a new hell began for them. The children, ages three to seventeen, were immediately taken into custody by the Child Protective Services and placed in foster care. Christina was granted temporary custody of John Junior and Rebecca, the oldest two. Soon after the teenagers arrived at her home, she realized the depth of her brother's insanity and his inability to be a loving parent. Both children had repeated nightmares. Rebecca wet her bed. John, teased at school about his parents' arrest, provoked fistfights with fellow classmates.

Shortly before John Junior confided in Christina about killing Christopher, her fourteen-year-old niece Rebecca informed her she disbelieved the story of Christopher living in Columbus with his grandmother, since she and the other children had not seen their grandmother for years. Rebecca claimed she and the other children came home one day from school to find Christopher gone. When she asked where he was, her parents came up with 'the grandma story.'

During the excavation of John's yard, authorities interviewed several neighbors concerning their suspicions of Christopher's absence. Through these interviews, authorities discovered Christopher had not been seen at the trailer by any neighbor for nearly two years. One such person was Registered Nurse Sarah Black.

She reported she had been Christopher's babysitter when he was younger and thought fondly of him, saying, "I'm gonna miss him." She recalled asking the older Engle children where the child was when she no longer noticed Christopher around the trailer. She said she received different stories, indicating to her the children did not know where Christopher was.

She told authorities that shortly before Christopher was believed to have disappeared, she was in her yard and noticed John Engle burning debris in his backyard. She described the odor as being "like burning flesh." She said she wished she had called the police then, but she never thought John was crazy enough to kill his own child. She said she had lived in the neighborhood her entire life, and all John and Edna Mae did was drink and hit one another.

Sarah claimed several of the neighbors complained to Children's Services about the children being abused, but the county never checked things out. The system failed those kids, she said. She claimed the landlord knew the kids were victimized but said all that drunk cared about was getting the rent money.

Christina agreed with Sarah. She was also given various stories about Christopher's whereabouts from John and Edna Mae. Each time she visited the trailer, no one mentioned Christopher, and she never saw him around the trailer. She even contacted his pre-school class and discovered he had not attended in ages. John and Edna Mae played dumb, as if he was never born, she said. She claimed that if she had suspected murder, she would have taken those kids out of the home.

She told authorities that John confided in her, telling her he was too big of a drunk for any woman to love. According to Christina, John told her he and Edna Mae drank to forget their problems, poverty, and their ever-growing brood.

During her interviews with Prosecutor Langdon, Christina recalled him telling her that everyone takes sides when it comes to going to court. She reassured him that she knew her brother committed a crime and must face his punishment. She was willing to testify against John and Edna Mae even if that meant his disowning her.

She explained that the main thing about John and Edna Mae's marriage was their constant fighting, saying, "They had no respect for one another." She claimed John belittled Edna Mae daily, for not cleaning the home or about her weight gain. He would argue over her cooking abilities or lack thereof, or her hair was not long enough. It was definitely a "love-hate" relationship, she said.

However, she claimed Edna Mae assaulted John while drunk, spewing obscenities at him such as "loser" and "bastard." She admitted Edna Mae's belittlement of her brother put a rift between them, but she knew John physically abused Edna Mae, with her abuse toward him more emotional, so "I guess it balanced."

She claimed she spoke with Edna Mae concerning divorcing John, but Edna Mae made it clear she would never leave John and raise all those kids by herself. However, to her knowledge Edna Mae left John twice, taking the children with her. John told Christina he could never leave Edna Mae because she knew something that would put him in prison for life. Christina said John begged her not to turn him in to police the night he confessed, but the secret ate at her, and she knew she must find justice for Christopher. She claims she hated herself for not intervening sooner, saying, "I can't help Christopher, but maybe I can save the other children."

Edna Mae's relatives gave interviews with one sister telling reporters that reading news accounts of the case was like a nightmare. John Engle, terrorizing his family, plus threatening neighbors and in-laws, was pure evil, the sister claimed. "I'm a God-fearing woman, but if anyone deserves to die, it's John Engle," she said. "Edna Mae and those kids ain't never gonna be right."

In an interview by the city newspaper, Steve Long, director of the County Welfare Department, tried to cover his hide. He claimed his agency became involved with the Engle family in 1999. He claimed the family moved in and out of the county for years, so the case file was opened and closed many times. He claimed to not know the true gravity of their situation. He said the primary goal now is the care of the remaining children, saying, they need a lot of attention.

Court records revealed Children's Services re-opened the file on the Engles when they returned to Fairfield County in 2006. The Franklin County Children's Services removed a child from the home and requested support services for the children still at home. According to Long, the Fairfield court wanted the Franklin County Children's Services to reunite the child with the family, but that was never done, the reason being that the child and foster parents had bonded, and the Franklin County Children's Services felt the child would be further traumatized if returned to the unstable home of John and Edna Mae.

The Engles case file was closed in August 2011 by the Fairfield County Children's Services but received more abuse reports in October of 2012, eight months after Christopher died. Three other referrals involving child neglect came in just weeks after Christina spoke with police. In the three years the case was open, a caseworker and case aide worked with the Engles on communication, discipline, and other family skills.

In addition, they made planned and unplanned family visits, acknowledging their futile efforts. Mr. Long added, "John Engle pulled the wool over our eyes. He fooled us and the people in this community. Though a slick operator, he was not an intelligent man, but he was able to terrorize his family to such an extent we could not notice what was going on. Nobody knew the depth of the family's problems until the sheriff declared his investigation a homicide."

The Ohio Attorney General's Offices stated at the time of Mr. Long's first interview with reporters, changes in the system were considered statewide. Everyone involved wanted to assure the Engle children received the care they needed. As a result, Mr. Long's agency received weekly reports from the foster families concerning medical and psychological assessments of the children. These required several months to conduct and process.

August 1, 2017, marked Christopher Frederick Engle's 7th birthday, if he had lived. The police unearthed twenty bone fragments from the burn pit in the Engles' backyard. During a press conference, Prosecutor Langdon stated, "I can't tell you how sorry I am about Christopher, but we want to help the remaining children develop a sense of security. They haven't been safe in their entire lives."

As the charges against John increased, authorities received more reports of the children's long-term abuse. One incident concerned Christopher. A witness reported Christopher's father hung him on a nail in the living room of their trailer, then beat him with a leather belt. Another case reported his being jabbed in the ears with a wooden spoon.

Mike Butterbaugh, who lived near the Engles, said he called Children's Services a number of times. On May 31, 2010, he persuaded Edna Mae to file domestic violence charges against John after she suffered a severe beating. Municipal court records showed Edna Mae received a protection order but withdrew it the next day.

The domestic violence charge was dismissed July 11, 2010, after Edna Mae wrote an affidavit saying, "John promised to stop drinking, and not hit me (Edna Mae) again."

On August 2, the grand jury met for approximately eight hours. They heard testimony from four of the children, Christina, several deputies and detectives, a few citizens, and Steve Long.

Doctor Valdez's evaluation of John Engle clarified the grand jury's understanding of him. The doctor opened his statement with "John Engle controlled his family with lies and violence, both verbal and physical."

From his observations with John, the physician described John as showing no remorse for killing Christopher or for abusing his wife or remaining children. He denied any wrongdoing, but denial was a part of manipulation in domestic violence, Valdez said. After reviewing John's military record and profile of abuse, including his raping his twelve-year-old daughter, Doctor Valdez was convinced Mr. Engle would have murdered again if his sister had not reported him.

Concerning the battle fatigue defense, John exhibited signs of depression and anxiety and had a difficult time adjusting to civilian life. According to Valdez, the Army physician's letter, expressing concern for John's mental state, will certainly hold some value as a defense.

John also pushed much of the blame of abuse against the children off on Edna Mae, which the doctor claimed was typical of abusers. They often blame their victims for the abuse. John insisted his wife killed Christopher and inflicted years of verbal and emotional abuse on John.

What was certainly determined was that John and Edna Mae suffered from alcohol and drug addiction. That certainly contributed to the family's poverty, said Valdez. Alcohol, drugs and poverty are main contributors to abuse and neglect in a family. These patterns of violence are passed from generation to generation, he said. If a person does not receive love, they do not know how to give love. Reliance on drugs and alcohol pushes normal inhibition out the window, and anger was a secondary emotion fueling abuse.

Often anger was the result of something deeper, like feelings of inferiority, shame or hurt, he explained. Misplaced or built-up anger becomes a leading factor in abuse. Men, especially, are taught to resort to violence when angered. As a society, we validate aggressiveness in males. When fathers behave aggressively, their sons inevitably learn the same things. Mr. Engle's actions are a multi-generational way of coping with stressful situations. "Abuse was a learned behavior," Valdez explained.

When a person was abused as a child, he or she then

builds up anger and resentment, then, in turn, takes it out on someone else when he becomes an adult, which was why the Engle children need extensive counseling on how to deal with their emotions. Feelings of shame, anger, abandonment, and blame take a long time to heal. Many children have a wrenching conflict between their love for their parents and their hatred of abuse, the doctor explained. Bad things that happen inside the home, stay in the home, and the abuse goes on and on.

Unfortunately, he said, no one else learns about the abuse. Dysfunctional families do not talk, do not trust, and do not feel. Even if communication was desired, family members are seldom able to put into words what they feel. They tend to stuff things inward until the point of explosion. They become frustrated with their inability to resolve conflicts in a rational way, so they resort to power, verbal threats, and insults. Dysfunctional families also tend to move often. Moving leaves the children no stability and unable to make friends.

According to Christina, the murder case and upcoming trial took its toll. She began experiencing frequent nightmares. She dreamed she was wearing a long white gown and running through the woods behind her brother's trailer as Christopher called for help. "Aunt Christina, Aunt Christina," the child called. "Help me, Aunt Christina."

However, she could not find him. She followed his voice, but it led to nowhere. All she saw was the darkness. She ran in circles calling for him. "Christopher, where are you?" she called. She was lost in the dark, cold woods running in circles. Christopher's voice guiding her into the darkness.

With each reoccurring nightmare, her nephew's voice became fainter. The cold and darkness increased. The nightmare abruptly ends the same way each time. She wakes screaming, bolting upright in her bed. Covered in sweat and trembling, she realizes it was another bad dream.

Eddie Newman testified that he served an eviction notice on the Engles in 2011, but they ignored it and stayed. He claimed he felt sorry for John and Edna Mae, and since they paid their rent on time, with many children to care for, he allowed them to stay. He said the government should not allow people to have that number of children, saying, "It's too big a hardship. No wonder he went nuts."

The Engle children detailed to the grand jury their years of abuse and fear of their father. They told them how their main food supply came from their meals at school and how they lived in their cramped, unsanitary trailer home. They testified how John ordered them to cover the ashes site — where Christopher's body was burned — with old tires and other debris.

When it was time for the children to testify, Deputies screened them from reporters as they were led to and from the grand jury room. When two brothers passed in the hallway, one admonished the other to "do a good job."

As a key witness for the State, Christina hugged each of her nieces and nephews as they left the witness rooms, one by one. She noticed the children had gained weight since their removal from their parents' care. She told each child she loved her or him and how happy she was to see all of them.

Aaron, then eleven years old, testified to being hit in the head with a screwdriver one afternoon after John returned home drunk from a card game. He recalled Christina and his mother preparing a cookout in the yard. The trailer, he said, was "as hot as an oven" during the summer, since it was not air-conditioned.

He said John complained of being cheated out of money by his friends and took his anger out on him, by throwing a screwdriver in his direction which lodged in the right side of his skull.

When he pulled out the screwdriver, he said blood gushed from the wound. His mother did nothing, but Christina helped. She wrapped his head in a towel and laid him down on his bed, staying with him until he fell asleep.

John Junior, now a tall, slender, handsome boy with brown hair and eyes like his namesake, testified that his father shot him in the foot with a .38 caliber pistol. It happened after an argument in the kitchen. He concealed the injury by saying he stepped on a nail. When asked the reason for the shooting, John Junior claimed his father accused him of drinking his beer. After the shooting, Edna Mae told him to wrap the wound in a towel filled with herbs. When the herbs failed to control the pain and swelling, John Junior pleaded to see a doctor. John refused for fear of being arrested. Unable to walk for days, John Junior missed school and suffered a permanent limp.

When asked to describe other details of the physical abuse, John Junior revealed assaults with broom handles, fly swatters, his father's fists, and any object his father could lay his hands on. "Dad even used shoes, a plastic ball bat, and a black leather belt with his initials on it," he said.

John Junior claimed the abuse was daily. He explained that he was unaware abuse was wrong until he noticed other children at school without bruises, scratches or cigarette burns. When asked why he thought John Engle beat his children, John Junior said he first believed it was his father's alcohol and drug usage, but now the teenager believed his father was just plain evil.

When asked what provoked the beatings, John Junior claimed that if one of the kids sneezed or coughed, John hit them. If they complained about being hungry, they were hit, and they were always hungry, he said. He admitted the parents received food stamps for the family, but he said John sold them to buy beer and cigarettes.

When John was not physically abusing one of his children, John Junior claimed he verbally abused them, routinely telling them and Edna Mae he hated them and wished them dead. He cursed them and called them vulgar names. John Junior believed his father would have murdered them all if he had not been arrested.

Both recalled the night Christopher was scalded. They remember being outside with their parents and younger siblings, including Charley. They said their father was entertaining two male friends with all three men drinking heavily. When Christopher dirtied himself in front of John's friends, it embarrassed and angered John, forcing his friends to leave.

John cursed Christopher, and that made him cry. He ran inside the trailer and hid. John Junior and Rebecca testified they knew Christopher would be spanked for soiling himself; they felt sorry for their baby brother, but helpless.

The next thing they heard was Christopher screaming. They all ran into the trailer and found Christopher naked in the bathtub, his entire body covered with large red blisters. John stood over him holding a large, steaming pot. Then John grabbed the screaming child and threw him on a blanket in John and Edna's bedroom.

The children described how Christopher drifted in and out of consciousness for days, whimpering. John Junior and Rebecca said they tried helping Christopher, but John hit them and forced them from the room. They said their mother pleaded with John to allow her to help the child.

John Junior and Rebecca both stated that their father beat Edna Mae, called her names, and threatened her continuously with further harm if she helped Christopher. They said their mother was unable to defend her children against John. They watched in horror as John raged, kicking her so hard she limped for a week.

According to John Junior, he last saw Christopher Wednesday morning before going to school. When he and the other children returned, Christopher was gone. They were told he went to live with relatives.

Rebecca said she was happy for Christopher, knowing he no longer lived with John. When she learned the truth, she cried for days. She said she hated herself for not having the courage to seek help from a neighbor or a teacher.

John Junior also felt he betrayed his mother and siblings. Not having the gumption to stand up to John by notifying the police, the teenager claimed he could not forget Christopher's screams.

Christina listened, aghast, as her niece and nephews described their fears and hatred for a man they should have loved and respected.

When the grand jury asked Rebecca to talk about her rape, she claimed it happened early on a Wednesday morning when her mother was at the store. John had sent her to get him a pack of cigarettes.

Rebecca recalled being in the bathroom washing up before school, when John pushed open the door and entered, completely nude and drunk. She said she was terrified to refuse him, so she closed her eyes and waited for it to end.

Then John told her if she ever told anyone, he would kill her like he did Christopher. She was devastated. All that time until then, she had believed Christopher was safe and happy. When John told Rebecca her little brother was dead, she wanted to die, too.

To be in heaven with Christopher sounded better than living with John, she claimed, saying she missed Christopher and all her brothers and sisters.

A teacher employed at the Forest Rose School for the handicapped, Judith Kramer, explained that her degree was in human behavior. She had five of the Engle children as students and, like others who knew the Engles, she was stunned by Christopher's death because she remembered one of the Engle boys saying Christopher had gone to live with an aunt. She did not think anything of the statement at the time, saying, "I felt the children must have been emotionally strong to live with daily abuse and still cope with school. They seldom missed class."

She described Christopher as "a darling child," saying she holds fond memories of him. She described her exercised home visit, which was customary with her position, with John and Edna Mae Engle when Christopher was one year old.

She explained that she likes seeing the environment the new pupil resides in. She knew the family was impoverished, so when she arrived, it came as no surprise that the living conditions were atrocious. The home was a very small two-bedroom trailer with all the children sleeping in the same bedroom.

Windows were broken out, and salvaged vehicles lay everywhere, she said. The entire family was present. There were six children then, and a very unsanitary family, with one child mentioning they no longer had running water. Their clothes were dirty and worn, and Mr. Engle smelled like a brewery when he introduced himself to her. Also she had the impression everyone was terrified of him.

According to her, the older children teased and taunted the younger ones. They picked at Christopher when she paid attention to him. Then, whenever Mr. Engle entered the trailer, the children immediately went quiet. They quickly took seats until he went outside, she said. "It's abnormal for children to act like that."

She explained that she visited the home to enroll Christopher, who just turned thirteen months, in a new daycare program for special needs children.

There are certain steps in evaluating a toddler, she said. For example, upper body mobility, which shows how easy or how difficult it was for the child to raise himself to a sitting or standing position.

Next was small and large muscle mobility, the ability to grasp and hold objects of various sizes, shapes and weight, such as a rattle or baby bottle. She explained that those tests guide her and her staff, showing them the area in which the student needs the most help.

In Christopher's case, she said, the tests revealed the child to be mildly retarded. She said John Engle became very angry, making it clear to her that he did not want a dummy for a son.

When asked what kind of student Christopher was, Judith explained that in the beginning, his parents seldom brought him to class, but he did learn to walk with the Forest Rose staff members, saying, "He was so proud of himself. We all miss him terribly."

She believed school was the children's only escape, their only sanctuary. She believed the children knew the teachers cared for them. She apologized for the children being too frightened to confide in her.

The newspaper reported nothing positive about John. Christina felt it important the public understand her brother's state of mind and granted an interview.

According to her, John was once a kind and loving man who took pride in being a husband and father. He was not the career alcoholic and drug addict he's labeled by the state, she said.

She described Edna Mae as equally culpable for Christopher's death as well as the abuse the other children suffered. She admitted her brother physically abused Edna Mae, but she insisted Edna Mae emotionally abused John for a long period. The brother she knows was not the monster the papers labeled him. She described John as being disturbed since returning from Vietnam and holds the county social agencies responsible for that abuse. If the county had investigated the reports they received, her brother's family might have been helped.

She, like most of the other female witnesses, cried throughout her testimony. She told the court the numerous excuses she received from both John and Edna Mae concerning Christopher's absence. Each time she visited, she claimed she was told the child was with a different relative. "It had been two years, and I missed him most of all," she said.

She described the atmosphere inside the trailer as being "bizarre." She claimed the children were strangely quiet around their parents but hyperactive when away from them. They all seemed tense whenever their father was around, especially Rebecca and John, she said. One day, during a visit, Rebecca came home from school crying, claiming her classmates said she smelled. It was apparent the children never bathed, she said.

She said Edna Mae had no response to Rebecca's plight, so she explained to the girl how to wash herself before going to school. From that day on, Rebecca rose early and heated a pot of water on the family stove carried it into the bathroom and washed off while standing up.

She said John and Edna Mae had deplorable hygiene, allowing their physical appearances to deteriorate with the passing years. They shrugged off important matters like water from a duck's back, she said, adding, "Edna Mae and John stopped caring about their appearance and home years ago."

Christina was the only relative who disclosed her name throughout the trial. All others remained anonymous. Whether at the grocery story, at work, or just running errands, her face was embedded in the minds of every citizen.

She explained to the court that Christopher was not submerged in water; it was deliberately poured on him. She cited the Sheriff's Department report stating Christopher was put in a tub of boiling water, but that statement was incorrect. The older children heard Christopher scream, then saw him by their parents' bed for two days. She explained how John confessed he burned Christopher's remains, but it bothers her to see all the blame put on him. "Everyone was pointing his finger at John and it was not all his fault. That's just not right," she claimed.

She addressed the domestic violence charges filed against John that Mike Butterbaugh encouraged her to file, saying, "Edna Mae asked for it."

She claimed John was not abused as a child and the siblings remained close, though some live in other counties. Before leaving the building, she told waiting reporters she will fight to keep those kids together as a family, saying, "That is the least I can do for them. They should not be divided up."

Asked by the grand jury members if she thought John and Edna Mae loved their children, Christina said, "I don't think you can love your children and abuse them like that."

Two of Edna Mae's sisters said, from the start, John controlled his wife. He told her how to dress, whom to associate with, forbade her piercing her ears, wearing makeup, and seeing her family. The sisters reported how the Engles moved to Escanaba, Michigan, soon after they wed, where their first two children, John Junior and Robin, were born.

In 1998, Edna Mae left John, taking her two children with her to her parents' home in Columbus. After John discovered Edna Mae's whereabouts, he went to his in-laws' home. Luring his son into the car, he threatened to disallow Edna Mae to see her son again if she did not return with him. Therefore, to be with her son, she went back with John.

The son removed from the home, Tim, was discussed. The sister said that incident was what made Mr. Engle antagonistic toward his in-laws. In 1984, the family moved to the small trailer in Rushville. Contact between Edna Mae and her family became even more sporadic. By 1988, there were eight children living in the two-bedroom home. Edna Mae's sisters talked to Edna Mae by phone, but said, "We couldn't go out there. When we did show up, Edna'd get a beatin' for it."

When Detective Jim Stasewich from Michigan took the stand, he told the court that in 1985, Michigan's Child Protective Agency investigated Mr. Engle for shoving one-year-old Robin into a refrigerator. However, there was insufficient evidence to remove the child from the home.

Three months later, he said he investigated Robin's death. He was suspicious of the family's story about how she died, yet they seemed remorseful and cooperative, saying John and Edna Mae even agreed to a lie detector test, only they fled the state instead. He explained there were problems with the case they could not overcome. Two-year-old John Junior obviously could not be interviewed, so the coroner ruled the death an accident.

A second sister of Edna Mae's gave a statement on Edna Mae's behalf. She said she had talked to Edna Mae since her arrest, and Edna Mae talked as if she and her sisters were still teenagers instead of their actual ages (mid 40's). "It's like Edna Mae was comin' out of a long, dark tunnel."

The sister went on to say it was very hard on her and other relatives to see Edna Mae behind bars facing a death sentence. However, the sister believed Edna Mae was better off in jail than being abused by John Engle.

Besides the two sisters, the court-appointed psychiatrist testified. In his opinion, Edna Mae Engle was a battered woman and victim, as were her children. Edna Mae clearly led a life of tremendous abuse, all of it at the hands of her husband, he said. Furthermore, when Edna Mae talked with him, she tended to lose her composure, crying uncontrollably. Because of that, important evidence might be overlooked, he said.

After five days of deliberations, the grand jury found there to be enough evidence to charge John and Edna Engle with a combined 56 counts. That following Monday, August 5, Edna Mae appeared before Judge Claris. With tissue in hand and answering in a whisper, she pled "not guilty" to all 26 felonies filed against her and the aggravated murder charge holding death penalty specifications.

Then, on her behalf, her attorney filed for divorce on the grounds of extreme cruelty and neglect. The court accepted her plea.

Because of Edna Mae's crying jags, she was referred to a second psychologist, Doctor Samuel Peter. After a two-week evaluation, he diagnosed her as mentally incompetent for trial. He agreed with the first mental evaluation. She suffered from the battered woman syndrome and was a victim of torture at John's hands.

With Doctor Peter's testimony, Attorney Lowe argued for Edna Mae to be dismissed as mentally incompetent, discounting her statements to authorities before and after her arrest. Prosecutor Langdon informed the court he had no quarrel with Doctor Peter's findings and noted it would not be in the State's best interests to try Edna Mae twice, saying, "We feel there are some problems with Mrs. Engle. We believe the judge made a wise decision in asking for the psychiatric examinations."

Subsequently, by court order for treatment, the police transferred Edna Mae from the county jail to a maximum-security mental health facility in Columbus for an indefinite period of time.

Prosecutor Langdon told reporters he hoped Edna Mae Engle would become competent within a year, assuming she receives treatment for her illness. In addition to the aggravated murder charge against Edna Mae, she faced three counts of theft as a result of accepting government funds for Christopher after his death. There were also two counts of perjury for lying to a special court concerning Christopher's whereabouts, and three counts of forgery for her signing government documents, receiving state benefits for Christopher after his death, and 19 counts of child endangering concerning all the children.

Two days later, on Wednesday, August 7, at 2 p.m., John's arraignment before Judge Claris took less than five minutes. Christina was present to hear the charges against her big brother.

The local newspapers printed daily reports of the case and the overwhelming evidence against John. Many, including Christina, wondered how John and Edna Mae could possibly receive a fair and unprejudiced trial in this county.

With John Junior's recent eighteenth birthday and with him employed full time, he now lived on his own. Rebecca settled in with foster parents and wrote Christina frequently, relating news of church, classmates, and her new home life. Each time Christina read Rebecca's letters, they gave her renewed strength. Unlike the sorrow she felt for

Amy and Ronny, the youngest of the Engle children who were not at all adjusting to their new surroundings and suffered emotionally.

The foster parents gave an interview and stated the children feared their parents. The foster mother described the murder case as "a media circus," saying she and her husband accidentally had the news channel on one evening, while Amy played with her dolls. She saw her father's picture and screamed, then she began hitting herself in the face and head. They were horrified to see the fear Amy had for her own father, claiming she was terrified of that man. According to the foster father, Amy had to be removed from the room to calm her.

In the year the New York Giants beat the Buffalo Bills, the Dead Sea Scrolls were made public, and Desert Storm began, the county's most heinous case against a child unfolded. Security was tight that hot humid day when police officers escorted the most hated man in Fairfield County, handcuffed and shackled, wearing dark green jail fatigues, through the back entrance of the courthouse.

Clean-shaven and handsome, when John passed Christina, he looked frightened and underweight. The leg-irons to prevent his escape looked too heavy for his frail body. Watching closely, she recalled sobbing quietly as John politely responded to the judge's questions with a series of very sober "Yes, Your Honor" answers to the following charges:

1. Three (3) counts of forgery pertaining to false applications for income, medical and food assistance to the County Department of Human Services, by representing that Christopher F. Engle resided with him, his wife, and seven other children, at their residence from the dates of June 2012 through August 2014.

2. Two (2) counts of abuse of a corpse, stemming

from the defendant John Engle's burying Christopher beneath the kitchen floorboards, then burning his remains in a pit.

    3. Three (3) counts of Felonious Assault pertaining to the defendant John Engle's shooting his son John Engle Jr. in the foot on the 4th day of March, 2010, in the kitchen (using a deadly weapon, a .22 caliber pistol), and refusing the boy medical treatment, assaulting Aaron with a screwdriver, then refusing the boy medical treatment, and scalding Christopher with water, then with broom bristles popping the blisters formed by his burns.

    4. One (1) count of Grand Theft, from John's accepting, by fraud or deception, grant monies from The State of Ohio and the County Department of Human Services, from June 2012 to August 2014, in the form of Aid to Dependent Children and food stamps, by deception for the defendant John Engle knew Christopher Engle was already dead.

    5. Count (I) Perjury in that the defendant John Engle on August 23rd, 2014, at the County Court of Common Pleas, Hall of Justice, did knowingly utter a false statement under oath, testifying Christopher Engle was alive, living at the Engle residence in Fairfield County, Ohio, and attending Pleasantville Elementary School for the 2013-14 school year, when he (John Engle) knew his statements were false.

    6. Count (II) Perjury stemming from the day of August 23rd, 2014, at the County Court of Common Pleas, Hall of Justice, when John Engle knowingly uttered a false statement under oath, stating that Christopher Engle lived in Michigan with the sister of John Engle when he knew said statement was false.

    7. Nineteen counts (19) of Child Endangering pertaining to defendant John Engle's previously scalding Christopher on at least one other occasion, frequently

abusing Christopher by hitting him with his fists, his belt, and a broom handle, then refusing to take Christopher for medical treatment, and his preventing Edna Mae Engle from taking Christopher for medical treatment, and for hanging Christopher Engle from a nail and on a doorknob by his shirt, and assaulting his other minor children frequently over an extended period of time, with full knowledge that such mistreatment would result in permanent harm, or retard said minors if mistreatment continued.

8. (1) count of Forcible Rape against defendant John Engle pertaining to Rebecca M. Engle, who at the time was 12 years old.

John protested the high bail against him. Following the grand jury session, the judge raised his bail to one million dollars.

When asked by Judge Claris if he wanted to make a statement, John clearly said, "I never said me and Edna Mae were perfect parents."

On leaving the courtroom after John's hearing, Prosecutor Langdon announced to reporters: "At this time Edna Mae Engle will not be tried due to health-related problems, but charges against Mrs. Engle remain open. Charges filed against John Engle earlier this month have been amended to include aggravated murder, felonious assault, and multiple counts of child endangering."

Upon hearing the news of John and Edna Mae's contradicting stories concerning Christopher's whereabouts, the public loathed them.

Nothing was more mortifying to Christina, though, than finding her name and photograph on the front page of the newspapers one morning. "Those heartless reporters!" she recalled saying. She confronted each rude stare, whisper, and sneer, which continued for months.

When Prosecutor Langdon received word of the

newspaper photograph, he told reporters that this case file suggests there will be a lot of finger pointing. He did not necessarily blame the county caseworkers for the neglect and abuse the Engle children suffered; he blamed society as a whole, saying, "It takes a whole village to raise a child." What happened to Christopher Engle was unforgivable, he said. He claimed John Engle's ability to conceal his crime makes them all appear foolish.

When asked by a reporter about the numerous complaints to Children's Services, the Prosecutor admitted they were ignored and Christopher Engle paid the ultimate price. He said he hopes everyone associated with the case learns a valuable lesson from this tragedy, saying, "It must never happen again in our community."

The trial for Edna Mae began on August 25. Although the defenses experts testified for Edna Mae during the grand jury concerning her mental incompetence, all testimony concerning the Battered Woman's Syndrome was disallowed during her trial. Her attorney informed the court that if she were found guilty, she would be appealing her conviction. For that matter, there was a recess and the attorneys and Judge retired to the Judge's chambers. When they reappeared, a new plea deal was in place. The Prosecutor agreed to dismiss all the charges against Edna Mae if she pled no contest to the aggravated murder charge. She agreed, and the trial was complete. She was immediately sentenced to fifteen years to life in prison and transferred to Marysville State Prison for Woman.

Upon learning of Edna Mae's fate, John accepted a plea deal of forty years to life with the possibility of parole. He was sent to Ross County Correctional Facility.

The bombast did not stop there. The children were still on everyone's minds. Many wanted to help, but the county social services turned persons away, which angered many.

From then on, letters from concerned citizens, poured into the local newspapers like daily tsunamis. Everyone condemned John, Edna Mae and the County Children's Services, similar to this letter:

"About three weeks ago on a Sunday morning, as I sat in church listening to Reverend Michael Harrah tell about the horrifying life of the Engle children. He asked us all to please keep these children in our prayers. I thought surely that we, as a church body, might help more. On the way home, I came up with the possibility of a gospel concert.

"The first four phone calls I made to local bands were met with overwhelming enthusiasm and positive response. By Sunday evening, the concert was arranged. What better mission project could we commit to, than one in our own backyard? Monday morning, I had phone calls from two more bands wanting to be in the concert.

"I then called a printing company. They agreed to donate 500 flyers. I thought, 'This was great. We can put some sunshine in these troubled lives,' but then the roadblocks began. I called Judith Kramer, thinking we could work together on the two projects, and she told me of her problems with Children Services. I was appalled. We were told we could not present these gifts to the children our funds had to be turned over to Children Services, and they would do the distributing. I sought legal counsel, and found this was not true. Steve Long finally agreed on August 23 that Judith could accompany a caseworker to the foster homes and present these gifts.

"On August 27, a caseworker called Judith and said they had changed their minds. She could not go. Steve Long told Judith her fund was only complicating the care of these children. In total frustration, I called Sheriff Norris who suggested I contact Prosecutor Langdon. Then Norris contacted him for me, and said Langdon wanted to meet with me. He arranged a meeting with the Children Services' Board of Directors.

"However, I decided it was time the public knows how Children Services are going out of their way not to assist us, but to block our every effort. Come on, Mr. Long get real! Even a prisoner has the right to accept a gift. Since when are we, as citizens of a free country, not allowed to give a gift to anyone we so choose?

"Please continue to give your support, and we will see the donations are not turned over to Children Services, but given directly to the Engle children. This tragedy should never have happened: however, the sad reality was it did happen, and we the public, need to show these children we love them and will give them our total support. This thought was contrary to Mr. Long's belief, who said, 'The businesses who have contributed are doing it for self-serving reasons.' Submitted by Norma Zambenee.

John's mother said that, soon after his arrest, he confessed that when he saw police cruisers entering his driveway, he wanted to run, but had no money, no car, and no one he trusted. He said nothing made any sense. His marriage had deteriorated. Neither he nor Edna Mae had any ambition to work or better their lives.

Christina learned through news reports the devastating news that many county agencies knew of the problems within the Engle family. Unfortunately, that information was not shared among the groups. The case pointed up a need for better communication between the agencies. When it was made public that the agencies did not communicate with one another, it infuriated the community.

Prosecutor Langdon immediately addressed the issue during a press conference on the courthouse steps, saying if the agencies had talked with each other, there would have been some red flags. He admitted the Engle family was on welfare for years. Mr. Engle had an apparent drinking problem. It was obvious, he said, serious changes governing children in Ohio must be made to assure this never happens again.

He stated that being understaffed, underpaid, uncaring, or just plain lazy was no excuse for disregarding a reported abuse case. He said he understood how a person cannot be paid to care, but if an employee of the Children's Services was without empathy, he or she had no place in the department.

The community's loathing for John and Edna Mae intensified. Someone burned down the now-condemned trailer on Market Street. The entire neighborhood turned out to cheer as the flames colored the dark skies into a canvas of bright red and orange, giving neighbors another opportunity to voice their opinion to the media. The arsonist was never found.

One neighbor claimed not knowing anything about the fire, but said whatever happened to John and Edna Mae, they deserved, saying, "They killed their kid. Blood don't run no colder than that." Others wanted John and Edna Mae sterilized, saying people like them were unfit to raise children.

Another claimed the only type of shopping the family did in area stores was the "five-finger discount," claiming the parents are thieves and taught their kids to steal. One store owner reported that John routinely sent one of his children inside the store with a dollar food stamp to buy a piece of candy while he waited outside for the change. Then when he had enough money, he would come in and buy a quart of beer for himself. Legally that was welfare fraud, but John got away with a lot of illegal behavior.

Appointed by Judge Claris and known for playing hardball, John's attorney gave the following interview once John's psychological evaluation was complete: "The killing of a child was the grimmest of crimes and, after reviewing the evidence, I anticipate a lengthy trial and a death penalty case. This trial was going to be difficult for everyone involved, since the deceased was a child, but John Engle was also a victim. A Vietnam veteran who suffered repeated emotional breakdowns . . . that were ignored. My client was also verbally and emotionally abused by his wife. I will prove that at trial."

The case was the talk of the town, generating more gossip than a pregnant nun does. It became unbearable for Christina to read a newspaper or watch television. Many wanted to fry John and Edna Mae in "Ole Sparky."

Whether it was Edna Mae's relatives, the attorneys assigned to the case, social workers in charge of the Engle children, or common citizens, everyone had horror stories concerning John and Edna Mae. One such person was Stanley Jones. "I lived down the road from the family but never allowed my kids to associate with any of them. None of them got along with the neighbors. The whole family was filthy. My daughter attended school with the Engle kids, and she said those kids always had dirt and bruises on them."

According to Christina, her relationship with some relatives turned bitter. She recalls a physical confrontation with a younger sister concerning her turning John in. The sister insisted that if John were executed, his death would be on Christina's hands.

With fingers pointing and relative acting against relative, facts concerning Christopher's death and how the abuse went undetected for two years became known. One evening, according to Christina, as she, Rebecca and John watched television, they listened as a sister of Edna Mae's gave an interview. "Watching and reading news accounts of the case has been a nightmare," said the sister. "We were all shocked at Edna Mae's appearance. I've never seen Edna Mae look so worn and exhausted."

The woman claimed the last time the family heard from Edna Mae, she called from a shelter for battered women after filing that domestic violence charge against John. According to the sister, Edna Mae believed John would not harm her or the kids again, but the sister said she knew he was lying.

The sister and her family tried to get Edna Mae to divorce John, but his hold on her was too strong. The sister then broke down and began sobbing before turning away from the camera, letting her brother finish the interview.

According to him, the family had no idea what Edna Mae was going through. He claimed Edna Mae stopped calling because things got worse between her and John if she talked to her family. He said John wanted Edna Mae to have no friends or communication with her relatives, saying, "We are just grateful Christopher's remains were found. That little boy deserved a decent burial."

Since no charges were filed against John and Edna Mae concerning neglect or abuse of their children, Steve Long said the Children's Services hands were tied. Also, the children all attended school regularly. "I assumed everything was okay," he told a reporter.

He chalked up the fact that even though those welfare recipients were required by law to have a face-to-face interview with their caseworker every six months, John and Edna Mae Engle simply "slipped through the cracks." He said it was unfortunate, but it happens. He blamed other reasons for his office's incompetence as being "overworked and understaffed."

Many of the excuses reported by social workers and

other county personnel angered many following the case.

As more evidence surfaced, county employees came under fire for their incompetent handling of the Engle case. The community demanded an explanation.

After the ruling, Prosecutor Langdon gave the following speech: "I don't know if there was any way to prevent Christopher's death, but we need to keep open lines of communication between the agencies involved."

It was apparent, he said, that various states and county agencies did not communicate with one another concerning the Engle family, and that disturbed him the most. Although John Engle may well be the only one serving prison time, he said the welfare system itself should be on trial.

Because of this case, the Ohio laws governing children were amended.

Afterword

Neighboring families adopted John and Edna Mae's children. Once they became adults, some, unfortunately, amassed criminal records. The State released Edna Mae from the sanitarium following two years of treatment. It then charged her, as well, with Christopher's murder. Found guilty, she went to Marysville State Prison. Her attorney never gave up, though. In February 2018, he successfully overturned her conviction based on the Battered Women's Syndrome. She lives in Lancaster with relatives.

Because of John's twisted love of sadistic control and torture, two innocent children died at his hands, and many others suffered emotional and psychological disorders for their remaining lives.

A Senseless Killing

It was a grand evening for all at Mario's Lakeway Lounge that Thanksgiving evening of November 25th, 2010. The country band kept everyone on the dance floor. The occasional smacking of pool balls was heard above the laughter, and the crowd's favorite barmaid, Ann McSween, was serving them. She had asked a co-worker to allow her to work the night shift to earn a little extra cash. This turned out to be a choice she would not live to regret.

"Better times are coming," said the bubbly blonde, who only began working for the small neighborhood pub four months earlier. According to patrons, Ann was looking forward to moving into her own apartment next to the pub in just a few days. Her forty-ninth birthday was just hours away.

Little did the joyful crowd realize, but that cool autumn evening would be the last time anyone saw Ann, except for her killer.

According to Ann's time card, she punched out at 3 a.m. Her last duties were washing glasses and ashtrays. Black Friday was on the horizon. Her birthday party would consist of her daughter and son as well as a few close friends. Everything was planned -- everything except what actually happened to the tall, slender grandmother.

Fifty-four-year-old Mario Cacic, the bar owner, said he returned to the bar at 8 a.m. and noticed Ann's car with flattened tires in the parking lot along with two other vehicles with flat tires.

The short, heavy, Albanian immigrant said he called police who searched the perimeter and canvassed the street but found nothing and soon left.

Shortly afterward, thirty-eight-year-old James Yager, a boat mechanic, noticed Mario and told him he had notified police because two boats at his business, located near the bar, were vandalized. According to the tall, slender man with sandy-colored hair, as he walked around surveying the damaged boats, he discovered a woman's shoe and underwear. He told Mario, "This doesn't look good."

The two then began looking around and discovered near Ann's car and scattered about the parking lot, her keys, a necklace and eyeglasses. Then Mario noticed one of Ann's shoes was jammed under the wheel well "like she kicked up there as somebody grabbed her," said Mario.

James noticed that shoe matched the one he found in the boat yard. Mario then noticed blood on the ground in splotches. They followed the blood trail and were led to the home beside the bar, which he owned, where blood was smeared on the outside wall of the house, on its steps, and the outside of its windows. A bloody hand mark was smeared near the door.

When he knocked on the door, his tenant and bar manager, forty-two-year-old Margaret March, answered.

The petite, red-haired Margaret said when Mario woke her around 8:30, she was half drunk and hung-over. When Mario told her about the blood on the house, she said maybe it was from a deer.

She said she and her boyfriend, Brian Williams, were watching television after leaving the Lakeway Lounge. They fell asleep but were woken around 4:30 a.m. when they heard thumps on the wall behind them. They thought someone was breaking in like nights earlier.

Brian Williams was of medium height and build with dark hair and eyes. According to Margaret, Brian looked out the window and asked her if she knew "a guy with long hair," and she said "no."

She then told Brian to check things out, and after pulling a knife from his buckle, he went outside -- "shoeless, shirtless and sockless." He returned soon saying he saw no one and "'whoever it was must have run away.'"

She said she slammed the door and locked it, and she and Brian went to bed.

Mario called the police again, waiting until two officers arrived. The four of them followed the blood trail, which led behind the home through a grassy area, then into a wooded area adjacent to the bar and boat yard.

James Yager looked into the woods and saw what he thought was a mannequin, but upon closer inspection, he realized it was the nude -- except for one sock -- and mutilated body of Ann McSween.

Mario said when he saw the blonde hair, "I knew it was Ann."

The men described the enormous amounts of blood throughout the parking lot and along the wall of the house on Park Avenue as horrifying.

Once investigators arrived with crime lab technicians, the bar and the entire perimeter, including the area of woods where the corpse was discovered, was cordoned off. Investigators from BCI swept surfaces inside the bar for fingerprints, including pool balls and cues.

David A. Green, an expert in trace evidence such as footwear and tool mark impressions, gathered evidence near Ann's vehicle, saying, "It appears a struggle occurred in that area."

Police Chief Joseph Doran remarked there was no sign of a struggle inside the bar, and Ann had obviously restocked the bar and washed glasses before leaving. Investigators said fingerprints of the assailant would be most unlikely.

"What kind of an animal would do this?" Mario said

when interviewed by police. He described Ann as being a nice person and a hard worker who did not drink alcohol. He said he could count on her to work whenever needed.

Mario said Ann was also employed at Breakwall Tavern as well as the Mentor Fraternal Order of Eagles. He said Ann had undergone financial difficulties causing her to "live here and there." She was happy to be finally moving into her own place, he said.

Ann's ex-husband, Richard McSween, said she was the mother of two grown children, Erica and Justin. He said he had not spoken to her in twenty years. He said she was originally from California, with her family involved with the Navy, adding, "Ann lived in Mentor most of her life."

Patron Matt Miller said he received a telephone call from another customer about the murder. He drove directly to the bar and spoke with police. He said he did not know Ann well but was at the bar the previous night and socialized with a man whose name he did not remember, whom he had seen at the bar just one other time. He said they watched a group of intoxicated women.

"They were dancing sexually, and the man said he liked it," recalled Matt. He claimed they commiserated about women while playing several games of pool. He said the man talked about meeting up with a woman, but the two had an argument and she broke up with him. The man told Matt he had spent seventy dollars on a meal, but it went to waste, so he came to the bar.

According to Matt, the man seemed distraught, so he bought him a shot of Yukon Jack. He recalled the man wore a stained white undershirt, a "weird-looking vest," and a knife clipped to his jeans.

He said he left the bar around 2:15 a.m. after the man approached Ann wanting to dance. He said Ann told him, "No, I don't dance." He then heard the man say something to the effect of, "That's odd because most bartenders like to dance."

Matt recalled Ann seemed like she wanted to leave. Matt said the man was highly intoxicated. He described the man as having a "messed-up tooth and a diamond earring in his left ear."

Once investigators identified the twenty patrons inside the lounge Thanksgiving night, they began interviewing. Some were asked to give DNA samples, including Mario and several men who were at Lakeway Lounge Thanksgiving night. They were all cleared.

All the patrons present on Thanksgiving night were accounted for except one, a man many remembered as being "strange" but known by name to none.

When asked of his recollection of Thanksgiving night at the Lakeway Lounge, Kevin Bonney said "there was absolutely nothing extraordinary about it."

Kevin thought he was the last patron to leave the bar. He said he went to the bathroom and, when he came back, only Ann was present. "I just noticed that she was packing up, putting beer in the cooler," he said.

Another Lakeway Lounge bartender, Lynette Brown-Keba said Ann refused to serve a customer named Jason after he accused her of overcharging him. The customer left in a huff soon thereafter.

Mario recalled that Jason was angry when Ann cut him off. He said he offered to buy Jason a beer the next time he came in, and there was no animosity between the man or anyone at the bar that evening.

Margaret March recalled bar patron and her ex-lover Allen Hewise Jr. was angry with her after she refused to allow him to crash at her home. She told police it was common for regulars to spend the night at her home if they had too much to drink. She also said Allen Hewise Jr. said

Lynette also recalled the man tried talking to Ann, but she was busy. She said the man did not seem angry about being rejected. She said everyone else inside the bar was a regular. He was the only one that stood out.

Matt Miller remembered the man asking Ann to dance and her declining. He said he and this man played pool, and the man carried a knife that evening and talked about how he and his girlfriend had a fight and broke up. Matt said he left the bar about two hours before closing and the man was still there.

According to several bar patrons, the man was loud and disruptive. They saw him playing pool, drinking heavily, and he complained too many times about being dumped by his girlfriend.

Within two days, the blood was gone. Mentor-on-the-Lake firefighters washed down the house and the blood pools. The pub, now called Hannah's Restaurant & Bar, re-opened to a somber group of mourners and an eager group of reporters.

Mario admitted persons were angry with him for allowing Ann to close the bar alone. His only answer to them was, "It's typical for the bartender to close up."

He said Ann was cheerful when she showed up. She had just had her hair and nails done by a friend to celebrate her upcoming birthday.

Mario said everyone seemed in high spirits, playing pool, pumping money into the jukebox, dancing and drinking. One regular brought a turkey dinner to share, and "I bought a round for the house," he said.

He said the place was exactly as Ann left it. The jukebox and arcade games were still illuminated, the bar spotless, the glasses clean, the cooler fully stocked with bottles of beer. The small blackboard in the corner still had "Happy Birthday Annie," written in colorful chalk.

something to the effect of "someone's going to jail tonight" before he left. When questioned by police, Allen said he made that comment while at Margaret's home earlier that day. He claimed houseguests were smoking marijuana and offered him some. He then made the joke, "I don't feel like going to jail tonight."

He said his argument with Margaret concerned sleeping arrangements. He said Margaret had offered him her couch, and he told her, "If I'm staying at the house, I'm not sleeping on the couch." He claimed he left the bar with friend Jimmy Webb.

Several patrons described the "mystery man" as white; between twenty-five and thirty-five-years-old; between five-foot ten-inches and six-foot one-inch tall. He had light-colored hair and a chipped dark right incisor. He was seen wearing a diamond stud earring and black boots, having a large head and hands and lusting after every woman he saw.

According to Margaret, she told police she only knew the "mystery man" by his preferred drink -- Miller Genuine Draft in a bottle.

The video surveillance system was not working on the night of the murder. Mario Cacic told police someone had climbed on the building's roof to cut the cable and phone lines.

When this mystery man told Mario he was having a real bad day and was dumped by his girlfriend, Mario told the man he was young, he'd find someone else. "He kept saying he was going home with a woman that night," said Mario.

Lynette Brown-Keba agreed with Mario. She told police the man bothered her and other women all night. She said he kept asking them to dance and stared at her all night. "He gave me the creeps," she said.

The next day, a press conference was held in front of the police station. Chief Doran said they were working with Mentor Police, the FBI and Bureau of Criminal Investigations. The Chief announced his department was awaiting results of tests for DNA or fingerprints found on other items in the bar. He said Ann was attacked by her car and taken by force.

Fox 8 News reported the finding of DNA, but Chief Doran said the report was inaccurate. According to an FBI spokesperson, the Bureau was investigating other homicides in Ohio for similarities.

Lake County Deputy Coroner Mark Komar stated that samples from Ann's body were collected but it could take weeks to determine whether or not those samples contain any DNA other than hers.

Ann's twenty-six-year-old daughter, Erica McSween, attended the conference. She said she was confident police would solve the mystery. "People say they can't imagine what I have been going through," she said. She called the feeling "horrible," saying no one should ever have to go through anything like this.

When the preliminary autopsy results for Ann were reported, the small community was horrified. According to Coroner Komar, Ann sustained a broken bone in her neck from manual strangulation, was stabbed multiple times in the neck and back, and was raped. He described the homicide as "a horrific killing."

Chief Doran said he and his men were "grasping at every straw we possibly can to try to develop a lead in this case." He said it was tough because, so far from talking with friends and family of Ann and people from the bar, nobody had any beef or gripe with her. He said he believed someone was waiting for her when she left her shift.

Immediately friends and family of Ann's placed a

memorial of flowers in front of the bar. One resident stopped by and dropped off a teddy bear. "There's a monster out there somewhere, and I hope they catch him," she told waiting reporters.

Meanwhile, some in Mentor-on-the-Lake worried whether a murderer might be in their midst. Even those unfamiliar to Ann showed empathy for her murder. One local bartender never met Ann but brought flowers because of occupational solidarity. She said what happened to Ann could happen to any bartender who worked the night shift. "We close bars and walk outside by ourselves all the time, and it's not safe."

On December 4th, "Benefit For Our Annie" took place at the Breakwall Tavern. Ann had worked there for ten years, and the benefit was to help with funeral expenses.

The *News Herald* reported the town had an area of less than two square miles, and Ann's homicide was the first in eighteen years. Many said anxiety, fear and paranoia grew with each passing day without an arrest.

Local reporters who attended the wake said some attendees recounted pools of blood found outside the bar the following morning. Other reports suggested Margaret March heard Ann struggling to get in and failed to help her, mistaking Ann as the "guy with long hair" seen by Brian Williams.

Margaret would later tell police Ann lived with her and others a few months before her death. However, she was asked to move out when other people in the house suspected her of using drugs.

Another ex-roommate, Cheryl Zahn, claimed Ann moved from Margaret's home because her roommates made her buy drugs for them. "She believed she had to buy the drugs or she would have been kicked out," she said.

Most who gathered that day still wore dark clothing

after paying their respects at Ann's wake earlier. According to reporters, they swapped their favorite Annie memories. Some slammed shots of Yukon Jack, tapping their glasses twice on the bar before lifting them skyward to her memory.

They all believed, though, the significance of a series of mystifying clues: A cable found severed and hanging from the bar's roof that knocked out TV and phone service; tires slashed on vehicles belonging to Ann and two other women; and boats vandalized in a neighboring boatyard.

They discussed the "mystery man." Seemingly anyone who fit that profile was a suspect in the eyes of the public.

Another attendee and ex-roommate, Tracy Bellman said Ann lived with her for six months, and she believed more than one person was involved. "That's just my gut feeling," she said. She said Ann never wanted to impose and was always worried about overstaying her welcome. She said Ann would often spent the night in a booth in one of the bars where she worked.

Some wrapped gift baskets to be auctioned at the benefit dinner being held that evening. Some recalled how Ann bought thoughtful gifts to cheer her friends when they were sick and was known to give away any of her possessions on a whim to a friend who admired it.

Her daughter listed among Ann's achievements twenty years of sobriety, a yearly milestone she celebrated every June, ironically by buying shots for the bar. She filled her own shot glass with Red Bull. The two told patrons who asked that they were doing as well as they could under the circumstances. "Our mother was proud of us," said Justin.

According to court records, an attempted methamphetamine possession conviction on Ann's record belies the story of her sobriety, but friends said she took the blame to keep a friend out of bigger trouble. That, they said, was the kind of person she was.

Ann moved to California briefly about three years earlier to be closer to her mother and find a fresh start. She missed her children and only grandchild, so she moved back one year before her death.

According to her children, financial trouble plagued Ann. She relied upon the hospitality of friends, who opened their homes to her.

Her friend Laura Biggs reported that hundreds of people attended the Breakwall benefit. She claimed the place was standing room only, forcing her flat against a wall as she sold raffle tickets to help defray the cost of Ann's funeral.

She recalled how Ann always had a smile and a hug for her from the first time she started coming here. "It's just strange to be here and not have her here," she said.

Breakwall Tavern manager Angela Dragas said her daughter, Ashlee, thought of Ann as a second mother.

"If Ann had a dollar in her pocket, you got 75 cents of it," Angela said. "She really cared about taking care of everybody." She said when her eighteen-year-old daughter Ashlee wanted to skip school one day, Ann picked her up from home with a case of Red Bull in tow as an incentive to go.

High school friend Dawn Ondo told police she lost touch with Ann over the years. Now, she regrets that. When asked what she missed most about her friend, she replied, "The years I lost, the years I would have spent with her."

Matthew Cortelli grew up next door to the McSween household and said he, too, thought of Ann as a second mom. "She could turn any situation into a laugh. She had a great perspective on life."

Many of the friends who gathered at the benefit recalled Ann's sense of humor, trading stories about her ability to make them laugh. Angela recalled one time when Ann was late to work and the bar's owner gave her a hard time. Angela recalled that instead of getting annoyed or defensive, Ann grinned and said, "Well, this was the earliest I've ever been late."

Officers found no one who knew the sought-after man's identity, only that he "looked familiar."

Later that month, according to Chief Doran, they received a tip concerning twenty-six-year-old Joseph Thomas.

Mentor-on-the-Lake Sgt. Scott Daubenmire led the interview. He said Joseph told him, "I don't dance," and never asked any women, including Ann McSween, to dance with him on Thanksgiving night. "I hardly ever talk to barmaids except to order a drink," said Joseph.

The Sergeant claimed Joseph told him he lived with a family and babysat their children. He said Joseph claimed leaving the bar around 2:15 a.m. and getting home at 2:30 a.m. He then stayed up and played Farmville on his computer before going to bed. The police did not connect Joseph with the description of the "mystery man," and after the interview, he was released.

Weeks later in early January 2011, Joseph was brought in for a second interview. According to Sgt. Daubenmire, Joseph admitted that he in the past carried a small knife for work but had not carried one "for months."

When questioned again about asking Ann MsSween to dance and what time he left the Lakeway Lounge, the Sergeant claimed Joseph gave the same answers he gave in his first interview.

When Sgt. Daubenmire told Joseph his answers differed greatly from statements by four witnesses, he said Joseph continued to deny what others said of him. During this interview, Joseph voluntarily submitted to a polygraph test, which he passed, and to a cheek swab. He was again released.

Three months later in March 2011, Chief Doran had police officers canvass the neighborhood where the murder occurred, hoping to find Ann's clothes.

One resident, Robert Jenkins, recalled seeing a man on Black Friday, standing in the rain and burning something in a barrel in the backyard of a home at 5589 Marine Parkway, the same address listed on one of Joseph Thomas's arrest records. "I thought it was kind of nuts," he told police.

According to Robert, the reflection of the fire's light awoke him. He said it wasn't unusual for his neighbors to be up late, but not at such an odd hour and to be starting a fire in the rain. He admitted that his neighbors displayed some weird behavior, but starting a fire at 5:30 a.m. was most unusual.

He said he told his girlfriend and a few others what he saw later that day, but he said they all chalked it up to the neighbor's sometimes weird behavior. He said after learning of Ann's death, he began connecting dots in his mind.

When police searched the backyard, they found the barrel containing charred clothing. A test later matched Ann McSween's DNA with blood found on a sweater.

Homeowner Susan Gorsha indicated Joseph was a tenant during the time of Ann's murder and frequented the Lakeway Lounge. In exchange for doing repairs and mowing grass, Joseph received free shelter and food. She said police had come to the home several times over the last several months to speak with Thomas, who was also her daughter's friend.

When asked by a NewsChannel5 reporter if she thought Joseph was guilty, she said, "I don't know. I'm going to leave that up to everybody else to decide. I'm not going to say he's guilty and I'm not going to say that he's not guilty. I don't know." The clothing was then sent to BCI for analysis.

Not wanting to depend solely on the testimony of the bar patrons and the evidence of the burn barrel, police relied on The Laboratory Corporation of America for DNA evidence to link Thomas to the crime.

Shawn Weiss, associate technical director of forensics identification for the North Carolina-based corporation, used an YSTR test to compare Joseph's DNA to male DNA found on Ann's underwear and on her body, saying, "Joseph Thomas cannot be excluded as the man who raped and murdered Annie McSween."

The DNA tests also matched blood belonging to Ann to that found on the sweater inside the burn barrel police confiscated.

He also took swabs of the victim's vaginal area, a sock, and the palm and finger of her right hand. He found three markers of male DNA on the underwear and on vaginal swabs and compared it to Joseph Thomas's Y-chromosome profile. "I saw the same profile consistent with Joe Thomas on everything I tested," he said.

Stephen G. Labonne, who heads up DNA testing for the crime laboratory, tested various blood stains for DNA, along with Ann's black underwear, her shoes, two cigarette butts, and a piece of denim found at the crime scene. The underwear did not contain any seminal fluid nor any type of genetic material from Joseph Thomas.

The cigarette butts found near Ann's car and the piece of denim recovered from the burn barrel also contained insufficient DNA data. "Very high heat would break down DNA fairly rapidly," he said.

He concluded that most of the blood found at the scene belonged to Ann McSween, and the remaining minor

DNA profile he called "touch DNA" contained DNA from one or more persons.

He did find Joseph's DNA on two Miller Genuine Draft bottles discovered outside the bar in the trash, along with a number of other bottles tested and linked to other bar patrons. Other than that, he found no DNA or genetic material of Joe Thomas linking him to the homicide.

In mid-May 2011, Chief Doran released the description of the "mystery man." Soon thereafter, the Chief announced his department and the FBI joined with Crime Stoppers to offer thirty thousand dollars for information concerning Ann's murder. They hoped the promise of monetary gain would jog someone's memory concerning the killer's identity.

Days later Christine Vanatta called Mentor-on-the-Lake police, giving them Joseph's name after seeing a TV media report that police were seeking someone matching his description. She claimed she had dated Joseph for four years ending in 2008.

Believing their case to be strong enough, Mentor-on-the-Lake and Madison Township police arrested Joseph on June 7th at his then-girlfriend Linda Roncalli's home. When searching the home, police discovered four knives inside Joseph's duffel bags.

Both individuals were taken to the police station and placed in separate interrogation rooms with Joseph's interrogation being taped.

According to Linda Roncalli, she began dating Joseph in August 2010 while she was married to another man. On Thanksgiving night of 2010, she planned on driving to Joseph's house to go with him to Ladies Night at Mario's Lakeway Lounge after she made dinner for her husband and six kids. However, she said she didn't go because her car wouldn't start and Joseph had no car to pick her up.

She recalled texting Joseph that evening telling him she did not want to see him again because they lived in different towns and the drive was too hard on her old car.

She said he became angry, not only because of the breakup, but because she broke up with him in a text. The next morning, Joseph called her asking if she seen the news about Ann McSween's murder.

Linda asked Joseph if he was at the bar because "it was a common haunt for him" since he lived within walking distance, and he repeatedly told her he was not there.

Over the next few months, she asked Joseph again if he had been at the bar, because a description of a bar patron police were seeking sounded like him. "He said it wasn't him." She said Joseph told her he did not own earrings, but she recalled seeing him wear one when she first met him.

She claimed Joseph routinely carried a knife clipped to his pants when he went to bars, but she never saw him with a knife after that Thanksgiving. "We never went back to Mario's," she said. "He said he didn't want to go back there, ever, because he didn't feel safe."

During Joseph's taped interview, he denied knowing how Ann's charred clothing ended up in the barrel behind the home on Marine Parkway where he once lived. He repeatedly denied he had anything to do with the murder.

Joseph told police, "No matter what I say, you guys aren't going to believe me. I don't appreciate being called a liar."

When asked if he killed Ann in a drug deal gone badly, he denied it. "I didn't even know she did drugs," he replied. "I didn't do this! I never hurt her! I never hurt a female," he said. "I never will. I raised myself a lot better than that."

The investigators disclosed that Joseph claimed he at

one time experimented with cocaine and crystal meth but had since quit. When he came home from Mario's the night of the murder, the couple he lived with, in exchange for taking care of their children, was already in bed for the night.

Officers confronted him about Jaclyn Miller's statement of returning home from an out-of-town Thanksgiving trip around 2:30 a.m. and he was not yet home.

Joseph admitted to using drugs with Jaclyn and Jasmine while living with them in the Marine Parkway home and admitted to having sexual threesomes with them, but insisted that he did not kill Ann McSween.

When the public discovered Joseph was interviewed twice before by police and then released, they wanted answers. Authorities gave no reason for not matching Joseph with the composite sketch bar patrons gave.

All Chief Doran said was, "The interviewing officer did not feel Joseph Thomas fit the description of the sought-after man."

David A. Green, the trace expert, later claimed one boot impression he found at the crime scene could have been made by a boot belonging to Joseph. "The boot had a unique shape to it," he said. He also tested four knives belonging to Joseph, but none were consistent with the damage to the tires.

According to court records, in 2003, Joseph was charged with aggravated menacing in Fairport Harbor. He was accused of pulling a knife on a pair of teenagers who had thrown snowballs at him. That charge was later dropped.

In 2006, he was found guilty of inciting violence and disorderly conduct.

In Painesville Municipal Court, he pled guilty to a

grand theft charge in 2007 while living on Marine Parkway, the neighborhood where Ann's body was found. He received sixty days jail time with fifteen days suspended and was ordered to complete a chemical abuse program. Thomas had prior convictions for inciting violence, disorderly conduct, criminal damaging, grand theft and OVI. He added another disorderly conduct conviction in 2008.

He previously was convicted of unrelated misdemeanor charges of criminal damaging, inciting violence, disorderly conduct and theft, but nothing in his criminal record portended a murder charge. However, they do show he sometimes got into trouble when drinking.

He was previously accused, but never convicted, of punching a pregnant teenager in the stomach. A few days later, he was accused of stealing a pen set, lottery tickets, a phone and Dell laptop from cars in Leroy Township.

According to Yahoo messenger, Joseph's screen name was "The One Dragon666."

When his arresting officer asked him why he stole the laptop, Joseph replied, "I really don't know. I was drunk and it sounded good."

Mentor Municipal court records showed thirteen charges filed against Joseph Thomas for offenses ranging from traffic violations and obstructing official business to disorderly conduct.

When his younger brother, James Thomas, learned of the arrest, he told a reporter he and Joseph and their siblings lived a troublesome and dysfunctional childhood. Their mother abandoned Joseph with strangers in an RV park when he was fourteen.

When learning of Joseph's arrest, ex-girlfriend Jaclyn Miller told police she and Joseph were roommates living with Susan Gorsha, and she learned of Ann's murder from Joseph on Black Friday when she woke.

According to Jaclyn, she returned home around 2 a.m. Black Friday morning. She had visited out-of-town relatives for Thanksgiving, and Joseph was not there.

She said when she woke hours later, around 10 am, Thomas was sitting at a table drinking coffee and using his laptop computer. He told her he was at Mario's Lakeway Lounge the night before until it closed, but he claimed to know nothing about the murder.

Then according to Jaclyn, when police released the description of the man wanted for questioning in mid-May, she told Joseph it matched him. "He said he would take care of it," she said.

When a few days passed without any action by Thomas, Jaclyn said her sister Justina contacted police and told them about Joseph. Police then brought him in for questioning.

She claimed when Joseph returned from talking with police, he appeared upset, saying, "Thanks a lot, Justina and Jaclyn, for turning me in before I even had a chance."

The day after Joseph's arrest, everyone at Mario's Lakeway Lounge, which was changed its name to Hannah's Bar and Grill, were glued to the television screen as information regarding the arrest was broadcast on the evening news.

After seeing photos of the suspected murderer, many patrons remarked they did not know him and had never seen him before at the bar.

Mike Kunz, who was at Mario's the night Ann was killed, said Thomas looked familiar, although he didn't remember seeing him at the bar that night. Mike said he knew Ann from her work at Mario's and a neighboring bar and believed the killing was a chance encounter. "I think it had to be a one-time thing," he said. "Annie had her circle of friends, and this guy wasn't part of it."

While his current address was listed as Madison Township, court records showed Joseph had lived in Mentor-on-the-Lake since 2007.

According to Ann's friends, many had mixed emotions after the arrest. Laura Biggs said she cried when she heard a suspect had been arrested. "It was the best possible moment I could have gotten." She said any joy coming from the arrest was bittersweet "because it doesn't bring Annie or Erica back."

Tim Dever, another regular at Breakwall, said he was excited the police arrested someone but still had unanswered questions. "We just want to know the truth," he told a reporter.

Erica Richards, another bartender at Breakwall, said she did not necessarily feel safer with the arrest. "Mentor's totally different than it used to be," she said. "I used to take the garbage out by myself. Not anymore." Many, though, said they did feel safer with someone in custody.

Robert Sylvester lived near Lakeway Lounge and said he recalled seeing Joseph at the bar on several occasions. "The police never interviewed me and I never stepped forward. I figured the cops had enough information to go on," he said.

June 9th, 2011, was the day of Joseph Thomas's first preliminary hearing. He entered no plea to the murder of Annie McSween. According to a reporter, he walked into the crowded courtroom filled with Ann's friends and supporters, including her son, head held high before temporary Judge John Trebet in Mentor Municipal Court.

His attorney was Chief Assistant Lake County Public Defender Christopher Grieshammer. Joseph waived a reading of the full complaint.

Friends Bob Kruk and Sherry Evans organized a group motorcycle ride to the hearing. They decided to do so as a tribute to Ann as soon as they heard the news that a suspect had been arrested. Kruk said he hoped for "a quick trial" that would ensure justice was done.

According to Sherry, she said she does not remember seeing Joseph Thomas in the area at all. "Other than my girlfriend knowing him from years ago, I don't think any of us had ever seen him before," she said.

On September 16th, 2011, it was official. Chief Doran, after twelve years at the helm of the Mentor-on-the-Lake Police Department, announced his retirement.

In a letter to Mayor John M. Rogers, Chief Doran wrote, "It has been particularly rewarding to have been in the company of so many remarkable law enforcement and communications professionals."

He said with the department running smoothly and efficiently, he felt now was the opportune time to hand the reins to the next generation of leadership and begin a new chapter in his life, retirement.

He planned spending retirement pursuing personal, family and volunteer interests. He called his time as police chief the "capstone" of his thirty-three years in law enforcement.

Doran was appointed chief in January 1999. Since taking the job, Doran said the department has worked to continually improve services and relationships within the department and throughout the community.

Mayor Rogers announced at a press conference that Chief Doran's professionalism and service are examples of how he served the city "with honor and distinction."

He described Chief Doran as a confidant, an adviser and a friend, saying, Joseph Doran's service to the community, along with his leadership to the police department, was very much appreciated and would certainly be missed.

Chosen as new Police Chief was Lt. John P. Gielink, who began his law enforcement with the department in 1986. He was promoted to lieutenant in May 1999.

According to Mayor Rogers, Lt. Gielink's accomplishments included completion of the FBI's National Academy and twice being named the department's officer of the year.

Joseph Thomas was official indicted for Ann's murder on October 11th, 2011. Additional charges of rape, kidnapping, tampering with evidence, and aggravated robbery were added. The indictment included death penalty specifications, alleging Joseph killed Ann while committing a total of eleven crimes.

Lake County Prosecutor Dwayne Coulson said the death penalty was appropriate because of the "nature of the crime." Judge Richard L. Collins Jr. was assigned to hear the case.

On October 14th, the now twenty-seven-year-old Thomas pled not guilty to all charges. He was quiet except when he answered the judge.

Justin McSween declined comment after the hearing, but his wife Erin spoke. "Annie would sit on the floor and read books to her grandson, Cody James," she said. "Now our son cannot share the drawings he made for his grandmother. Instead of putting them on her refrigerator, he leaves them on her grave. How can I explain such evil to our son?"

Christmas came and went for friends and family of Ann McSween. Many said they missed her ever-present smile. She always had a small gift for her special friends, even when she couldn't afford to buy anything, some said.

When 2012 arrived, the biggest event would be Joseph Thomas's murder trial. According to reporters, Mentor-on-the-Lake residents waited for their chance to give Ann's killer a piece of their mind.

Thomas appeared in Common Pleas Court with his court-appointed public defenders on July 3rd to motion for many requests, including a change of venue, that the potential jurors be questioned individually and in private, and that the court authorize a $3,500 payment so the defense may hire William Evans, an Akron-based polygrapher known as one of the best in the field.

On January 23rd, 2012, Joseph was back in court requesting Judge Collins Jr. to eliminate death as a possible punishment. The defense attorneys claimed the death penalty was cruel and unusual punishment and offended the Eighth Amendment.

The lawyers also requested defense expenditures to hire James Eisenberg, a Painesville clinical neurophysiologist, for no more than $7,500.

Judge Collins Jr. previously approved requests to appoint private investigator Thomas Pavlish for the defense up to five-thousand dollars.

The prosecution was arguing over the expenses that had accumulated so far and the defense's motions for expenditures. Other expenses for sequestering jurors would include hotel rooms, meals and transportation, as well as paying for extra security.

According to Lake County Commissioner Raymond E. Sines, the trial was likely to cost taxpayers $100,000.

The second shock for the residents came on January 22, 2012, when the lifeless body of Erica McSween was found inside her home just before 10:30 p.m. According to Coroner Mark Komar, there were no obvious signs of trauma.

While rumors floated that Erica's death was related to her mother's, those rumors were proved unfounded. Her toxicology tests revealed she died from an accidental overdose of drugs, including OxyContin and heroin.

When residents learned of Erica's death and that there were drugs involved, they rallied to her and Ann's defense. One said solving Ann's murder should be top priority instead of insinuating the mother and daughter were "drug addicts."

On August 9th, Judge Collins Jr. denied the defense's motion for change of venue, believing an impartial jury would be found. The jury pool consisted of 250 jurors.

Jailhouse records showed the only visitors Joseph received the entire time he was incarcerated in the county jail were his mother, Verna Rodriguez, and younger brother, James Thomas.

Court records indicate September 1st was Joseph's final pretrial. Judge Collins Jr. ordered the attorneys to put the final touches on witness lists and spoke of rules for media coverage, such as only one TV and one still camera in the courtroom at a time.

The first two weeks of the estimated four-week trial took so long to pick a jury, in part, because of the high-profile nature of the case, reported *The Plain Dealer*.

More details of Ann's murder surfaced. Her face was severely beaten to the point of her nose being sunk in. She was choked. Her neck was slashed. She was stabbed five times in the back.

Joseph sat in jail nearly a year, but on September 18, 2012, his first day of trial in Painesville, Ohio, began. Jurors were taken to the crime scene that morning. On their return, Assistant Prosecutor Charles Cichocki made his opening statements by explaining why the State believed Thomas beat, raped and stabbed Ann McSween in the early morning hours of November 26, 2010, her forty-ninth birthday.

"Joseph Thomas lured Ann McSween outside by

cutting power to the building," said Cichocki. He contended that once Ann was outside, Joseph beat her, breaking bones in her face.

He told the jury on the night Ann McSween was murdered, Joseph was seen intoxicated at Mario's Lakeway Lounge complaining that his girlfriend had just dumped him.

He stated the victim's sweater, pants, bra, and shirt were found in a burn barrel in a Marine Parkway home Joseph lived in. He talked of Ann's injuries and defensive wounds and that it appeared she briefly escaped her attacker and tried to get inside a neighboring home.

Defense Attorney David Doughten began his opening statement by saying Joseph's DNA was not found on any evidence confiscated by forensic experts.

He argued the homicide occurred around 4:20 a.m. two hours after Joseph was seen leaving the bar. "There was no motive. The evidence will show that Joseph did not commit this crime," he said.

Three witnesses were called that day. The first was boat mechanic James Yager for the State. He explained how he discovered Ann's body. "I just figured she was dragged to the back of the lot, so I just walked straight back, like a diagonal from the car to the back corner behind the sailboat and behind the equipment, and I just looked in the woods and there she was, mostly unclothed. I was pretty shook up."

Mario was called to the stand. Under cross-examination by the defense, he admitted he had once gone to police to report having stopped a man named George from punching Ann.

The defense suggested that man was waiting in the woods for Ann that night.

Police Chief John Gielink testified to the fact that police were searching for a man with a gap in his teeth, and that Joseph Thomas fit the description several gave to police.

Prosecuting Attorney Dwayne Coulson spoke with reporters after that day's trial. He said the McSween family were having a very hard time with her death. He compared the family's pain with shoving "something in an open wound and wiggling it around."

News Channel 5 reported the prosecution were pushing for the death penalty, saying "the severity of the victim's injuries calls for capital punishment." Joseph was facing a minimum of twenty-five years to life in prison.

On day two, videos of Joseph being interviewed by police were played for the jury.

Margaret March testified to her friendship with Ann and Ann's suspected meth use, saying, "We didn't want to be mean because we loved her," she said. "So we told her we didn't have enough room and that she had to leave."

She recalled hearing thumps on the outside wall of her home and admitted on cross examination she was a bit "fuzzy" about when she heard the noise.

Robert Jenkins, who uses a cane, took the stand to state he saw someone matching Joseph Thomas's description burning clothing the morning of Black Friday.

Doctor Daniel Galita, medical examiner at the Cuyahoga County Coroner's Office, took the stand. He told of Ann having hydrocodone and amphetamine in her system. The combination of the blunt force blows to her head and stab wounds had killed her, he said.

Matt Miller testified to his socializing with Joseph on Thanksgiving night. He talked of how intoxicated Joseph was and that he saw a knife clipped to Joseph's pants.

Under cross examination, defense attorney David Doughten argued that Miller could not have been certain that the clip he saw contained a knife.

"It was a knife, for sure," said Matt.

When re-questioned by Assistant Prosecutor Cichocki about how he noticed the knife, Matt replied, "Whenever drinking is involved, people get irate if they get beat in pool. I've heard of people getting stabbed or even shot over games, so I tend to keep an eye on that type of stuff."

Lynette Brown-Keba testified that Ann was not dating anyone she knew of, and she seemed "aggravated" and "out of sorts" the entire Thanksgiving evening. She stated she saw Joseph at the bar and "had a bad feeling" about him.

Steven G. Labonne, who headed The Lake County Crime Laboratory, testified about the items he tested for DNA.

Special Agent Daniel Winterich for the Ohio Bureau took the stand Thursday. He recalled how Agents were called to the Mentor-on-the-Lake police station in April 2011 to analyze the items found in the burn barrel. In addition to clothing, police found melted makeup compacts and makeup remover mixed in with the barrel's ash.

When news of Ann's alleged drug use was released, it angered many. Persons vented their outrage and opinions on Facebook and other networking channels.

The next day, Robert Jenkins and Patrolman Scott Daubenmire testified.

Patrolman Daubenmire testified to his questioning of Joseph before he was officially charged. When asked on cross if Joseph passed his polygraph test, the officer said "yes."

Immediately, the judge stopped the proceedings and ordered the jury to disregard the officer's statement, for the polygraph test had already been ruled inadmissible.

Mentor-on-the-Lake Police Detective Gerri Deutsch

testified to Joseph being caught in multiple lies when interviewed. On cross examination, he admitted Joseph voluntarily talked with police.

On the fourth day of trial, Special Agent Mark Kollar identified two folding knives and one serrated blade as belonging to Joseph.

Afterward, two of Joseph's ex-girlfriends took the stand against him. When shown photographs, Jaclyn Miller positively identified the burn barrel the police confiscated from her backyard.

Defense attorneys claimed the clothes were placed there by someone else. And, if Joseph was the killer, he would have destroyed that evidence instead of leaving it for police to find.

Susan Gorsha was called as a rebuttal witness. She testified that Joseph was living in her home on Maine Parkway when Ann was murdered.

Cheryl Zahn testified to being certain the clothes found in the barrel were Ann's and were the clothes Ann had worn when bartending on Thanksgiving night.

She also testified that it was common for Ann to stay out until 4 a.m. or later because Ann did not want to wake her before her day as a bus driver began. "She never wanted to be in my way or be any inconvenience for me," Cheryl said.

On cross examination, Cheryl admitted Ann won a lawsuit while she lived in California. She said Ann expressed concern that the people she sued were upset about the ruling, but she did not know if Ann was actually frightened for her life.

Defense Attorney Doughten pointed out that the charred clothing was not found until months after Joseph had moved away.

While Joseph did not take the stand, the sixth day of

trial began with jurors hearing his taped police interviews. His answers to police contrasted with testimony that jurors had already heard from bar patron Matt Miller.

Robert Jenkins and Forensic Expert Shawn Weiss gave testimony before Christine Vanatte testified. Crying through most of her short testimony, Christine admitted she also called police suspecting Joseph was involved with Ann's murder.

The next day opened with the defense calling their witnesses, starting with Joseph's mother, Verna Rodriguez. She testified in an effort to spare her son from the death penalty. She told the jury she was a crack addict, an alcoholic who abandoned her three small children, then secretly moved to Seattle with a boyfriend

According to the *News Herald*, Verna admitted to being hooked on crack and said, "The kids were taking care of themselves."

Joseph's younger brother, James Thomas, testified that, as a child, he was dropped off by his mother to spend the weekend with relatives, and his mother never came back, saying, "We pretty much raised ourselves."

Joseph's sister, Tessa Rodgers, testified their father abandoned them, saying, "I consider him a sperm donor."

Other family members told the jury Verna Rodriguez went from one bad relationship to another, had many relationships with different men, and that all three of her children were exposed to violence, drug abuse, and excessive drinking.

During his closing argument on September 26, Attorney Grieshammer, presented several scenarios. "Annie McSween could have been murdered by someone stealing scrap from the bar and nearby boat yard," he said, recalling how the phone lines of the bar were cut, suggesting that person wanted the wire to sell.

He reminded the jury of Ann sending a text to her ex-boyfriend asking him to get her methamphetamine for her birthday. "Did she meet up with someone that night and that's why she had drugs in her system?" he said.

Assistant Prosecutor Cichocki called the defense's theories "boogeymen" alternatives in his closing statement.

He reminded the jury of Thomas's denials and the inconsistencies between his recollections of what happened that night and those of everyone else point to his guilt. "If you're not the guilty person, why would you lie?" he said to the jury.

On September 29, even with the knowledge Joseph Thomas endured a loveless and neglectful childhood, the jury unanimously recommended the death penalty.

When asked by Judge Collins Jr. if he had anything to say to the jury, Joseph stood and said, "Honestly, there's not much I want to say to you people."

He then accused the prosecution of hiding facts about the case that favored him. He talked of his passing the polygraph test in January. He insisted he was innocent, saying another man failed his polygraph.

After the proceedings, Joseph stormed out of the courtroom into a shower of flashbulbs, loudly answering reporters who lined the hallways each day of the trial with, "I passed the polygraph test proving I didn't do this s---. I didn't do this s---."

October 3 marked the penalty phase at the Lake County courthouse. Nine defense witnesses took the stand in the sentencing phase. Many were called just to testify that Joseph, now twenty-eight-years-old, was not a regular at Mario's Lakeway Lounge.

Also taking the stand that day were Mark McCool, Allen Heise Jr. and Kevin Bonney.

Mark McCool told the jury he heard a scream coming

from Lakeway Lounge sometime around 2 a.m. the morning Ann was murdered. He explained it was common for it to be noisy around the bar near closing time. He said he thought the screams came from the goofballs at the bar. He then heard a second scream later that occurred before his wife, who worked at a department store, left for work at 4:10 am. "I heard the second scream, and I thought, 'How strange.' This was late even for the bar.'"

He said he went outside to see if he could locate the source of the scream and peeked into the bar's parking lot but saw nothing.

The next day brought testimony from an assistant psychologist for the Lake County Juvenile Court.

Judy Jackson testified that, before Joseph Thomas was a twenty-eight-year-old accused killer, he was a fourteen-year-old child who got in trouble for hitting his mother. She said Joseph, at fourteen, told her he punched his mother because she and her then-boyfriend were hitting him and he decided to fight back.

She talked of her psychological evaluation of Joseph, telling the court he had a nomadic, sometimes violent, childhood. She said he grew up with a lot of violence and a lot of chaos in the house.

She stated even at fourteen, Joseph had already been to several different schools because his family kept moving. She explained that having that nomadic lifestyle tends to lend itself to children who act out.

Judy stated her evaluation of Joseph revealed he had problems with anger management and a very low tolerance for frustration. When it came time for fourteen-year-old Joseph to return home, Judy said he would have preferred to stay in the juvenile jail because of the violence in his home.

The last defense witness was Walter Robert Blare, an

ex-boyfriend of Rodriguez's who lived with the family for a time. When asked if Joseph had a temper or fancied himself a ladies' man, he said "yes" on both counts.

He recalled how Joseph once made a twenty-dollar bet with him that he could get any woman. When Joseph failed to pick a woman up, he got angry. "I got slapped upside my head by a cold-cocked fist," he said.

He admitted Joseph was not always angry, but then he compared Joseph when he drank to Dr. Jekyll and Mr. Hyde.

However, on October 15th, the jury, which consisted of the same persons throughout the trial, decided Joseph deserved death. The following day at 3 p.m., Judge Collins Jr. agreed, saying, "Ann McSween tried to get away from you, Joseph Thomas," he said, "leaving a 165-foot trail of blood behind her. Her death was senseless and brutal."

According to a reporter, Joseph mumbled a few inaudible words and shook his head when the judge read the sentence. When asked if he had anything to say, Joseph replied, "Nope."

Instead he stared into space and rocked in his chair as Judge Collins Jr. carefully explained his legal rights before handing down the death sentence. Collins also sentenced Joseph to thirty-three additional years for the remaining offences including the rape and kidnapping.

The only emotion Joseph showed during the hour-long court appearance was a smirk when the judge said his execution would affect his family, described as abusive and dysfunctional.

Afterward, Ann's family and friends spoke their piece. Valerie Cortelli told the newly convicted killer, "You committed the most heinous crime possible and you show no remorse."

Erin McSween, the wife of Justin McSween, told

Joseph he showed no remorse throughout the entire trial, which speaks to "the narcissistic monster you are."

Cheryl Zahn of Mentor said she sat at the kitchen table of her home the morning of November 26th, waiting for her best friend. "Look at me," she said to Joseph, who refused to turn her way. "You killed my best friend. I was waiting for her to come over so we could celebrate her birthday. Instead, I got the call that she was dead. You got the sentence you deserve."

In the end, no one got what they wanted. Joseph lost his freedom, Ann lost her life, and everyone who loved Joseph and Ann lost them to prison and death, all because of Joseph's twisted love for sadistic sex, control, and violence.

About the Author

JoAnne currently lives in Irving, Texas and is a Recording Arts graduate. Besides being a cross-genre writer JoAnne canvas paints and writes alternative song lyrics. She is currently working on her 8th book titled *"Murder Most Foul 2: Batya"* and her 9th, *"Invaded by the Galaxy"*, which is a SyFy comedy.

You can discover more about JoAnne here:
http://facebook.com/authorpage.joannemyers
www.booksandpaintings.com

Made in the
USA
Monee, IL